Catalan

Catalan: An Essential Grammar is a concise and convenient guide to the basic grammatical structure of Catalan.

Presenting a fresh and accessible description of the language, this engaging grammar uses clear explanations and sets out the complexities of Catalan in short, readable sections clarified by examples. Quick reference overviews are also provided in the appendix.

Catalan: An Essential Grammar is the ideal reference grammar for all learners of Catalan, whether class-based or independent, looking to progress beyond beginner level.

Nicolau Dols lectures as Professor Titular d'Universitat in Catalan at the University of the Balearic Islands. He is also a full member of the Philological Section of *Institut d'Estudis Catalans*, the official academy for the Catalan language.

Richard Mansell is Senior Lecturer in Translation at the University of Exeter.

Routledge Essential Grammars

Essential Grammars are available for the following languages:

Arabic
Chinese
Czech
Danish
Dutch
English
Finnish
Modern Hebrew
German
Greek
Hindi
Hungarian
Korean
Latvian
Norwegian
Polish
Portuguese
Romanian
Serbian
Spanish
Swedish
Thai
Turkish
Urdu

Catalan

An Essential Grammar

Nicolau Dols and Richard Mansell

LONDON AND NEW YORK

First published 2017
by Routledge
2 Park Square, Milton Park, Abingdon, Oxon OX14 4RN

and by Routledge
711 Third Avenue, New York, NY 10017

Routledge is an imprint of the Taylor & Francis Group, an informa business

British Library Cataloguing-in-Publication Data
A catalogue record for this book is available from the British Library

Library of Congress Cataloging-in-Publication Data
Names: Salas, Nicolau Dols, author. | Mansell, Richard Michael (Lecturer) author.
Title: Catalan : an essential grammar / Nicolau Dols Salas and Richard Mansell.
Description: Milton Park, Abingdon, Oxon ; New York, NY : Routledge, [2017] | Series: Routledge essential grammars
Identifiers: LCCN 2016032227 | ISBN 9781138921283 (hardback) | ISBN 9781138921290 (pbk.) | ISBN 9781315686462 (ebook)
Subjects: LCSH: Catalan language—Grammar.
Classification: LCC PC3822 .S25 2017 | DDC 449/.982421—dc23
LC record available at https://lccn.loc.gov/2016032227

ISBN: 978-1-138-92128-3 (hbk)
ISBN: 978-1-138-92129-0 (pbk)
ISBN: 978-1-315-68646-2 (ebk)

Typeset in Sabon and Gill Sans
by Apex CoVantage, LLC
Printed and bound by CPI Group (UK) Ltd, Croydon, CR0 4YY

Contents

Abbreviations

Conventions used in this book

An asterisk (*) before a word or sentence denotes that it is incorrect. A question mark (?) before a word or sentence means that it would sound strange to a native speaker, and should be avoided.

When 'lit.' appears before an English example sentence, it means that it is a literal translation of the Catalan, sacrificing fluency in English to be able to show more clearly the point of Catalan grammar being explained.

A tick symbol (✓) indicates a correct version of a sentence, normally compared to an incorrect version with an asterisk.

Pronunciation guides follow the International Phonetic Alphabet.

We have not used the inclusive forms 'he/she', 's/he', or 'him/her' and so on throughout examples in the text unless necessary, simply to make it easier to read. So, even though an example says 'he' or 'she', the other may also be possible. Unlike English, Catalan frequently does not use subject pronouns, and so the gender of the third person is often understood from context, or from other factors such as any adjectives agreeing with the human referent.

PART I

What is Catalan?

Chapter 1

Catalan-speaking areas

Catalan is spoken in the eastern part of the Iberian peninsula (Catalonia, Valencia, a small part of Aragon close to the Catalan border, and a much smaller part of the Murcia region close to the Valencian border), in the Balearic Islands, in a region between the two eastern branches of the Pyrenees (Albera and Corbera Massifs) normally called 'Northern Catalonia', in Andorra, and the city of Alghero in Sardinia. This distribution includes four states (Spain, France, Andorra, and Italy), and a different status in every state and region. Catalan is the only official language in Andorra according to its constitution, and it is co-official with Spanish in the autonomous regions of Catalonia, Valencia, and the Balearic Islands in Spain. It is also a protected language according to the Law of Cultural Heritage (2016) of the autonomous region of Aragon, due to its presence in the most eastern part of this region, known as 'La Franja' ('The Strip'). Co-officiality in Catalonia, Valencia, and the Balearics is unbalanced. According to the Spanish constitution, all citizens must know Spanish; according to the regional constitutions, citizens also have the right to use Catalan (also called Valencian – the Spanish High Court recognises Valencian and Catalan as two different names for the same language). In 2006, the new Catalan autonomy statute (effectively the constitution for the region) made knowing Catalan a legal requirement, but this was dismissed in 2010 by the Spanish Constitutional Court, leading to the current institutional crisis (as we write in 2016) and giving new impetus to the Catalan independentist movement.

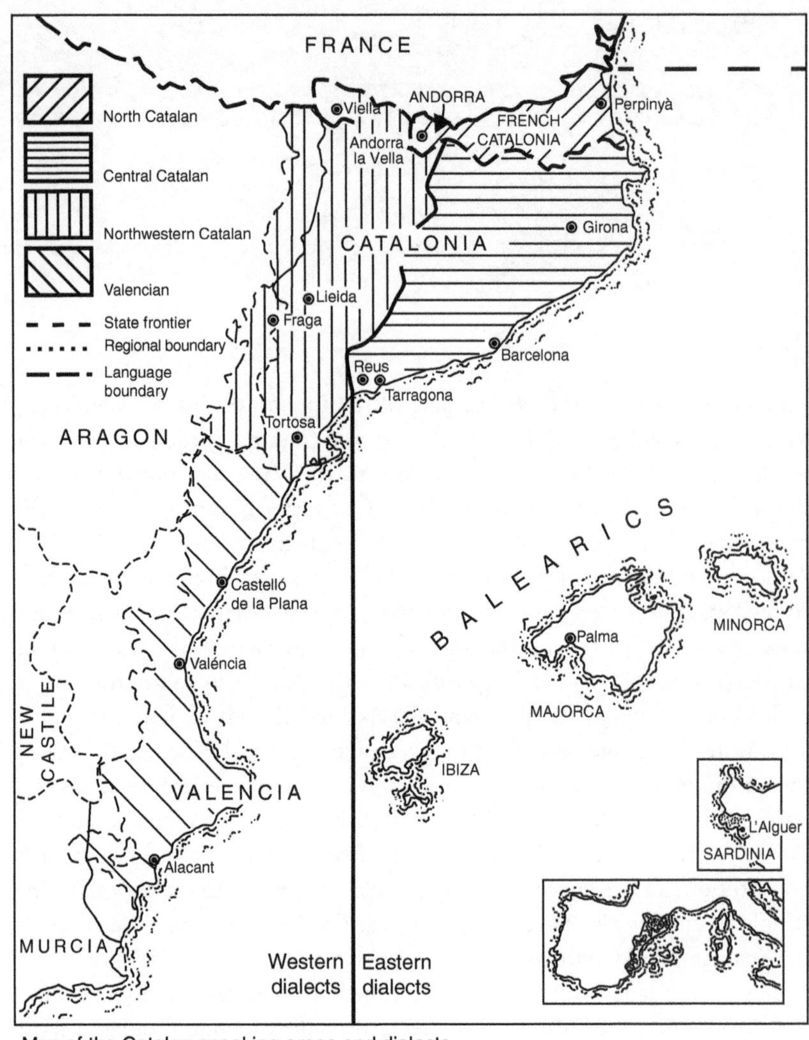

Map of the Catalan-speaking areas and dialects

Chapter 2

Catalan among the other Romance languages

The Catalan language has been shaped by the region's history, and each stage has left a mark on the modern language: there are the pre-Roman languages surviving the Roman invasion of 218 BC, such as Basque and Iberian, especially in the North-West (Pallars, Ribagorça, and Vall d'Aran escaped initial Romanisation); there is the Germanic invasion in 415 which led to the establishment of the kingdom of Toulouse (Tolosa by its Occitan name); then the Arabic invasion after 711 which affected in various degrees the whole of the mainland Catalan-speaking territories and the Balearics, and north of the Pyrenees reached the Roussillon, occupying that northern territory for 40 years (719–759). As a reaction, the Franks fought back, reaching Barcelona (801). Frankish counties were established over half of present-day Catalonia and Northern Catalonia. These counties were eventually unified, and the Catalans enlarged their territories by annexing the Arabic kingdoms of Tortosa and Lleida, a process complete in the 12th century. In the following century, the Balearics and Valencia followed. In the 14th century (1354), Alghero was populated with Catalans after a victory over Genoa.

All this contact together with the influence of indigenous peoples in the territories where Catalan is spoken gives the language its particular shape among all of the other Romance languages. Occitan is its closest relative. Indeed, Catalan troubadours used Occitan for their work up to the 15th century. However, Occitan poetry in Catalonia was seen as a courtly activity, detached from real language, and thus requiring constant attention to preceptive books on poetics. Vocabulary in non-literary works shows the influence of a language already different from Latin by the 10th century. The first texts in Catalan appeared in the 12th century, such as the *Llibre jutge*, a translation in vulgar language of a Visigothic law code. Also in the late 12th or early 13th century, the *Homilies d'Organyà* was written, a fully developed text in Catalan, probably used as a help for delivering sermons in the vulgar language. The 13th century is undoubtedly the century of Ramon Llull (Majorca, 1232–1315), who wrote novels, philosophy, and theology works in Catalan. It is also the century when historiographic texts in the language began, with books translated from Latin (*De rebus Hispaniae*, 1268; *Gesta comitum Barcinonensium*, 1267–1283) and others written in Catalan (*Llibre dels fets*, 1274; *Crònica de Bernat Desclot*, 1288). In the 15th century, Ausiàs March opened new paths for poetry, in Catalan and bridging the troubadour tradition and new, Renaissance verse.

Catalan maintained its role as a full national language even after the Aragonese and Castilian crowns united under Isabella of Castile and Ferdinand II of Aragon. Ferdinand himself was of Castilian origin, after the last king of Aragon belonging to the House of Barcelona, Martin, died without an heir in 1410, and Ferdinand I, grandfather to Ferdinand II, was elected king. The decline of Catalan as a national language began in 1659 in Northern Catalonia when under the Treaty of the Pyrenees the territory was annexed by France. South of the Pyrenees, the decline began after defeat in the War of Succession (1715), when the Spanish crown was consolidated and the laws and customs of Castile were progressively imposed on Catalan territories. Even so, Catalan remained the only language of everyday (albeit non-official) usage until the arrival of mass internal migration from Spanish-speaking territories in the second half of the 20th century.

After 1834, a strong movement to recover the Catalan language took hold in literature and other artistic fields, leading to the restoration of Catalan identity, and to the modern standardisation of the language. Antoni Maria Alcover (1862–1932) and Pompeu Fabra (1868–1948) are the two main linguists who worked to recover and restore the language. In 1911 the Philological Section of Institut d'Estudis Catalans was founded as the language academy of Catalan. This institution is in charge of the official dictionary and grammar of the language, and it also issues surveys and other research matters on the use of Catalan.

In recent times, the greatest obstacle to normalising Catalan has been Franco's dictatorship (1936/1939–1975). After the transition of Spain to democracy, Catalan-speaking territories under Spanish control have recovered official use of the language, and this is explored below.

Chapter 3

Catalan in the twenty-first century

According to the latest official reports (2013–2014) on language skills in the main speaking areas (data from the 2011 official census in Catalonia, Valencia, the Balearics, and the Aragonese Catalan-speaking area, known as 'La Franja'), knowledge of Catalan is as follows[1] (Graph 1.1), with precise figures in the following table:

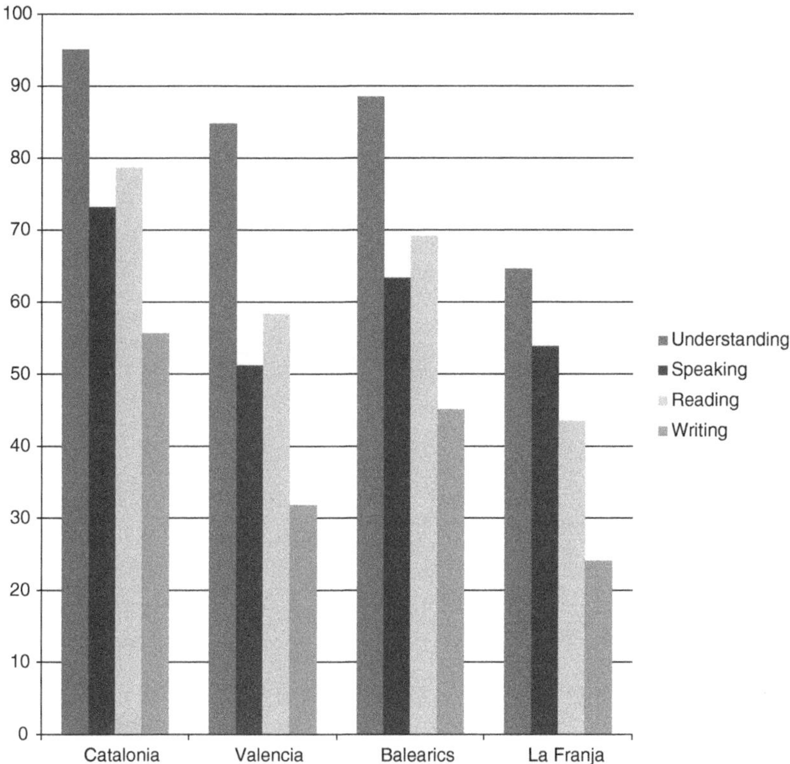

Graph 1.1 Percentage of inhabitants who can understand, speak, read and write Catalan, by geographic area

	Catalonia	Valencia	Balearics	La Franja
Understanding	95.1	84.8	88.5	64.6
Speaking	73.2	51.2	63.4	53.9
Reading	78.7	58.4	69.2	43.5
Writing	55.7	31.8	45.1	24.1

The population of all the Catalan-speaking areas reached 13,497,830 inhabitants in 2013, distributed by territories[2] as:

Catalonia	7,509,000
Valencia	4,252,000
Balearics	1,103,000
Northern Catalonia	465,000
Andorra	76,950
La Franja	47,630
Alghero	43,510
El Carxe (in Murcia)	740

Learning Catalan in primary and secondary education is compulsory in Catalonia, Valencia, the Balearics, and Andorra, and possible in the rest of territories (except in the tiny area of El Carxe, Murcia). Catalan can be studied to degree level in the universities of these three main territories, and in the University of Perpinyà (Perpignan), in Northern Catalonia.

5,966 books and pamphlets were published in Catalan in Spain in 2014, making 27.15% of the total production in Catalonia, Valencia, and the Balearics (5,381 out of 19,818). 54 were published in Aragon and 531 in other parts of Spain:

Area	Books in Catalan	Total books	Proportion
Catalan	4,482	16,079	27.87%
Valencia	607	3,178	19.10%
Balearic Islands	292	561	52.04%
Aragon	54	1,376	3.92%
TOTAL	5,435	21,194	25.64%[3]

Written mass media in Catalan has a daily circulation of 189,345 copies, of which 146,064 are effectively bought. The most important newspapers edited in Catalonia (*La Vanguardia, El Periódico, Segre*) are printed in two editions, Catalan and Spanish, and along with them, other daily newspapers like *Ara, El Punt Avui, Diari de Girona*, and *Regió 7* exist only in Catalan. *Ara* has a Balearic edition, *Ara Balears*, online from Monday to Friday and printed on Saturday and Sunday. *Ara* also has digital editions in Andorra, Valencia, Girona, and Tarragona. *Diari de Balears* was a printed newspaper completely in Catalan edited in Palma between 1996 and 2013. It exists now in its online edition only. With a current daily circulation of 19,000 copies, *Diari d'Andorra* has appeared in Catalan since 1991.

The presence of Catalan on the internet is important, not only in the field of digital newspapers (*Vilaweb, Nació Digital, El País* in its Catalan edition since October 2014, etc.) but in general, as shown by the number of companies operating in Catalan-speaking countries with a website in Catalan (63.58%), the position of Catalan in Wikipedia (17th in number of articles), or the fact that Catalan merited the first generalistic domain granted by ICANN to a language community <.cat>, which occurred in 2005. In February 2016 the number of <.cat> domains was 98,359.

Radio broadcasting in Catalan is especially followed in Catalonia, where in 2014 listeners of stations in Catalan outranked those of stations in Spanish by 1,468,000 to 754,000. In Valencia and the Balearics, broadcasting in Catalan and the reception of channels from Catalonia have been a main political issue, often blocked in the periods when the right-wing party Partido Popular has been in power, which is true not only for radio but also for television. Ràdio Nacional d'Andorra and Andorra Música broadcast in Catalan.

TV3 Televisió is the leading channel in Catalonia. Belonging to the autonomous public broadcasting corporation, it broadcasts solely in Catalan, as do the rest of Catalan public channels. However, the amassed audience of all TV channels in Catalan only adds up to 20% of viewers. The situation in the Balearics and in Valencia is similar to that of the radio. The Balearic public TV channel IB3 has broadcast mostly in Catalan under right-wing governments, and completely in Catalan during left-wing or coalition governments. Canal 9, the Valencian public channel, with a greater presence of Spanish than Catalan, finally closed in 2013, after broadcasting for 24 years, a casualty of the financial crisis. ATV (Andorra Televisió) broadcasts in Catalan.

Notes

1. Xarxa CRUSCAT (2015) *VIII Informe sobre la situació de la llengua catalana (2014)*. Barcelona: Observatori de la Llengua Catalana, http://blogs.iec.cat/cruscat/wp-content/uploads/sites/15/2011/11/Informe-2014.pdf
2. This excludes territories in Valencia that historically have only spoken Spanish, and the Vall d'Aran in Catalonia, where Occitan is spoken.
3. This general average is skewed by the Aragonese statistics, whose low percentage stems from its language distribution.

Chapter 4

Main dialects

The main dialectologic division in Catalan runs from north to south and produces two main groups of dialects: east and west. The dialects of Northern Catalonia, half of Catalonia, and the Balearics belong to the eastern group, and those of Andorra, the western and most southern part of Catalonia, the Aragonese Strip, and Valencia belong to the western group. The most important differences between east and west are phonetic and focus on the unstressed vowel system, which is more reduced in the eastern than in the western due to the fact that stressed /a, e, ɛ/ turn into [ə] in the east, and the same vowels show up as [a, e] in the west:

set 'seven' [ˈsɛt] → *setè* [səˈtɛ] 'seventh' (E) ([səˈtə] for most Balearic speakers)

set 'seven' [ˈsɛt] → *setè* [seˈte] 'seventh' (W)

In a similar way, /o, ɔ/ reduces to [u] when unstressed in the east (except in Majorca), and to [o] in the west and Majorca:

Roma 'Rome' [ˈromə] → *romà* 'Roman' [ruˈma] (E)

Roma 'Rome' [ˈroma] → *romà* 'Roman' [roˈma] (W+M)

Also discrepancies between stressed vowels are important in different dialects. However, other limits appear here, more precise than the E–W division. Words originating from Latin turn an original long *e* (Ē) or short *i* (Ĭ) into [e] in Western dialects, [ɛ] in Central Catalan, [ẹ] in Northern Catalan, and [ə] in Balearic (the only dialect with tonic [ə]):

lat. rēs > cat. *res* ([ˈrɛs], [ˈres], [ˈrẹs], [ˈrəs])

lat. fĭde > cat. *fe* ([ˈfɛ], [ˈfe], [ˈfẹ], [ˈfə])

Apart from phonetics, another field of dialectologic distinction is verbal morphology (verb endings). Central Catalan, Valencian, Balearic, north-western, and northern Catalan show different systems, although this is only seen in some persons, tenses, and conjugations. The most distinctive example is the first person singular ('I' form) of the present indicative tense of the first conjugation:

1st pers sg pres ind of *cantar* 'I sing':

Central	North-western	Valencian	Balearic	Northern
canto	*canto*	*cante*	*cant*	*canti*
['kantu]	['kanto]	['kante]	['kant]	['kanti]

Also, the definite article is an important source of differences. Balearic dialects and also the speech of certain spots of Costa Brava use a form of the definite article called the 'article salat', derived from Latin IPSE, consisting of *es* (masculine sg) / *sa* (feminine sg) / *s'* (masculine and feminine sg followed by a word initial vowel) / *es* (masculine pl) / *ses* (feminine pl), and, in Majorca and Eivissa, also *so* (masculine ablative sg) / *sos* (masculine ablative pl) after preposition *amb*. However, there is a long tradition of avoiding the 'article salat' both in written and in formal spoken language. Evidence of a greater extensive use of this article is visible in place names out of the domain where it is currently used, as *Sant Joan Despí* (<des Pi), *Coll Sacabra* (< sa Cabra), *Sant Climent Sescebes* (< ses Cebes). The rest of Catalan makes use of the definite article deriving from Latin ILLE: *el* / *la* / *l'* / *els* / *les*, with *el* / *els* being substituted by *lo* / *los* in informal north-western Catalan.

Although all these forms and all verbal systems are seen as correct, the greater circulation of central Catalan forms makes them good candidates for the standard language when used for an unknown audience. These are the forms to be found in this grammar.

In any case, all dialects are mutually intelligible and native speakers are accustomed to hearing the main ones.

Chapter 5

Pronunciation and spelling

The only Catalan sounds that are not used in standard English are the following:

/r/, spelled <r> at the start of a word or after a consonant other than <p, t, c, b, d, g, f>, and <rr> between two vowels: this is a strong *r*, produced by a vibration, not just one flap, of the tongue tip against the alveolar ridge, i.e. the area just between the upper teeth and the palate: *carro* 'cart', *rosa* 'rose'

/ɾ/, spelled <r> between two vowels or after <p, t, c, b, d, g, f>: it is a soft, single flap of the tongue tip against the alveolar ridge: *cara* 'face', *tres* 'three'

/ɲ/, spelled <ny>: pronounced as a nasal, but with the tongue blade against the palate. It is similar to English <ny> in *canyon*, but compressed into one sound: *canya* 'cane, rod', *seny* 'sanity, common sense'

/ʎ/, spelled <ll>: pronounced as an <l>, but with the tongue blade against the palate, as a fusion between /l/ and /j/ in a single sound: *llar* 'fireplace', *colla* 'group, gang', *pell* 'skin'

Also some vowels differ due to the fact that Catalan has only short vowels, some of which coincide only with the onset of English diphthongs, as explained below.

5.1 Vowels

All vowels in Catalan are short, and are 'pure', which means that they do not have rounded endings, unlike what often happens in English. There are seven tonic vowels (eight in Balearic):

/i/ as in 'me', and the start of English 'feel'. *Pi* 'pine tree', *sí* 'yes', *dir* 'to say'.

/e/ as in English 'café', but shorter and pure with no [ɪ] ending. *Sé* 'I know', *més* 'more', *déu* 'god'. It is also the same as in French *les* 'the (feminine pl)' or Spanish *tres* 'three'.

/ɛ/ as in English 'bed'. *Verd* 'green', *tècnic* 'technical'.

/a/ as in the start of English 'time' and 'out'. *Pa* 'bread', *àcid* 'acid'. As in French *las* 'tired' or Spanish *da* '(s/he / it) gives'

/ɔ/ as in English 'fall', although shorter. *Or* 'gold', *port* 'harbour'

/o/ as in English 'go', but shorter and pure, with no [ʊ] ending. *Sóc* '(I) am', *dos* 'two'

/u/ as in English 'boot', although shorter. *Tu* 'you', *comú* 'common'

(And Balearic Catalan adds /ə/ as in English *verb*, but a bit raised, as in the second syllable of *teacher*. *Verd* 'green', *seny* 'sanity, common sense'.)

A grave accent is used on open vowels /a, ɛ, ɔ/ <à, è, ò> as explained below, while an acute accent is placed on closed vowels /i, e, o, u/ <í, é, ó, ú>. The accent, grave or acute, is used according to the following rules:

a. in words where the last syllable is stressed when they finish in a vowel, a vowel followed by -s, or in -en/-in: *català* 'Catalan', *camí* 'way', *repàs* 'review', *vermellós* 'reddish', *Berlín* 'Berlin', *comprèn* '(s/he / it) understands'
b. in words where the penultimate syllable is stressed, when they do not finish in in any way listed in (a) above: *plàcid* 'placid', *còmic* 'comic', *ségol* 'rye'
c. all words where the antepenultimate syllable is stressed: *ràpida* 'fast (feminine)', *múltiple* 'multiple', *pàtria* 'homeland'

It is important to bear in mind that Catalan does not consider it a diphthong when a consonant is followed by 'i' or 'u' and then another vowel. In such cases the vowels are two separate syllables, as in the last example above: *pà-tri-a*. In reality and in spoken language, the vowel cluster is often being pronounced as a single syllable, especially when it appears after the word stress. Nevertheless, Catalan normally does consider it a diphthong when a consonant is followed by a vowel and then 'i' or 'u'. In this case the final vowel is not considered as a full vowel, and, for this reason, words like *anàveu* '(you pl) went' receive graphic accent, and *aneu* '(you pl) go', with tonic last syllable, does not – following rule (a) above.

Some words receive a diacritical accent, meaning that the accent is there just because otherwise they would be identical to another word. See the following list:

bé 'well, good (n.)'	*be* 'lamb'
déu 'god'	*deu* 'ten', '(s/he / it) must'
és '(s/he / it) is'	es (3rd pers reflexive or impersonal pronoun), (definite article)
mà 'hand'	*ma* 'my' (for a sg feminine possession)
més 'more'	*mes* 'month', 'my' (for a pl feminine possession), 'but'
món 'world'	*mon* 'my' (for a sg masculine possession)
pèl 'hair, fur'	*pel* (contraction = *per* + *el*)
què 'what' (an interrogative pronoun, also a relative pronoun after a preposition)	*que* 'that (a relative pronoun)'
sé 'I know'	*se* (3rd pers reflexive or impersonal pronoun in certain combinations)
sí 'yes'	*si* (3rd pers reflexive tonic pronoun), 'bosom', 'B note'
sol 'sun', 'alone', 3rd pers. sing. present indicative of *soler*	*sòl* 'soil'
són 'they are'	*son* 'his/her/their' (for a sg masculine possession); 'sleep' (noun), 'sleepiness'
té '(s/he / it) has', 'have it!' (2nd pers sg imperative)	*te* 'tea', 'you' (sg object or reflexive pronoun in certain combinations)
ús 'usage'	*us* 'you' (sg object or reflexive pronoun)

vós 'you' (polite treatment)	*vos* 'you' (sg object or reflexive pronoun in certain combinations)

Open and closed *e* and open and closed *o* are easy to distinguish by their written form, when there is an accent mark on them:

<é> is for closed /e/ as in *consomé* 'broth', *seré* '(I) shall be', *Dénia* (place name)

<è> is for open /ɛ/ as in *ciència* 'science', *herència* 'inheritance', *serè* 'serene'

(<è> also stands for /ə/ in Balearic Catalan, and there is no easy way to figure out from the written form how to pronounce it, whether /ə/ or /ɛ/: *serè* is pronounced with an [ə], while *herència* is pronounced with an [ɛ])

<ó> is for /o/ as in *canó* 'canyon', *meló* 'melon'

<ò> is for /ɔ/ as in *còmic* 'comic', *ressò* 'echo'

When no written accent is present, then there are no clear rules to decide whether the vowel is open or closed: *bec* [e] 'beak' / *bec* [ɛ] '(I) drink', *moc* [ɔ] '(I) move' / *moc* [o] 'mucus'. However, certain tendencies can be observed, bearing in mind that only experience (and a good dictionary) can supply the learner with the real pronunciation; there are many exceptions to the following:

i. suffixes *–er*, *–ment*, *–or* have closed vowels: *argenter* 'silversmith', *ametller* 'almond tree', *agraïment* 'thanks', *lentament* 'slowly' ([e]), *actor* 'actor', *professor* 'lecturer', *menjador* 'dining room' ([o])
ii. the presence of <i> in a following syllable contributes to openness: *misteri* 'mystery', *tebi* 'warm', *col·legi* 'school' ([ɛ]), *borni* 'one-eyed', *foli* 'sheet of paper', *boira* 'fog' ([ɔ]). A significant exception is in subjunctive forms – *i* does not change the vowel in the verbal root, which appears unchanged: *regui* [e] 'water' (1st and 3rd pers sg pres subj) / *segui* 'sit' (1st and 3rd pers sg pres subj) ([ɛ]), *donin* [o] 'give' (3rd pers pl pres subj) / *posin* [ɔ] 'put' (3rd pers pl pres subj)
iii. a following <rr> or <l> usually forces <e> to be open ([ɛ]): *ferro* 'iron', *terra* 'ground', *serra* 'saw', *desferra* 'debris'; *vel* 'veil', *cel* 'sky, heaven', *mel* 'honey'

Unstressed vowels are a smaller set in comparison with stressed ones, as observed in I.4 above. In central Catalan, unstressed <e, a> are read as a schwa ([ə]), and unstressed <o> as [u]. The exceptions to this are certain combinations in which contrast would be lost if vowel reduction was performed, as in *teatre*, where the first <e> is pronounced [e], or *camaleó*, where <e> is also pronounced [e]. Acronyms and words formed with initials tend to avoid reduction, as in UNESCO or OTAN (Catalan for NATO). Also Latin or foreign borrowings can avoid it: *Boston, Washington, Salve* (lat.), *judo, soprano.*

When a word begins or ends with an unstressed <e> or <a> it is generally omitted when in contact with another vowel (ending or starting the previous or following word): *última hora* 'last hour' is pronounced as *últim' hora* (<h> is always unpronounced), and *espera una hora amb aquesta amiga* ('wait one hour with this (female) friend' as *esper' un' hor' amb aquest' amiga.* The same can happen between two identical vowels (again, across a word boundary): *dono un poc de pa* '(I) give some bread' as *don' un poc de pa* (remember that *dono* is pronounced *donu* due to vowel reduction), *passi immediatament* 'come in (polite) immediately'. However, stress on one of the two vowels can avoid elision, as in *canti himnes* (both <i>'s pronounced) 'sing (polite) hymns'.

5.2 Reading and pronouncing consonants

Catalan plosives are never pronounced as aspirated – aspiration is the puff of air escaping between the consonant sound itself and the beginning of the vowel in stressed syllables in English, as in *tea, pea, cake.* In contrast, voiced plosives, <b, d, g> (when a hard 'g' as in *gat* [g] 'cat' (and like English 'goat'), and not a soft 'g' as in 'girar' [ʒ] 'to turn', (as in English 'measure') sound softer than in English, especially between two vowels or between vowels, fricatives, and trills (in any order): *acabar, cada dia, agradar*, as if the closure making the sound were not complete.

All plosives at the end of words are pronounced as unvoiced. For this reason <b, d, g>, when at the end of words, are read the same way as if they were written <p, t, c>, as in *tub enorme* 'huge tube', *record amarg* 'sour memory', *mag anglès* 'English magician'.

<bl> and <gl> between two vowels are reinforced as if they were <bbl>, <ggl> (except for when a word begins with groups <abl> or <agl>: *agradable* 'nice' is read as if *agradabble*, and *segle* 'century' as if *seggle.*

<mp>, <mb>, <nt>, <nd>, <nk>, <ng> lose their second element (<p>, <t>, <d>, <k>, <g>) when at the end of words, except in the word *amb* 'with' when a vowel follows *amb alegria* 'with happiness, happily'.

<s> is pronounced unvoiced, as in English 'soap' or 'classic', when it is at the start of a word or after another consonant: *sabata* 'shoe', *cansat* 'tired'.

Between two vowels, the same sound is written with <ss>: *passa* 'step', *fossis* 'you were (2nd pers sg past subj)'. The same sound can appear written in certain words as <ç> (before <a, o, u>) or <c> (before <e, i>) due to etymology: *caça* 'hunt', *peça* 'piece', *cera* 'wax', *ciri* 'candle'.

<s> is pronounced voiced, as in English 'reason' or 'zero' when it appears between two vowels, even if the first is the final vowel of a diphthong: *cosa* 'thing', *Àsia* 'Asia', *causa* 'cause'; and also in words derived from *dins* 'inside' and *fons* 'bottom, fund': *endinsar* 'to insert', *enfonsar* 'to sink'. <z> stands for the same sound: *zebra* 'zebra', *zero* 'zero'.

<j> is pronounced as <s> in English 'measure' or 'treasure' as in *rajar* 'to flow' or j*ove* 'young', and the same sound is pronounced when reading <g> before <e, i>: *girar* 'to turn', *ragen* 'they flow'. Notice that as the vowel changes in the verb ending, the consonant changes too so that the soft 'g' sound is retained (rajar > ragen). <tj> and <tg> are read as the <g> in English 'region' or even with a greater emphasis on the initial closure: *desi*tg*en* 'they wish', *desi*tj*ar* 'to wish' – again, notice that the change in the consonant is caused by the changing vowel.

<x> is pronounced as <sh> in English: *xai* 'lamb', *anxova* 'anchovy', and the same sound is written as <ix>, with an unpronounced <i> when following a vowel: *caixa* 'box', *peix* 'fish'. Only when the <i> is the only vowel preceding <x> is it pronounced: *ix* '(s/he / it) goes out', *Flix* (a place name). When not preceded by <i> between vowels, <x> is pronounced as in English: *òxid* 'oxid', *examen* 'exam'. <tx> [ʧ] is pronounced as English <ch> in 'chocolate': *retxa* 'stripe', *cotxe* 'car', *despatx* 'office'. The combination <ig> at the end of a word is the same [ʧ] sound, where <i> is not pronounced except when preceded by a consonant: *maig* [maʧ] 'May', *mig* [miʧ] 'half'.

<h> is never pronounced in Catalan.

All fricatives are read as voiced when they come at the end of a word and are then followed by a vowel at the start of the next word: *do*s *amics* 'two friends' (with a [z]), *mate*ix *home* 'same man' (with a [ʒ]).

See above on <r>, <rr>, <ny>, and <ll>, and bear in mind that the final <-r> is normally not pronounced in endings *–er* (*ferrer* 'smith') and *–or* (*corredor* 'corridor, runner'), and infinitives (except when followed by an unstressed pronoun) (*menjar* 'to eat', *témer* 'to fear)'

<l·l> is a distinctive spelling in Catalan to avoid confusion between two /l/ sounds and the palatal sound /ʎ/ (written <ll>). In fact, most of the words showing <l·l> are pronounced as with a single <l>, and <l·l> remains only due to etymological reasons.

PART II

Words, word groups, and word formation

Chapter 6

Word classes

6.1 Nouns

Decades ago grammars would describe nouns as words describing people or things, but there are many examples that go beyond this: abstract concepts such as 'love' and 'hate', actions such as 'slap' and 'run', and more. Here we shall look at properties of nouns that will help us to understand how they work, and what we can do with them:

- In terms of **syntax**, nouns can either be the subject, object, or complement of a clause. They are also the head of a noun phrase, which means they will often be preceded by a determiner (such as an **article, see p. 32**) and can be qualified by **adjectives** and **adjectival phrases** (**see p. 24**).
- Nouns have different forms, and in Catalan these changes denote singulars and plurals, as well as masculine and feminine gender.
- Nouns can be created from other words, whether these are verbs, adjectives, or even other nouns (**see p. 121**).

In Catalan all nouns are marked for grammatical gender, as opposed to English, which only has natural gender. This means that all nouns in Catalan are either masculine or feminine, and this might have nothing to do with the gender of what they refer to (and so *persona* (person) is always feminine whether it refers to a man or a woman, and *jovent* (youth) is always masculine whether it refers to boys, girls, or a mix of both). This means that all determiners (including articles) and all adjectives qualifying a noun have to agree with it in both gender and number. See below for specific agreement rules for mixed genders and numbers in lists.

Nouns can be divided into different categories: first, they can either be **proper** nouns or **common** nouns. Proper nouns refer to specific places, people, times, events, and so on. As in English, these are written with a capital letter. Common nouns can be divided again into **count** and **mass** nouns. Count nouns are things that can be counted; as opposed to mass nouns (you can say 'one book, two books', but not 'one music, two musics'). Count and mass nouns can both be divided further still into **abstract** and **concrete** nouns. Concrete nouns are concepts that can be observed and measured (such as 'cow', 'computer', 'petrol'), whereas abstract nouns cannot ('love', 'beauty', and 'ease'). There are some nouns that allow both abstract and concrete usage, and so the division is not clear-cut.

6.1.1 Marking nouns for gender

There are no set noun endings in Catalan for different forms, but some are more common than others.

Final consonant, –e, –o and diphthongs tend to be masculine: *cap, braç, ull; ase, frare, conte, batlle, desembre, diable; mosso, carro, amo; peu, altaveu, europeu;* also suffixes *–atge, –isme, –aire: guiatge, abordatge, ultratge; absolutisme, cristianisme, cinisme; drapaire, cantaire, dansaire*. But, there are feminine words with the same endings: *flor, paret, font; mare, base, piràmide, imatge; moto, foto, libido; veu, creu, deu.*

The most typical feminine ending is –a. The following suffixes are also feminine: *–ió, –or, –itud, –edat, –etat*: *dona, cadira, ombra*; *unió, comissió, alteració*; *fredor, calentor*; *solitud, inquietud*; *pietat, brevetat*; *soledat, fluixedat.* However, some of these endings are shared by masculines: *papa, profeta, problema*; *guió, tió, milió*; *dolor, amor.*

In short, as a rule of thumb, if a noun ends in an 'a' it is probably feminine (with some very common exceptions), and in any case it is best to check in a dictionary when not sure. Also, see p. 139 for gender agreement with multiple nouns.

6.1.2 Marking nouns for number

As a basic rule, the plural of nouns (as well as determiners, pronouns, and adjectives) is made by adding a final -s. However, some peculiarities need to be born in mind:

a) an unstressed final -a turns into -es when followed by an -s ending, both for masculines and feminines: *casa – cases*, *dona – dones*, *grossa – grosses, vermella – vermelles, meva – meves, poeta – poetes, papa – papes, problema – problemes*. This may alter the consonant to be used before the -es ending to maintain pronunciation (see page 17), as in *paga – pagues, roja – roges, mitja – mitges, caça – caces, coca – coques*.

b) words ending in -s, -ç, -ix add an 'o' between this stem-final consonant and plural -s so it is clear the word is a plural: *cas – casos, avanç – avanços, peix – peixos*. At the end of a word in the singular, there is no way of knowing whether an 's' is related to a voiced consonant [z] or to an unvoiced one [s], since 's' is unvoiced in this final position. So, some words ending in -s in the singular end in -ssos in the plural, while others end in -sos, such as *gas – gasos, nas – nassos*. A good dictionary will always provide the answer. The same can be said about masculine/feminine alternations in adjectives and nouns, such as *ras – rasa, rus – russa*. Such alternations are not found when the final -s is preceded by a consonant. In this case, a single 's' is written and pronounced as unvoiced [s]: *pols – polsos, ascens – ascensos, cors – corsos*. Feminines ending in -ç add an -s when nouns and -es when adjectives, making the ending -ces to maintain pronunciation, as in *falç – falçs, feliç – felices*. Those ending in an -x when pronounced as English 'x' just add a final -s with no change to the sound of the word, such as *apèndix – apèndixs, esfinx – esfinxs, índex – índexs*.

c) masculine words ending in -tx add -os for the plural, such as *despatx – despatxos, cartutx – cartutxos*. Those ending in -ig, read as an affricate (similar to English '-tch' or '-itch', see page 18), also add -os, turning the final -ig into -jos or -tjos (depending on the word and without any clear rule, so check the dictionary), or conserve the 'i' if it is preceded by a consonant, as in *faig – fajos, lleig – lletjos, desig – desitjos*. In these -ig cases, the plural can also be achieved by simple addition of -s: *faigs, lleigs, desigs*. However, the feminine form of adjectives ending in -ig always become -(t)ja for the singular, and -(t)ges for the plural: *lletja – lletges, mitja – mitges*.

d) masculine words ending in -sc, -st, -sp, and -xt usually add an 'o' between the stem and the plural -s. However, this is not compulsory: *discs – discos, costs – costos, cresps – crespos, mixts – mixtos*. The rule is blocked in *aquest*, admitting only *aquests* (not **aquestos*). The feminine nouns *forest* and *post* do not add an extra vowel: *forests, posts*.

e) many nouns end with a stressed vowel, and also many adjectives in their masculine singular form. In general, these words are made out of stems ending with an -n, which, although not seen in the masculine, reappears in the plural: *germà – germans, alè – alens, pi – pins, raó – raons, comú – comuns*. This 'n' is also found in the feminine: *català – catalana, bru – bruna*. However, many loanwords or words not derived from Latin lack this underlying 'n'. So, we see *sofà – sofàs*, *cafè – cafès*, *consomé – consomés*, *bisturí – bisturís*, *bambú – bambús*, as well as *fe – fes*, *mercè – mercès*, *nu – nus*, *cru – crus*, and also the names of letters, musical notes, and grammatical words (conjunctions and adverbs: see page 124): *tres ces*, *dos las*, *massa perquès*, *quants demàs*.

f) some words do not change between the singular and plural. They end with an -s in the singular, and many of them, although not all, are either stressed on either the second or third from last syllable or end in two consonants: *plebs*, *urbs*, *dilluns* (see page 202), *llapis*, *atles*, *pàncrees*, *pelvis*.
g) in some dialects (Western and Ibizan), there are some words stressed on the second from last syllable that have an underlying 'n' that emerges in the plural: *ase – ases/àsens*, *jove – joves/jóvens*, *home – homes/hòmens*, *cove – coves/còvens*, *rave – raves/ràvens*.

See also Section 10.2 for the behaviour of compounds in the singular and plural.

6.2 Adjectives

The function of adjectives in Catalan does not differ from their function in English; they indicate some kind of quality or feature of a noun. They are used differently though, since they agree in gender and number with the noun they qualify, they frequently come after the noun, qualifying suffixes can be added to adjectives (see p. 114), pronominal use is different, and there is a more restrictive use of nouns as adjectives (such as in the English 'junk food').

For gender and number, the normal ending for the feminine is -a (and if the masculine adjective ends in -e, then -a takes its place), and an -s is added for the plural. Be sure to look at 6.1.2 above for all of the combinations and spellings – notables, a feminine plural adjective will normally end in -es. Two notable endings not covered above are when the masculine adjective ends in -au, -iu or -ou, where the 'u' normally becomes a 'v' in the feminine, and also when the masculine adjective ends in an unvoiced plosive -t or -c, which becomes voiced with the addition of the feminine -a. So, we get *blau – blava*, *viu – viva* and *nou – nova*, as well as *mut – muda*, and *cec – cega*. There are, however, exceptions, where the consonant does not change. Also, some adjectives are invariable for gender. In any event, a good dictionary will always show whether or not an adjective is invariable for gender, and what the spelling of the feminine should be, so it is best to check each case there.

6.2.1 *Placing adjectives*

The normal place for a qualifying adjective in Catalan is after the noun:

M'agraden les cases grans
I like large houses

Les coses importants no poden esperar
Important things cannot wait

Posi'm dues llibretes vermelles
Give me two red notebooks

El meu germà és l'ovella negra de la família
My brother is the black sheep of the family

No hi ha pa blanc, només hi ha pa negre
There isn't any white bread, only brown

The above applies when the adjective is restrictive, that is, it identifies the noun more specifically through an inherent characteristic. When the usage is non-restrictive the adjective can appear before the noun. In this sense, it is either giving additional information, emphasising an aspect of the noun, or expressing an attitude on the part of the speaker. This usually occurs with *bo* (adopting the form *bon* for masculine singular in this position):

En Miquel és un bon amic
Miquel is a good friend

Sa mare és bona persona
His mum is a good person

The same could be said about other non–restrictive adjectives (epithets): *gran, magnífic, excel·lent, òptim, previsible*, and so on.

The opposite of *bo* is *dolent*. As an epithet, however, it changes to *mal, mala, mals, males*:

En Miquel és un mal amic
Miquel is a bad friend

Sa mare és mala persona
His mum is a bad person

Compare now the sentences above with others showing a contrastive use of the same adjectives:

La xocolata bona és més cara que la xocolata dolenta
Good (i.e. good quality) chocolate is more expensive than bad (quality) chocolate

Gran, grans changes its meaning according to its position: after the noun it means 'large' or 'elderly' (the latter only applied to people); before the noun it means 'great':

És una gran dona
She is a great woman

És una dona gran
She is an elderly lady

Pobre, pobra, pobres means 'poor' (lacking financial means) when placed after the noun; before the noun it means 'miserable', 'worthy of compassion'. Again, in English different words are often used to make a distinction, since in the following example 'poor' would be ambiguous in both cases:

Es veia que la casa pertanyia a una família pobra
It was apparent that the house belonged to a family with little money

Es veia que la casa pertanyia a una pobra família
It was apparent that the house belonged to an unfortunate family

It is not rare to find adjectives preceding the noun in poetry and in other marked uses of languages, as in titles:

els gegantins turons d'Andalusia (Verdaguer)
the great hills of Andalusia

sol i de dol, i amb vetusta gonella (Foix)
Alone and in mourning, and in ancient robes

el Molt Honorable President de la Generalitat de Catalunya
The Right Honourable President of the *Generalitat* of Catalonia

la noble vila de Perpinyà
The noble town of Perpignan

When articles, possessives, demonstratives, or quantifiers are added to a noun phrase, the adjectives maintain their position by the noun:

algun home bo / algun bon home
any arbitrator / any good man

aquests homes grans ja no condueixen / aquests grans homes han fet grans coses
these elderly men no longer drive / these great men have performed great deeds

un parell de sabates vermelles
a pair of red shoes

When the noun phrase is introduced by a quantifying expression, as in the last example above, the adjective can qualify either the grouping noun (i.e. the noun in the quantifying expression) or the main noun. It is important to ensure that the adjective agrees with the appropriate noun:

una colla d'estudiants ben selecta / una colla d'estudiants ben selectes
a very select group of students / a group of very select students

un parell de sabates vermell / un parell de sabates vermelles
a red pair of shoes / a pair of red shoes

'*un parell vermell de sabates*' is also possible, and a good solution when both nouns are the same number and gender, and so agreement does not help to resolve any ambiguity. This would be so with the following case, where the difference in meaning may be not completely futile:

dos parells d'amics ben avinguts / dos parells ben avinguts d'amics
Two pairs of friends that get on well (i.e. the friends get on well) / two pairs of friends who get on well (i.e. the pairs of friends get on well)

6.2.2 *Modifying adjectives (for comparison, see p. 182; for consecutive clauses see p. 154)*

The meaning of adjectives can be accentuated or mellowed by means of a preceding adverb, as in English 'very'. Usual modifiers of adjectives in Catalan are: *molt / no gaire, poc, ben, massa,* (*no*) *gens, gairebé*, together with many intensifiers and moderators. Here are some uses of this type of adverb in non-attributive sentences:

Dues senyores *molt* resolutives ens han solventat el problema.
Two very decisive women have solved the problem for us.

Dues persones *no gaire* intel·ligents no poden atendre el public.
Two rather unintelligent people (lit. not very intelligent) cannot see to customers.

Un got *ben* ple de vi és el que necessito.
A good glass of wine (lit. a very full glass of wine) is what I need.

En vaig pagar un preu *massa* alt.
I paid too high a price for it.

Uns preus *(no) gens* alts servien per atreure els turistes.
Low prices (lit. not at all high prices) were good to pull the tourists in.

Ens van rebre amb una actitud *gairebé* servil.
They welcomed us with an almost obsequious attitude.

Ens van asseure en uns bancs *completament* molls.
They sat us on some completely soaking benches.

Has escrit unes històries *fortament* inspirades per les teves experiències.
You have written some stories inspired strongly by your own experience.

It is important to realise that when used as adverbs, *molt, poc*, and *gaire* do not change to agree in gender or number (see p. 83 and p. 85).

6.2.3 *Pronominal uses of adjectives*

Adjectives in Catalan can appear with no mention of the noun they qualify when this can be inferred from the context. This is a frequent problem for English-language learners of Catalan, since English requires either a repeat of the noun or the insertion of a token pronoun such as 'one':

Quins pantalons t'agraden més, els blaus o els blancs?
Which trousers do you like best, the blue ones or the white ones?

Les flors grosses són per a la sala, i les petites per al rebedor.
The large flowers are for the living room, and the small ones for the entrance.

When the inferred construction (i.e. the use of the adjective with the noun omitted) is not introduced by a definite article or a demonstrative, and the adjective alone takes the place of a noun in the role of subject or object, the preposition *de* is needed, and the unstressed pronoun *en/-ne* is also called into action (see the use of *en/-ne* in p. 95):

– Com són les teves camises? – *En* tinc *de* primes i *de* gruixudes *(two coordinated objects)***.**
'What are your shirts like?' 'I've got thin ones and thick ones.'

Li va donar una carta oficial i una *de* particular. *('particular'* *not alone as an object***)**
She gave him an official letter and a private one.

– Que tenen vi? – Sí, però *de* negre ja no *en* queda *('en' – 'de negre'* *as subject***)**
'Have you got any wine?' 'Yes, but there's no red left.'

When no noun can be inferred, the adjective stands for a noun meaning a quality in absolute terms:

Sempre m'ha agradat més el salat que no pas el dolç.
I've always preferred savoury food to sweet.

L'important és no perdre el ritme.
What matters is not to lose (our) rhythm.

El barat a la llarga surt car.
Cheap things turn out expensive in the long run.

When an adverb is used to modify the adjective, then the demonstrative pronoun *allò* can appear instead of article *el*:

Sempre m'ha agradat més allò fortament salat que no pas allò massa dolç.
I've always preferred truly savoury food over really sweet things.

Allò més important és no perdre el ritme.
The most important thing of all is not to lose (our) rhythm.

Allò molt barat a la llarga surt car.
Really cheap things turn out expensive in the long run

6.2.4 *Adjectival use of nouns*

In English it is common to use nouns as adjectives, such as in 'junk food', 'library books', or even 'man hugs'. The adjectival use of nouns is more restricted in Catalan than in English: prepositional phrases (see p. 106), or adjectives created from nouns by suffixation (see p. 123) are the usual translations into Catalan of this type of construction:

faculty members – **membres de la facultat**

bank account – **compte bancari**

university degree – **títol universitari**

house insurance – **assegurança de la llar**

There are no rules on whether a derived adjective or a prepositional phrase is to be chosen. In addition, in certain cases, midway between compounds and adjectival nouns, we find

jutge àrbitre / jutges àrbitre or jutges àrbitres (arbitrating judge)

dona policia / dones policia (female police officer)

camió cisterna / camions cisterna ((lorry) tanker)

sofà llit / sofàs llit (sofa bed)

bar restaurant / bars restaurant (bar and restaurant)

where a tendency is observed for limiting number inflection to the first element (see p. 128 on compounds).

English also easily derives adjectives from verbs by using a present participle ('the coming year') or a gerund ('a changing room', i.e. a room where one can change, not a room that changes). Only the first option is available in Catalan, and limited to certain collocations. It requires the noun to be the subject of the verb, and the sense of the verb to be intransitive:

un món canviant – a changing world (from 'el món canvia', the world changes)

a sol ixent – at sunrise (from 'el sol ix', 'the sun rises')

aigua bullent – boiling water

aigua corrent – running water

compte corrent – current account

la Bella Dorment – Sleeping Beauty

l'any vinent – next year (lit. the coming year)

Thanks to combinations such as those above, certain present participles such as *avinent, coincident, divergent, provinent*, or *vistent* have become adjectives in their own right.

Most English adjectival constructions using a gerund or present participle can be turned into Catalan by means of prepositional or relative clauses, or a single adjective where available:

the road leading to the university – **el camí de la universitat** (prepositional phrase) / **el camí que va a la universitat** (relative clause)

waiting room – **sala d'espera** (prepositional phrase)

drinking water – **aigua potable** (single adjective)

cooking wine – **vi per a cuinar / vi de cuinar** (prepositional phrase)

drinking time – **temps per a beure / temps de beure** (prepositional phrase)

6.2.5 *Complements of adjectives*

Certain adjectives admit complements, such as in English 'sure' ('I'm sure of that') or 'easy' ('A door not easy to open'). Below is a short list of common adjectives allowing this classified according to the preposition usually appended to them:

- *a*
  al·lèrgic, aficionat, atent, contrari, destinat, disposat, favorable, fidel, idèntic, inferior, interessat, obert, tancat, superior, semblant, tendent
- *de*
  agradable, bo, capaç, còmode, content, culpable, desitjós, diferent, difícil, dur, fàcil, farcit, gelós, incapaç, innocent, interessant, mal, orgullós, partidari, ple, terrible
- *per a*
  llest, preparat, útil
- *amb*
  enfadat

The preposition *de* can also introduce adjective complements in constructions as *curt de vista* ('short-sighted'), *afavorit de nas* ('having a big nose'), *ample d'espatlles* ('with wide shoulders'), *fort de caràcter* ('of a strong character, strong-willed'), *viu de potències* ('lucid, energetic', applied to a person), *alt de sostre* ('with a high ceiling'). In all cases these constructions alter the logic relationship between nucleus and complement: *de vista curta* ('of a short sight'), *de nas afavorit, d'espatlles amples*, etc. seem more logical. However, inversions giving the adjective a complement such as those above are possible and usual when the quality described is unable to be detached from the person or object qualified by the adjective. For this reason, constructions such as **un home fosc d'ulleres* or **un quadern blanc de pàgines* are not possible.

6.3 Articles

Articles are part of a wider group of constituents of a noun phrase called **determiners**, which all together help to 'determine' what type of noun is being used in the noun phrase: proper or common, count or non-count, and definite or indefinite. The main use for articles is to indicate whether a noun is being used in a specific or generic way.

The usage of the definite and indefinite articles is broadly the same in both Catalan and English, although the principal differences will be covered below. Chief amongst these is the usage of the article when talking about nouns in a generic or indefinite way.

6.3.1 *Definite articles*

6.3.1.1 Formation

	Singular	Plural
Masculine	*el, l'* (and *en, n'* for the personal article, preceding names)	*els*
Feminine	*la, l'*	*les*

The definite article must agree in number and gender with the noun it determines, although see below for cases where there is more than one noun in a phrase.

A shortened form of the article (called a **contraction**) is used depending on the word that precedes or follows it:

6.3.1.2 Masculine singular el > l'

The masculine singular article is always contracted to **l'** when it is followed by a vowel (or an **h**, which is silent in Catalan): *l'helicòpter* (the helicopter), *l'oceà* (the ocean). In the case of initial rising diphthongs (*ia, ua, ie, ue*, etc.), the article remains in its full shape: *el iot* (the yacht), *el uadi* (the wadi). When the noun has an initial fricative followed by a consonant (typically a loanword or a Latinism), the masculine article behaves as if an initial <e> was found: *l'statu quo*, *l'striptease*, *l'ftalat* (the phthalate).

6.3.1.3 Feminine singular la > l'

The feminine singular article is contracted to **l'** when it is followed by a vowel (or an **h**) except:

- When the noun begins with an unstressed **i** or **u**, such as in *la universitat* (the university), *la unitat* ('the unity'), *la història* (the story), *la ironia* (the irony); but: *l'ungla* (the nail), *l'illa* (the island) because in these nouns the initial vowels are stressed. In common pronunciation in fact there seems to be no difference for the same reason as a final unstressed <a> is normally omitted before an initial vowel, as in *aquesta illa, una universitat* (pronounced as *aquest' illa, un' universitat*) (see p. 13).
- When the noun is the name of a letter: *la u* (the letter u), *la i* (the letter i), *la efa* (the letter f);
- With the three nouns *ira*, *host*, *una*.

The rule observed by masculines before a noun begun with a preconsonantal fricative, is not observed in the feminine, as the final <a> in the article becomes a support to build up the syllable: *la schola cantorum*.

Both articles, masculine and feminine, also contract before acronyms, initials, and numbers where their pronounced form begins with a vowel: *l'ONU* (pronounced *lonu*, with an open o, 'the UN', Catalan initials for *Organització de Nacions Unides*), *l'IEC* (pronounced *li-ec*, initials for *Institut d'Estudis Catalans*), *l'1 de desembre* (pronounced *lu de desembre*, 'the 1st of December').

6.3.1.4 Contractions with prepositions

Both the masculine singular and plural articles contract when placed after the prepositions *a*, *de*, *per*, and *ca*.

Preposition	Definite article el	els
a	al	als
de	del	dels
per	pel	pels
ca	cal	cals

This contraction is not used when the article is already contracted with the word it precedes.

Vaig al poble.
I'm going to town.

Vaig a l'altre costat del poble.
I'm going to the other side of town.

It is important to remember regional variations of the article, such as the 'article salat' in the Balearics and some parts of the Costa Brava. These are mentioned on p. 12.

6.3.1.5 Position of the definite article

The definite article precedes the noun it determines, and also any adjectives or qualifiers if these are placed before the noun:

la casa blanca – the white house.

la fredíssima ciutat d'Hèlsinki – the very cold city of Helsinki.

l'interessantíssim llibre del professor – the lecturer's very interesting book.

When there is a list of more than one noun, the article can be omitted for the second noun onwards, even if there results a lack of gender agreement:

els jugadors i els entrenadors = els jugadors i entrenadors – players and coaches.

les mares i les àvies = les mares i àvies – mothers and grandmothers.

el pare i la mare = el pare i mare – father and mother.

les imatges i quadres – images and pictures.

6.3.1.6 Usage of the definite article

The definite article is mostly used to make the noun more specific.

- Referring to something specific from somebody's immediate context or general knowledge:

  Has vist la nova pel·lícula de James Bond?
  Have you seen the new James Bond film?

- Referring back to a noun that has already been mentioned (called **anaphoric reference**), and so becomes specific:

  Tinc un cotxe i una bici, i m'agrada més la bici.
  I have a car and a bike, and I prefer the bike.

- Referring forwards, when the noun is qualified later (called **cataphoric reference**) and made more specific:

  Va veure l'home pel carrer. No sabia que aquell home era el seu pare
  He saw the man in the street. He did not know that man was his father. (Notice that as in English, this is more specific than saying *va veure un home pel carrer* – he saw a man in the street).

- Catalan also uses an article before people's names. In the masculine there is the special form *en* (or *n'*) depending on the region:

  Has vist en/el Marc?

  Have you seen Mark?

  In Central Catalan, the *en* article is mostly used before names that begin with consonants, and *l'* used before names beginning with vowels: en Miquel / l'Ignasi. For the feminine the form *na* exists, but only for the Balearic Islands – everywhere else uses *la / l'*. *La Margalida és amiga meva* – Margalida is a friend of mine.

  The personal article is avoided before the names of authors, classical figures, and famous names:

  Això ja ho va dir Aristòtil.
  This was already stated by Aristotle.

  Chomsky és el lingüista contemporani més influent.
  Chomsky is the most influential linguist of our times.

There are two instances here where English uses an article and Catalan does not: ordinals with popes and kings, and some set adverbial phrases such as *a llarg termini* 'in the long run'.

El papa Joan Pau II (read as **El papa Joan Pau Segon**). Pope John Paul II.

Felip V va acabar amb les llibertats dels catalans (read as **Felip Cinquè**). Philip V took away the Catalans' rights.

6.3.1.7 Generic nouns and noun phrases

In the vast majority of cases, Catalan uses the definite article with nouns used generically, whereas English tends not to use the article. Also, Catalan can use the singular of count nouns to refer to things generically, whereas English tends to use the plural:

El gat és un mamífer (or **Els gats són mamífers)** – Cats are mammals

Els drets del treballador (or **Els drets dels treballadors)** – Workers' rights

L'amor és molt important en la vida. – Love is very important in life.

Here a distinction needs to be drawn between generic and indefinite usage. **Generic** usage is where the noun is understood to include all instances of the noun (the examples above refer to **all** cats, **all** workers, and love as a whole concept). Indefinite usage refers to certain undefined members of a group.

L'equivalència entre llengües no existeix, segons els especialistes.
Equivalence between languages does not exist, according to specialists (i.e. all specialists).

L'equivalencia entre llengües no existeix, segons alguns especialistes.
Equivalence between languages does not exist, according to some specialists.

6.3.2 *Indefinite article*

6.3.2.1 Formation

	Singular	Plural
Masculine	un	uns
Feminine	una	unes

6.3.2.2 Position of the indefinite article

Like the definite article, the indefinite article precedes the noun, as well as anything that qualifies that noun and comes before it:

un despatx petit – a small office.

una gran empresa – a great business.

6.4 Personal (stressed) pronouns

Personal pronouns, also called stressed pronouns and strong pronouns, are those used as the subject for a sentence and those used after prepositions.

Catalan, like some of the other Romance languages, does not always use the relevant subject pronouns, and instead the subject is worked out from the verb ending (see **inflection**).

6.4.1 *Formation*

There are two ways to classify personal pronouns. One is by their meaning, in the sense of which person they refer to. The other is by **morphosyntax,** which is the form of verbs and possessives they take. For example, the formal singular form of you, *vostè*, is second person in its meaning but takes a third person verb form. Here are the pronouns in full:

By meaning

	Person	Gender	Subject	Prepositional object
singular	1st		jo (I) nós (we, i.e. the 'royal we'))	jo, mi (me) nós (us)
	2nd		tu (you, informal), vostè, vós (you, formal)	tu (you) vostè, vós (you)
	3rd	m.	ell (he)	ell, si (him)
		f.	ella (she)	ella, si (her)

	Person	Gender	Subject	Prepositional object
Plural	1st		nosaltres (we)	nosaltres (us)
	2nd		vosaltres (you, informal), vostès (you, formal), vós (you, formal)	vosaltres, vostès (you), vós (you, formal)
	3rd	m.	ells (they)	ells, si (them)
		f.	elles (they)	elles, si (them)

By morphosyntax (i.e. by word formation)

	Person	Subject	Prepositional object
singular	1st	jo	jo, mi
	2nd	tu	tu
	3rd	ell, ella, vostè	ell, ella, vostè, si
Plural	1st	nosaltres, nós	nosaltres, nós
	2nd	vosaltres, vós	vosaltres, vós
	3rd	ells, elles, vostès	ells, elles, vostès, si

See p. 189 for the selection of polite forms.

6.4.2 *Personal pronouns as prepositional objects*

In most cases the form of the pronoun is the same for both the subject and the prepositional object.

> **Tenen una cosa per a tu, per a ell, per a ella, per a vostè, per a nosaltres, per a vosaltres, per a ells, per a elles i per a vostès.**
> They have something for you, for him, for her, for you, for us, for you, for them (masculine), for them (feminine) and for you.

The only cases where they change are in the first-person singular, and some cases with the third person.

6.4.2.1 Mi

Mi is the correct form for the first-person singular after all prepositions except **segons** (according to):

Vine amb mi.
Come with me.

És un regal per a mi?
Is that a present for me?

Aquest llibre és molt bo, segons jo.
This book is very good, in my opinion.

When *mi* is introduced by a compound preposition ending in *de*, *de* and *mi* can form *meu*, but this is optional. This applies to other strong pronouns too:

No copiïs davant de mi. / No copiïs davant meu.
Don't copy in front of me.

When there is more than one object of the preposition (and so the elements are **conjoined**), **jo** is used and not **mi**.

Està contra tu i jo.
He is against you and me.

Se'n riu de jo i les meves opinions.
He laughs at me and my opinions.

In Balearic usage, it is not uncommon to hear *jo* used instead of *mi*. This is acceptable in informal speech and after stressed pronouns (p. 108), but not in a formal context.

A jo, no m'agrada carregar bales.
I don't like loading hay bales.

Vine amb jo i veuràs.
Come with me and you'll see.

6.4.2.2 Si

The form *si* is used for both singular and plural third person reflexive objects, that is, where the noun that the preposition governs refers back to the subject of the sentence. This is often (but not always) followed by *mateix*, which in turn agrees with the subject of the phrase.

Ho fa per a si mateix / Ho fa per a si mateixa.
He is doing it for himself / She is doing it for herself.

The usage of *si* is not obligatory: in the above cases *ell mateix* or *ella mateixa* could also be used, and the meaning would be the same.

6.4.3 *Subject pronouns: When to include them and when to omit them*

Since subject pronouns do not have to be used in Catalan, you only need to use them either to add emphasis or avoid confusion. The emphasis gained from including the subject pronoun would often be conveyed by a different structure (such as a **cleft structure**) in English, or by stressing the subject pronoun with your voice:

Jo te'l donaré.
I will give it to you / I'm the one who will give it you / It's me who will give it to you.

However, confusion can arise in Catalan where the same verb form could take different subjects, and this cannot be resolved from the context. For example, when asking about a boy and a girl playing in the garden, if a parent asked *Què fa?* it could mean 'What is he doing?' or 'What is she doing?', so the subject pronoun would be added (*Què fa ell? / Què fa ella?*). However, if there was just one child outside, there is no confusion, and so the subject pronoun would be omitted.

The one time when the subject pronoun is obligatory is if the verb has been elided (omitted):

Preguntes si sabem conduir? Jo no.
Are you asking whether we can drive? I can't.

6.4.4 *Pronouns and human referents*

The third-person pronouns *ell*, *ella*, *ells*, and *elles* are almost always used exclusively with human referents, not to things or concepts – to use these with non-human (or inanimate) objects is often to personify them.

6.5 Possessives and demonstratives

There are two sets of possessives in Catalan, stressed and unstressed. Stressed possessives (also called analytic possessives), are by far the most common.

6.5.1 *Stressed possessives*

Stressed possessives are a compound form – the first part of them is the definite article. Usage of the article is compulsory when the possessive is followed by a noun. There is a significant difference between Catalan and English in the form of the possessive: in English only the gender and number of the possessor is taken into account (i.e. the person possessing the object, e.g. 'his cat' vs. 'her cat'), while in Catalan both the possessor and the possession itself affect the choice of possessive. This is shown in the following table:

Possessor	Possession		Possessive
I	singular	masculine	**el meu** gos
		feminine	**la meva** mestra
	plural	masculine	**els meus** amics
		feminine	**les meves** companyes
you (familiar, singular)	singular	masculine	**el teu** cap
		feminine	**la teva** esquena
	plural	masculine	**els teus** braços
		feminine	**les teves** mans
he / she / they (and relating to *vostè*(s))	singular	masculine	**el seu** llapis
		feminine	**la seva** goma
	plural	masculine	**els seus** llibres
		feminine	**les seves** pintures

we (and forms relating to *nós*)	singular	masculine	**el nostre** fill
		feminine	**la nostra** cosina
	plural	masculine	**els nostres** veïns
		feminine	**les nostres** col·legues
you (familar, plural, and realting to *vós*)	singular	masculine	**el vostre** punt de vista
		feminine	**la vostra** opinió
	plural	masculine	**els vostres** sentiments
		feminine	**les vostres** sensacions

6.5.1.1 Possessives and articles

The article is omitted in possessives when they are used as adjectives, especially in attributive constructions, mostly with the verb *ser*, and only when the topic under focus is possessive. The possessive works as a normal adjective:

Aquest llibre no és teu.
This book does not belong to you (lit. this book is not yours) (note that **aquest llibre no és teu llibre* would be incorrect).

Aquella casa era nostra.
We used to own that house (lit. that house was ours).

However, the article reappears when possession is not the topic, but identification. The possessive then works as a pronoun:

Aquest llibre no és el teu (note that you could say *aquest llibre no és el teu llibre*, even though the repetition sounds clumsy).
This is not your book.

Aquella casa era la nostra.
Our house was that one.

When possessives work as adjectives, they can qualify a noun. In this case they do not require an article, although most times the nouns are determined by other means. The normal place for possessives used as adjectives is after the noun, as with most other adjectives in Catalan:

He conegut dos amics teus.
I have met two friends of yours.

Aquelles dites seves que tant enyorem.
Those sayings of his that we miss so much.

Crec que algunes coses nostres us servirien.
I think that some of our things will be of use to you.

6.5.1.2 Under-use of possessives

There are contexts where English would use a possessive, but Catalan would not. When possession is clear in a given context, possessives tend to disappear:

Va alçar la seva mà would mean 'S/he raised her/his (=someone else's) hand'

but **Va alçar la mà** 'S/he raised her/his (own) hand' (see below for dative replacing possessives).

Va deixar els diners dins la seva cartera would mean 'S/he left the money in her/his (=someone else's) purse'

but **Va deixar els diners dins la cartera** 'S/he left the money in her/his (own) purse'.

When the possessor and the subject of the verb coincide, and the verb is an action applied on the subject, a reflexive construction is the right solution to translate English possessives:

'I can't reach my toes.' → **No m'arribo als dits dels peus.**

'He is rubbing his eyes.' → **Es frega els ulls.**

'Spread this cream on your face.' → **Escampa't aquesta pomada per la cara.**

Dative pronouns (see p. 100) make possessives unnecessary, especially when possessives are not contrastive:

Amaga-li els llibres.
Hide her/his books.

Et prendré la targeta de credit.
I'll take away your credit card.

La perruquera els tallava els cabells.
The hairdresser trimmed their hair.

Fermeu-vos les sabates.
Tie your shoelaces.

Possessives are normally avoided when the possessor would be an inanimate object. When this is the case, other solutions are preferred:

Agafo el llibre per fotocopiar-ne el primer capítol – 'I'm taking your book to photocopy its first chapter' (lit. to photocopy the first chapter of it), preferred to *Agafo el teu llibre per fotocopiar el seu primer capítol.*

Va llogar la casa i les dependències annexes – 'He rented the house and its annexes', preferred to *Va llogar la casa i les seves dependències annexes.*

6.5.2 *Unstressed possessives*

The second set of possessives in Catalan are the unstressed possessives, which take the following forms:

Possessor	Possession		Possessive
I	singular	masculine	**mon** pare
		feminine	**ma** mare
	plural	masculine	**mos** avis
		feminine	**mes** ties
you (singular)	singular	masculine	**ton** pare
		feminine	**ta** mare
	plural	masculine	**tos** avis
		feminine	**tes** ties
s/he	singular	masculine	**son** pare
		feminine	**sa** mare

	plural	masculine	**sos** avis
		feminine	**ses** ties
they	singular		**llur** dret **llur** casa
	plural		**llurs** comptes **llurs** pertinences

The use of *mon, ton, son* is restricted to close relatives, as in the examples above, although they can also appear in texts that either aim to be archaic or that follow dated forms of writing (such as old-fashioned styles of poetry). *Llur(s)* appears only in highly formal styles. They all can be replaced by their corresponding possessives from the stressed series.
Unstressed possessives can only appear before the noun they determine:

> *__Aquesta foto és de mon pare, no de ton.__ → ✓__Aquesta foto és de mon pare, no del teu__

> *__Aquests llibres són nostres, no llurs.__ → ✓__Aquests llibres són nostres, no seus__

6.5.3 Demonstratives

Like English, Catalan has (in most cases) two levels of demonstratives, indicating 'this' and 'that'. These can act both as adjectives and pronouns ('this one', 'that one'), and are inflected for gender and number. The forms for 'this' and 'these' are *aquest*, *aquesta*, *aquests* and *aquestes*, and the forms for 'that' and 'those' are *aquell*, *aquella*, *aquells*, and *aquelles*. Note that the first 's' of *aquests* is always silent, and the 's' in *aquest* is only pronounced if the demonstrative is followed by a noun beginning with a vowel, such as *aquest home* 'this man'.

There is a difference in usage between English and Catalan, where Catalan uses *aquest* and English 'that'. This is when the object being referred to is held by the second person (the person being addressed by the speaker). So, *Què fas amb aquest llibre?* would be 'What are you doing with this book?' if the person speaking is holding the book, and 'What are you doing with that book?' if the book is being held by the person spoken to.

There are also the neuter demonstrative pronouns *això* 'this' and *allò* 'that', such as in *Vols un poc d'això o d'allò?* 'Do you want a bit of this or that?'. See page 29 on usages of *allò* in pronominal adjectives, and page 92 on how *això* and *allò* relate to the neuter pronoun *ho*.

6.6 Quantifiers

6.6.1 *Numbers*

0	zero				
1	u / un / una	7	set	13	tretze
2	dos / dues	8	vuit	14	catorze
3	tres	9	nou	15	quinze
4	quatre	10	deu	16	setze
5	cinc	11	onze	17	disset
6	sis	12	dotze	18	divuit
19	dinou	23	vint-i-tres	32	trenta-dos / trenta-dues
20	vint	29	vint-i-nou	33	trenta-tres
21	vint-i-u / vint-i-un / vint-i-una	30	trenta	40	quaranta
22	vint-i-dos / vint-i-dues	31	trenta-u / trenta-un / trenta-una	50	cinquanta
60	seixanta	70	setanta	80	vuitanta
90	noranta	100	cent	101	cent u / cent un / cent una
121	cent vint-i-u / cent vint-i-un / cent vint-i-una	139	cent trenta-nou	200	dos-cents / dues-centes

300	tres-cents / tres-centes	428	quatre-cents vint-i-vuit / quatre-centes vint-i-vuit	572	cinc-cents setanta-dos / cinc-centes setanta-dues

1.000	mil
2.000	dos mil / dues mil
3.125	tres mil cent vint-i-cinc
1.000.000	un milió
1.357.862	un milió tres-cents cinquanta-set mil vuit-cents seixanta-dos / un milió tres-centes cinquanta-set mil vuit-centes seixanta-dues
2.000.000	dos milions
1.000.000.000.000	un bilió (an English trillion)
1.000.000.000.000.000.000	un trilió

6.6.1.1 Remarks

- *u / un / una*
  un / una works as a determiner or as a pronoun: *he comprat un quilo de patates* 'I have bought one kilo of potatoes', *He comprat una bossa de patates* 'I have bought a bag of potatoes'. *U* is used in abstract quantities, as in arithmetical operations: *Vint-i-u més trenta fan cinquanta-u*, but either *u* or *un* can be used when counting: *un, dos, tres, quatre . . ., u, dos, tres, quatre.*
- *u, un / una* and *dos / dues*
  These quantifiers differ in gender: *u / un* and *dos* for masculine, and *una* and *dues* for feminine, depending on the gender of the noun (see p. 22 on this). The distinction applies also to compounds: *dues-centes imatges* 'two hundred pictures', *vint-i-dues coses* 'twenty-two things', *cinquanta-una històries* 'fifty-one stories'. However, the gender distinction is cancelled when numbers are used with an ordinal sense, i.e. when the word 'number' may be supposed: *Viu a la planta dos* 'She lives on the second floor', *Això apareix a la pàgina trenta-u* 'This appears on page thirty-one'.

- A mnemonic for the use of a hyphen is Tens-Units-Hundreds (T-U-H). On the other hand, try to remember that no hyphen is attached to the words *mil*, *milió*, *miliard*, *bilió*, *trilió*, etc., or after *cent*.

6.6.2 Ordinals

From one to four, the form of ordinals is different to cardinal numbers:

1r/1a *primer / primera / primers / primeres* 'first'

2n/2a *segon / segona / segons / segones* 'second'

3r/3a *tercer / tercera / tercers / terceres* 'third'

4t/4a *quart / quarta / quarts / quartes* 'fourth'

For five and beyond add *è / ena / ens / enes* with certain graphic adaptations:

5è/5a *cinquè / cinquena / cinquens / cinquenes*

9è/9a *novè / novena / novens / novenes* (but *dinouè*, *vint-i-nouè*, etc.)

10è/10a *desè / desena / desens / desenes*

For those numbers ending in <e> replace it with a stressed <è>:

Onze 'eleven' → *onzè*

Dotze 'twelve' → *dotzè*, etc.

The rule is constant: *vint-i-unè* '21st', *quaranta-dosè* '42nd', *seixanta-tresè* '63rd' (and not **vint-i-primer*, **quaranta-segon*, **seixanta-tercer*, **cent quaranta-quart*), except for the final *–s* of the number's plural: *200è dos-centè* and not **dos-centsè*

The following forms are also possible instead of the regular ones:

quint / quinta / quints / quintes '5th'

sext / sexta /sexts / sextes '6th'

sèptim / sèptima / sèptims / sèptimes '7th'

octau / octava / octaus / octaves '8th'

dècim / dècima / dècims / dècimes '10th'

centèsim / centèsima / centèsims / centèsimes '100th'

mil·lèsim / mil·lèsima / mil·lèsims / mil·lèsimes '1000th'

milionèsim / milionèsima / milionèsims / milionèsimes '1,000,000th'

etc.

The number after the name of a monarch or a pope is normally pronounced as an ordinal up to 10, and as a cardinal from 10 on:

Jaume I (primer)

Isabel II (segona)

Joan XXIII (vint-i-tres)

6.6.3 *Partitives*

mig / *mitja* / *mitjos* (or *migs*) / *mitges* is 'half' when used as an adjective:

M'ha donat mig pa.
She has given me half a loaf of bread.

M'ha donat tres mitges pomes.
She has given me three half apples.

meitat 'half' (when used as a noun):

M'ha donat tres meitats de poma.
She has given me three apple halves.

When 'a half' is to be added to a quantity, the adjective is preferred, unlike what occurs in English:

L'he esperat dues hores i mitja (*L'he esperat dues hores i meitat).
I've been waiting for him for two and a half hours.

mitjan is an invariable adjective for gender used in the phrase *a mitjan* meaning 'in the middle of, halfway through', normally used for ways and temporal units. When used in a temporal sense, it can alternate with 'a mitjans de':

A mitjan camí – at halfway, *a mitjan vol* – at halfway of flight, *a mitjan tornada* – at halway of return, *a mitjan setmana* – in the middle of the week, *a mitjan novembre* – in mid-November, *a mitjan segle XX* – in the mid-20th century; *a mitjans de 1955* – in mid-1955

With the sense of a partitive, *terç* means 'third', a noun just as the rest of partitives, which from *quart* 'fourth' show the same form as ordinals:

Aquesta reforma només es pot aprovar per majoria de dos cinquens /
Aquesta reforma només es pot aprovar per majoria de dues cinquenes parts.
This reform can only be approved by a majority of two fifths.

In general, partitives are inflected in the masculine when they are not accompanied by the noun *part*:

Posa-hi només dues parts de ginebra i t'agradarà més.
Mix it with just two parts of gin and you will like it better.

Dos vuitens de la població comparteixen aquesta opinió.
Two eighths of the population share this opinion.

However, in scales of measure decimal partitives tend to be feminine:

Ara no té febre: té trenta-sis amb nou dècimes.
He has no fever now: his temperature is 36.9 degrees.

El segon classificat ha arribat cinc centèsimes després que el primer.
The second finisher has arrived five one-hundredths of a second after the first one.

6.6.4 Multiples

From 2 to 10, and with 100, the following multiples exist:

2 *doble*

3 *triple*

4 *quàdruple*

5 *quíntuple*

6 *sèxtuple*

7 *sèptuple*

8 *òctuple*

9 *nònuple*

10 *dècuple*

100 *cèntuple*

However, above *triple* it is more common to find *quatre vegades*, 'four times', etc.

6.6.5 Sets

The following are ways to name sets of elements:

un parell (de) – a pair (of), **una parella (de)** – a couple (of) (esp. of people living or working together, also a couple formed by son and daughter; ***una parella*** also means 'a marital partner')

un trio (de) – a trio (of) (normally of people or cards)

un quern (de) – a set of four (archaic)

un grapat (de) – a handful (of)

una embosta (de) – a double handful (of)

uns quants / unes quantes – a few

mitja dotzena (de) – half a dozen

The suffix *–ena* is used not only with *dotze* 'twelve' (→ *dotzena* 'dozen'), as with any round number and 7, 8, 15:

una setena, una vuitena, una quinzena, una vintena, una trentena, etc.

Vuitada and *novena* mean 'eight days' and 'nine days', used in liturgy.

Centenar, and *miler* or *milenar* are the set nouns for 100 and 1000.

6.6.6 *Indefinite qualifiers*

Identification	Quantity (from less to more)
cert, certa, certs, certes certain	*cap* no
altre, altra, altres other	*poc, poca, pocs, poques* little / few
qualsevol, qualssevol any	*algun, alguna, alguns, algunes* some
cada every	*tant, tanta, tants, tantes* so much / so many
	quant, quanta, quants, quantes how much / how many
	bastant, bastanta, bastants, bastantes enough
	prou enough
	força rather, many
	mant, manta many
	molt, molta, molts, moltes many
	tot, tota, tots, totes all
	massa too much / too many

- *Cert, certa, certs, certes* – certain. This works as an adjective, and it can be preceded by the indefinite article *un*:

(Una) certa persona que jo conec m'ha dit això.
A certain person that I know has told me this.

- *Altre, altra, altres* – other. Its determining function is weak, thus normally requiring the presence of un / una / uns / unes (like 'another' in English, but note the plural use of *uns altres / unes altres*):

Un altre home i una altra dona.
Another man and another woman.

Jo li vaig comprar unes altres estovalles.
I bought him another tablecloth.

In fact, *altre* admits the three degrees of definition, the first of them or degree zero, only in plural:

Jo tenc altres idees – I've got other ideas.
Jo tinc unes altres idees – I've got some other ideas.
Jo tinc les altres idees – I've got the other ideas.

It is difficult to find *altre* (in singular) with no article preceding it, only in fixed idioms as (*Una*) *altra vegada* 'another time', or (*Una*) *altra cosa* 'another thing' as in:

(Una) altra vegada ha passat el mateix.
The same thing has happened again.

(Una) altra cosa et vull dir.
I want to say one more thing to you.

The personal pronoun related to *altre* is *altri*, only used in the phrase *d'altri* in formal registers:

Jo no vull pagar deutes d'altri 'I do not want to pay other people's debts' (more normal: **Jo no vull pagar deutes d'altres / Jo no vull pagar deutes d'altra gent**).

- *Qualsevol*, *qualssevol* 'any'

This is used in singular as an indefinite, but it can receive number inflection when in adjectival usage, meaning 'of any sort', 'ordinary'. The plural is *qualssevol* (not **qualsevols*):

Qualsevol feina m'anirà bé.
Any job will suitt me.

Això pot passar a qualsevol família.
This can happen in any family.

Agafa una cadira qualsevol i vine al jardí.
Grab a chair (i.e. any chair) and come to the garden.

No té importància: eren unes anotacions qualssevol.
It doesn't matter: they were just ordinary notes.

As a pronoun (used only in singular) *qualsevol* means 'anybody'. Followed by a relative sentence it translates 'whoever':

Qualsevol pot fer aquest exercici.
Anybody can do this exercise.

Qualsevol que digui això, menteix.
Whoever says so is lying.

- *Cada* 'every, each'

Invariable in pre-nominal position, it agrees only with singulars as English 'every':

Cada terra fa sa guerra. (Proverb)
Every land makes its own war.

Poseu cada llibre al seu lloc.
Put every book in its place.

The pronoun for *cada* is *cadascú* (with no referent) or *cadascun* / *cadascuna* / *cadascuns* / *cadascunes*, and the latter can be followed by a partitive construction that can also remain implicit (*de* + the set of elements implied):

Cadascú és lliure de pensar el que vulgui.
Everyone is free to think whatever he or she likes.

Cadascuna (de les cambres) està equipada amb aire condicionat.
Every room is equipped with air conditioning.

Tots aquests escriptors m'agraden, encara que cadascun té un estil diferent.
I like all these writers, although each of them has a different style.

- *Cap* 'no, any'

Invariable, meaning 'no', 'any'. It needs the co-occurrence of *no* in negative sentences. In questions or doubts it means 'any'.

Cap restaurant no m'agrada com aquest.
I don't like any restaurant the way I like this one.

Hi ha cap restaurant que no t'agradi?
Is there any restaurant that you don't like?

Dubto que hi hagi cap altra regla com aquesta
I doubt there is any other rule like this one.

- *Poc, poca, pocs, poques* 'little, few'

When singular, it accompanies mass nouns, and is countable when plural:

Queda poca llet dintre de la nevera.
There isn't much milk left in the fridge.

Avui fa poc vent.
There is little wind today.

Poques coses són tan importants com aquesta.
Few things are as important as this one.

Poc can be modified by *molt* and *tan* – 'so'. In this case, *molt* is an adverb and cannot be inflected. In this position, *tan* is not to be replaced by *tant, tanta, tants, tantes*:

Queda molt poca llet dintre de la nevera (*Queda molta poca llet dintre de la nevera)
There is very little milk left in the fridge.

Queda tan poca llet dintre de la nevera (*Queda tanta poca llet dintre de la nevera)
There is so little milk in the fridge.

- *Algun, alguna, alguns, algunes* 'some'

This is preferably used in the plural. It can mean 'a certain' in singular:

Algun dia et vindré a veure.
Some day I'll come to see you.

En alguna sabateria encara trobaràs sandàlies d'aquestes.
In some shoe shop you will still find that type of sandals.

Alguns països encara apliquen la pena de mort.
Some countries still apply the death penalty.

Algú is a pronoun, meaning 'somebody':

Algú ha entrat al pis i n'ha robat les joies.
Somebody has broken into the apartment and has stolen the jewellery (from there).

Also *qualcun* can be used with a pronominal function, but when gender- or number-inflected, it can only be a pronoun, never an adjective:

Pel·lícules de por? N'he vistes algunes (or qualcunes) i no m'han agradat.
Horror films? I've seen some and I haven't liked them.

**He vist qualcunes pel·lícules de por → He vist algunes pel·lícules de por.*

Rarer and dialectal, *qualque* is the adjective related to *qualcun*. It can only apply to singulars, which can be understood as generalising:

He llegit qualque llibre d'aquest autor.
I have read some book(s) by this author.

- *Tant, tanta, tants, tantes* 'so much / so many'

This is used in exclamations or followed by a consecutive subordinate (see p. 154), and in both cases optionally followed by preposition *de* (*d'*):

Hi havia tanta (de) gent!
There were so many people!

Hi havia tanta (de) gent que no hi cabia ningú més.
There were so many people that no one else fitted in there.

- *Quant, quanta, quantes, quantes* 'How much, how many'

Used in questions and exclamations. Optionally followed by preposition *de* (*d'*):

Quanta (de) violència!
How much violence!

Quantes (de) vegades t'ho he de dir?
How many times must I tell you this?

- *Bastant, bastanta, bastants, bastantes* 'quite a lot of'

In formal usage it can be used without gender inflection (but this is not obligatory). It can be followed by the preposition *de* (*d'*), in which case agreement for gender and number is optional:

Hi ha bastant a (de) menjar. / Hi ha bastant de llet.
There is enough milk.

He llegit bastantes (de) novel·les aquest estiu.
I have read quite a lot of novels this summer.

- *Prou* 'enough, quite a lot of'

Always invariable, although in informal speech in some areas it can generate *prous, prouta*, and *proutes*:

Sempre deien que no guanyaven prou diners.
They always said they did not earn enough money.

- *Força* 'rather, many'

Invariable. Rarer than *molt*. It can also be used as an adverb. As an adjective it always appears in the singular, even when accompanying a noun in the plural:

Avui hi ha força aficionats al camp del Barça.
There are rather a lot of supporters today at Barça's ground.

- *Mant, manta, mants, mantes* 'many'

Rare. It is normally used only in singular, although plural is not completely unknown as in *mantes vegades* 'many times' (also *manta vegada* exists, with the same meaning):

Al camp hi ha manta casa que no té telèfon.
There are many houses in the countryside that do not have a telephone.

- *Molt, molta, molts, moltes* 'many'

As an adjective it appears in the singular before mass nouns and in the plural before countable ones. It is optionally followed by preposition *de* (*d'*):

Ha menjat molt (de) pa.
He has eaten a lot of bread.

Té molta (de) febre.
She has a high fever.

Molts (d')estudiants es queixen dels preus de les matrícules.
Many students complain about tuition fees.

Moltes (de) vegades els accidents són deguts al mal temps.
Accidents are often due to bad weather.

In non-affirmative constructions, *molt* is replaced by *gaire*, although it remains an option:

Que queden gaires seients lliures.
Are there many free seats left?

No tenia gaires parents.
She did not have many relatives.

Dubto que això ho sàpiga gaire gent.
I doubt many people know this.

Molts can stand for a noun as in:

Molts diuen que és millor no guardar els diners al banc.
Many (people) say that it is better not to keep money in the bank.

- *Tot, tota, tots, totes* 'All, every'

When singular, *tot / tota* can work as an indefinite alone with the sense of 'every', as in *Tot cuiner sap fer una beixamel* – Every cook knows how to make a béchamel; *Tota llei té excepcions* – Every law has exceptions.

Referring to the totality of a given set, it requires a definite article preceding the noun:

Tot el pa que tenim és sense sal.
All the bread we have is salt-free.

Totes les guitarres s'han d'afinar.
All the guitars need to be tuned.

Used in the singular with a countable noun it means 'the whole of':

Tota la ciutat fa olor de fum.
The whole of the town smells like smoke.

The negation of *tot* means the negation of the whole sentence: *Tots els professors no fan exàmens orals* equals *No tots els professors fan exàmens orals* – 'Not all lecturers give oral exams' and not *'No lecturer gives oral exams' (this last sentence to be translated into Catalan as *Cap professor no fa exàmens orals*).

- *Massa* 'Too much / too many'

This is invariable:

Hi ha massa sal a la sopa.
The soup is too salty (lit. there is too much salt in the soup).

Avui ja he rebut massa visites.
Today I have received too many visitors.

The non-standard plural form *masses* can be heard in informal speech.

Chapter 7

Verb phrases

7.1 Verbs

7.1.1 *Verb conjugation*

Verb conjugation in Catalan is complex for speakers of English. There are many tenses, a lot of endings, and then a lot of irregulars too. However, verb conjugation is also very important. Since Catalan doesn't normally use subject pronouns (as a **pro-drop** language), then the verb ending includes the vital information of who is doing something (**person**), how many are doing it (**number**), as well as when the action takes place (**tense** in the strictest sense), how the action relates to the time around it (**aspect**), and the attitude of the speaker to the action expressed by the verb (**mood**). Compared to this, verb conjugation in English is incredibly simple, since the verb is only marked for present or past tense (e.g. play vs. played), the third-person singular present (play vs. plays), and everything else is delivered by extra words: subject pronouns, modal verbs, and more. So we need to get it right.

There are three main groups of verbs in terms of their conjugation: verbs whose infinitives end in –ar, called conjugation I, those mostly ending in –er and –re, as well as verbs such as *dir* (to say) and *dur* (to carry), which make up conjugation II, and those ending in –ir, which make up conjugation III. These –ir verbs also split into two groups: those that add –eix– or another element into some of the conjugation, known as **inceptive verbs** or **inchoative verbs**, and those that do not. The vast majority of verbs in Catalan (over 75%) end in –ar, and this (and occasionally -ir) is the preferred ending that can be used to create new verbs, too.

In most cases the infinitive ending is taken off to leave the **stem**; verb endings are then added to this to conjugate the verb (some tenses use different stems, as explained below). It is important to remember that sometimes spelling changes are necessary at the end of the stem as the endings change between **front** vowels (e and i) and **back** vowels (o, and u, as well as a) to maintain the sound of the consonant at the end of the stem. This is the case with stems ending in c, ç, g, and j. So *començar* becomes *tu comences*, but *ella comença.*

There is also variation across the different Catalan-speaking territories. As with other cases of regional variation, you will be understood in most places using the general conjugation, but in some cases regional conjugations might not be understood outside of their region. Regional variations are covered in the appendix (p. 209) together with all of the irregular forms.

7.1.1.1 Present indicative tense

–ar verbs, e.g. muntar (to climb up)

jo	munto
tu	muntes
ell, ella, vostè	munta
nosaltres	muntem
vosaltres, vós	munteu
ells, elles, vostès	munten

–er / –re verbs, e.g. perdre (to lose)

jo	perdo
tu	perds
ell, ella, vostè	perd
nosaltres	perdem
vosaltres, vós	perdeu
ells, elles, vostès	perden

–ir inceptive verbs (with –eix– addition), e.g. assistir (to assist)

jo	assisteixo
tu	assisteixes
ell, ella, vostè	assisteix
nosaltres	assistim
vosaltres, vós	assistiu
ells, elles, vostès	assisteixen

–ir non-inceptive verbs (without the –eix– addition), e.g. sentir (to feel)

jo	sento
tu	sents*
ell, ella, vostè	sent
nosaltres	sentim
vosaltres, vós	sentiu
ells, elles, vostès	senten

*Verbs with a stem ending in –ix–, –g–, –ç–, –ss–, –s– and –z– have a 'tu' form ending in –es, simply for reasons of pronunciation, such as *cuses*, *fuges*, and so on.

7.1.1.2 Past indicative tenses

Imperfect

There are only two sets of imperfect endings for regular verbs.

	–ar verbs	–er/–re and –ir verbs
jo	muntava	sentia
tu	muntaves	senties
ell, ella, vostè	muntava	sentia

nosaltres	muntàvem	sentíem
vosaltres, vós	muntàveu	sentíeu
ells, elles, vostès	muntaven	sentien

Simple preterite

There are two ways to conjugate the preterite in Catalan, the simple and periphrastic forms. They have the same meaning and are used interchangeably. The *jo* form of the simple is rare outside of Valencia.

	–ar verbs	–er/–re verbs	–ir verbs
jo	muntí	perdí	sentí
tu	muntares	perderes	sentires
ell, ella, vostè	muntà	perdé	sentí
nosaltres	muntàrem	perdérem	sentírem
vosaltres, vós	muntàreu	perdéreu	sentíreu
ells, elles, vostès	muntaren	perderen	sentiren

Periphrastic preterite

This is possibly the easiest of all tenses to conjugate, since there are no irregular forms. It is formed by an auxiliary verb preceding the infinitive of the main verb.

	all verbs
jo	vaig muntar, vaig perdre, vaig sentir
tu	vas muntar (*or* vares muntar), etc.
ell, ella, vostè	va muntar, etc.
nosaltres	vam muntar (*or* vàrem muntar), etc.
vosaltres, vós	vau muntar (*or* vàreu muntar), etc.
ells, elles, vostès	van muntar (*or* varen muntar), etc.

7.1.1.3 Future tense

The future tense is formed by adding the endings –é, –às, –à, –em, –eu, and –an to the future stem, which is in most cases the infinitive (notable exceptions are *anir–* for *anar*, to go, and *far–* for *fer*, to do). If the infinitive ends in an 'e', this is removed, as in the case of *perdre* below, and if the –er ending of the infinitive is stressed then the –er is replaced with –r.

	–ar verbs	–er/–re verbs	–ir verbs
jo	muntaré	perdré	sentiré
tu	muntarás	perdràs	sentiràs
ell, ella, vostè	muntará	perdrà	sentirà
nosaltres	muntarem	perdrem	sentirem
vosaltres, vós	muntareu	perdreu	sentireu
ells, elles, vostès	muntaran	perdran	sentiran

7.1.1.4 Conditional tense

The conditional uses the same stem as the future (even if it is irregular) and the –ia endings of the imperfect tense.

	–ar verbs	–er/–re verbs	–ir verbs
jo	muntaria	perdria	sentiria
tu	muntaries	perdries	sentiries
ell, ella, vostè	muntaria	perdria	sentiria
nosaltres	muntaríem	perdríem	sentiríem
vosaltres, vós	muntaríeu	perdríeu	sentiríeu
ells, elles, vostès	muntarien	perdrien	sentirien

7.1.1.5 Perfect indicative tenses

Perfect tenses are formed by conjugating the auxiliary verb *haver* (to have) in the appropriate tense, and then adding the past participle of the main verb. *Haver* is conjugated as follows:

	Perfect (present of *haver*)	Pluperfect (imperfect of *haver*)	Past anterior (preterite of *haver*)	Future perfect (future of *haver*)	Conditional perfect (conditional of *haver*)
jo	he	havia	haguí *or* vaig haver	hauré	hauria *or* haguera
tu	has	havies	hagueres *or* vas/vares haver	hauràs	hauries *or* hagueres
ell, ella, vostè	ha	havia	hagué *or* va haver	haurà	hauria *or* haguera
nosaltres	hem	havíem	haguérem *or* vam/vàrem haver	haurem	hauríem *or* haguérem
vosaltres, vós	heu	havíeu	haguéreu *or* vau/vàreu haver	haureu	hauríeu *or* haguéreu
ells, elles, vostès	han	havien	hagueren *or* van/varen haver	hauran	haurien *or* hagueren

7.1.1.6 Present subjunctive

present subjunctive
–ar verbs

jo	munti
tu	muntis
ell, ella, vostè	munti
nosaltres	muntem
vosaltres, vós	munteu
ells, elles, vostès	muntin

–er/–re verbs

jo	perdi
tu	perdis
ell, ella, vostè	perdi
nosaltres	perdem
vosaltres, vós	perdeu
ells, elles, vostès	perdin

–ir inceptive verbs

jo	assisteixi
tu	assisteixis
ell, ella, vostè	assisteixi
nosaltres	assistim
vosaltres, vós	assistiu
ells, elles, vostès	assisteixin

–ir non-inceptive verbs

jo	senti
tu	sentis
ell, ella, vostè	senti
nosaltres	sentim
vosaltres, vós	sentiu
ells, elles, vostès	sentin

7.1.1.7 Imperfect subjunctive

The imperfect subjunctive, also called the past subjunctive (since technically it can be used 'perfectively',), uses the same stem as the simple preterite indicative. This then helps to account for many irregular verbs.

–ar verbs

jo	muntés
tu	muntessis
ell, ella, vostè	muntés
nosaltres	muntéssim
vosaltres, vós	muntéssiu
ells, elles, vostès	muntessin

–er/–re verbs

jo	perdés
tu	perdessis
ell, ella, vostè	perdés
nosaltres	perdéssim

vosaltres, vós	perdéssiu
ells, elles, vostès	perdessin

–ir verbs

jo	assistís
tu	assistissis
ell, ella, vostè	assistís
nosaltres	assistíssim
vosaltres, vós	assistíssiu
ells, elles, vostès	assistissin

7.1.1.8 Past periphrastic subjunctive

There is a less-frequently used form of the past subjunctive, modelled on the periphrastic preterite indicative. As with that, there is a special auxiliary used before the infinitive of the main verb:

	General	North-western and Valencian
jo	vagi	vaja
tu	vagis	vages
ell, ella, vostè	vagi	vaja
nosaltres	vàgim	vàgem
vosaltres, vós	vàgiu	vàgeu
ells, elles, vostès	vagin	vagen

So, it would be *vagi muntar*, *vagis muntar*, and so on.

7.1.1.9 Perfect subjunctive tenses

Like their indicative counterparts, perfect subjunctive tenses are formed by conjugating the auxiliary verb *haver* in the appropriate tense, and then adding the past participle of the main verb.

Perfect subjunctive

	General	North-western and Valencian
jo	hagi	haja
tu	hagis	hages
ell, ella, vostè	hagi	haja
nosaltres	hàgim	hàgem
vosaltres, vós	hàgiu	hàgeu
ells, elles, vostès	hagin	hagen

Pluperfect subjunctive

	General	North-western and Valencian	Valencian
jo	hagués	hagués	haguera
tu	haguessis	haguesses	hagueres
ell, ella, vostè	hagués	hagués	haguera
nosaltres	haguéssim	haguéssem	haguérem
vosaltres, vós	haguéssiu	haguésseu	haguéreu
ells, elles, vostès	haguessin	haguessen	hagueren

Periphrastic past anterior subjunctive

	General	North-western and Valencian
jo	vagi haver	vaja haver
tu	vagis haver	vages haver
ell, ella, vostè	vagi haver	vaja haver
nosaltres	vàgim haver	vàgem haver
vosaltres, vós	vàgiu haver	vàgeu haver
ells, elles, vostès	vagin haver	vagen haver

7.1.1.10 Imperative mood

The imperative mood is the verb form for giving orders ('Do this!' 'Open the door!'), and its conjugation borrows from other forms:

Tu imperative takes the form of *ell*, *ella*, *vostè* present indicative.

Vosaltres / *vós* imperative takes the form of *vosaltres* / *vós* present indicative.

All other persons take the form of present subjunctive.

So, 'Open the door!' is '*Obre la porta!*' for *tu*, '*Obri la porta!*' for *vostè*, '*Obriu la porta!*' for *vosaltres*, and '*Obrin la porta!*' for *vostès*. Likewise, where there are regional variants for the forms above, they carry across into the imperative.

7.1.1.11 Past participle

Past participles are created by removing the infinitive ending to leave the stem, and adding the correct ending. All past participles can be inflected for number and gender, but check the relevant sections for when this is done.

	Masculine singular	Feminine singular	Masculine plural	Feminine plural
–ar verbs	muntat	muntada	muntats	muntades
–er/–re verbs	perdut	perduda	perduts	perdudes
–ir verbs	assistit	assistida	assistits	assistides

A lot of conjugation II (–er/–re verbs) have irregular past participles – these are listed in the appendix.

7.1.1.12 Gerund

Gerunds are created by adding the following endings to the stem:

	Gerund
–ar verbs	muntant
–er/–re verbs	perdent
–ir verbs	assistint

7.1.1.13 Irregular verbs

Catalan has a long list of irregular verbs, and there are many books (and now apps and websites) that list all of these. Some are irregular only in certain tenses. Many of the more commonly used verbs are irregular, and so it is vital to remember these to write and speak the language accurately. These are covered in the appendix on p. 209.

7.1.2 *Tense and aspect*

Along with time, **aspect** also matters in Catalan. Aspect refers to whether or not actions or states are completed (**perfective**) or unfinished or ongoing (**imperfective,** also called continuous in English). This is quite similar to English verb system, except for the presence of a preterite imperfect tense:

		Aspect	
		Imperfect	Perfect
Tense	Present	*canto* (present tense)	*he cantat* (perfect tense)
	Preterite	*cantava* (imperfect tense)	*vaig cantar* (simple and periphrastic preterite tenses)
	Pluperfect		*havia cantat* (pluperfect tense)
	Anterior		*vaig haver cantat* (past anterior tense)
	Future	*cantaré* (future tense)	*hauré cantat* (future perfect tense)

7.1.2.1 Imperfect vs. perfect

The difference between the imperfect and preterite tenses is a routine area of difficulty for English-language students learning Catalan, since in many cases the English simple past tense (I went, you did, etc.) covers both meanings. Importantly, the imperfect is used for two main reasons in Catalan:

- when an action was usual or repeated in the past. In English this meaning is often reinforced with 'used to':

  De petit jo cantava al cor de l'església.
  As a child I used to sing in the church choir.

- when the action is continuing, especially in contrast with a non-continuing one; or to put it another way, when from the point of view of the sentence one action is not completed but another one is. In this case the continuous form (to be + gerund) is often used in English:

  Ahir jo cantava i de cop vaig sentir un tro.
  I was singing yesterday when suddenly I heard a clap of thunder.

This same continuous form exists in Catalan, with *estar* + gerund, although it is much less common than in English, and it is used to reinforce strongly the idea of an ongoing action:

No puc venir a la festa perquè estic preparant-me per als exàmens.
I can't come to the party because I am preparing for my exams.

Els meus pares estan pensant si canvien el cotxe.
My parents are thinking about changing their car.

7.1.2.2 Perfect vs. preterite

The division between the present perfect and simple and periphrastic preterites is clear-cut: the present perfect is used for something that has occurred in a unit of time that is still running, while the use of preterite shows that the unit of time has already ended:

Aquest curs hem estudiat molt (the year has not finished yet)**, però el curs passat no vam estudiar gaire** (last year is over).
We have studied a lot this year, but we didn't last year.

Aquest segle hem tingut sis presidents; el segle passat en vam tenir vuit.
This century we've had six presidents; last century we had eight.

There is only one exception to this rule (something that many non-native speakers of Catalan get wrong): events that have occurred in the same day as when the speaker is talking **must** be referred to by the present perfect, even if they happened in the morning and the speaker is talking in the evening (even if you have had an afternoon nap!):

Aquest matí he sentit tres ambulàncies.
I've heard three ambulances this morning (if said in the morning) /
I heard three ambulances this morning (if said later in the day).

7.1.2.3 Usage of other tenses

The pluperfect places a completed event prior to another event also in the past:

Jo ja havia pescat tres peixos quan vaig perdre la canya.
I had already caught three fish when I lost my rod.

Elles havien dut el regal a les seves cosines abans de preparar-se per a la festa.
They had taken their present to their cousins before getting ready for the party.

The pluperfect can also convey a sense of contradiction, i.e. that somebody had already thought of something else. In any case, remoteness in the past is also to be understood:

– **Anem al cinema?** 'Shall we go to the cinema?'
– **Jo havia pensat anar a passejar.** 'I was thinking of going for a walk.'

The future perfect works in the same way, by placing an event before another one, both of them in the time to come:

Quan tu arribaràs a Berlín, ja farà dos dies que jo hi hauré arribat.
When you arrive in Berlin, I'll have been there for two days.

Li farem la tramesa quan haurem cobrat la factura.
We'll send your order when we have received payment.

Note that in Catalan you cannot use the present continuous to indicate something happening in the future:

They say it's raining tomorrow. → **Diuen que demà plourà.**

He's coming next week. → **Vindrà la setmana que ve.**

However, the present can be used to indicate the future, especially in conditional clauses, where the future is not allowed (and note as well the present subjunctive is never used in conditional clauses):

*__Si demà estaràs bé anirem al cinema.__
✓**Si demà estàs bé anirem al cinema.**
If you are alright tomorrow, we shall go to the cinema.

Also when intention, certainty, cause, or presupposition are implied, the present can replace the future tense. In such cases, though, time must be expressed by means of an adverb:

Que bé: demà anem a la platja = Que bé: demà anirem a la platja

Oh good: we're going to the beach tomorrow.

Dilluns que ve dinem amb l'avia, o sia que no feu tard = Dilluns que ve dinarem . . .
Next Monday we're having lunch with your grandmother, so don't be late.

Diumenge segur que plou = Diumenge segur que plourà.
Of course it will rain on Sunday.

L'any que ve acabes la carrera, no? = L'any que ve acabaràs la carrera, no?
You're graduating next year, aren't you?

Observe how the pluperfect is formed after the auxiliary *haver* ('to have') conjugated in the imperfect *(havia)* followed by the past participle. A stronger sense of accomplishment is achieved by using the past anterior, formed using the auxiliary *haver* in the preterite. The past anterior appears only in temporal clauses, usually after *quan* or *després que*:

Quan vaig haver acabat l'examen, vaig anar a trobar els companys.
Once I have finished the exam, I went to join my classmates.

7.1.3 Mood

7.1.3.1 Indicative / Subjunctive

The subjunctive is not a tense, but a **mood**. Unlike aspect above, which indicates completeness, incompleteness, and continuity, mood indicates factuality, possibility, uncertainty, and likelihood. All of the tenses in section 7.1.2 are in the **indicative** mood, which is the mood of factuality. The subjunctive is a mood of non-factuality, as in the expression of wishes or possibilities (wanting something that is not considered to be real). For comparison, look at the following conditional sentences:

i. **Si véns, dinarem plegats.** If you come, we'll have lunch together (and I'm sure you can since it is in your power to do so).
ii. **Si venies, dinaríem plegats.** Should you come, we'd have dinner together (and I'm not sure you can, but it is still in your power to do so).
iii. **Si vinguessis, dinaríem plegats.** If you came, we'd have dinner together (but I know it's quite difficult for you to come, perhaps because you have already said no).

All three sentences are correct. However, the contexts in which they are used (i.e. their **pragmatic meanings**) differ: in (i) the present indicative imperfect is used when the possibility is easily attainable, and the main verb is conjugated in the future; in (ii) and (iii) the main verb is conjugated in the conditional, thus pointing at a greater remoteness, to which (iii) still adds a new degree of uncertainty by conjugating the verb *venir* in the preterite imperfect subjunctive – in (iii) something significant needs to change for the person to come.

7.1.3.1.1 *Noun clauses*

The subjunctive is compulsory in object or complement clauses depending on verbs of wishing, liking, or fearing. Note that the subject of the main verb has to be different to the subject of the subordinated verb:

Vull que siguis aquí a les quatre.
I want you to be here at four (as opposed to *Vull ser aquí a les quatre*, I want to be here at four).

El client desitja que li ampliïn la garantia.
The customer wants the guarantee to be extended.

M'han prohibit que conti com va anar la reunió.
They forbade me from saying how the meeting went.

Tinc por que vinguin i no em trobin.
I'm afraid they'll come and not find me.

Also clauses with conjugated verbs acting as subject or copulative predicates and starting with conjunction *que* require the subjunctive:

Que vinguis no és obligatori, però seria important.
It is not compulsory that you come, but it would be important.

Que es venguin tants llibres d'aquest autor no vol dir que sigui bo.
Just because this author has sold lots of books, it doesn't mean he's good.

Although the subjunctive is the mood of non-factuality, verbs conveying the idea of imagining normally require a verb in a subordinate noun clause to be in the indicative (indicating that the thought is real in the subject's mind):

Ens pensàvem que eres el porter de l'equip de futbol.
We thought you were the football team's goalkeeper.

Ahir vaig somiar que em feia ric.
Yesterday I dreamt I became rich.

When the main clause is negative, the verb in the subordinated noun clause appears in the subjunctive (indicating that the thought was not real in the subject's mind, because they did not think it):

No ens pensàvem que fossis el porter.
We didn't think you were the goalkeeper.

No he somiat mai que em fes ric.
I have never dreamt I became rich.

However, the indicative can persist in 'no' oppositions, when cancelling previously known or presupposed content, such as in 'It's not that . . .' sentences.

No, no vaig somiar que em feia ric, vaig somiar que sempre ho havia estat.
No, I didn't dream I became rich, I dreamt that I had always been so.

Verbs in clauses being pondered usually appear in the subjunctive:

Va ser molt injust que l'àrbitre pités un penalty.
It was very unfair that the referee awarded a penalty.

7.1.3.1.2 *Adverbial clauses*

In adverbial clauses the verbal mood can determine the meaning, as in the distinction between causal and final *perquè*:

perquè + indicative = causal ('because')

Et dic això perquè estàs tranquil.
I'm telling you this because you are calm.

perquè + subjunctive = final ('for', 'to', 'so that')

Et dic això perquè estiguis tranquil.
I'm telling you this so you don't worry.

Temporal clauses introducing events that occur in the future use either the indicative or subjunctive according to certainty, although in current usage priority seems to be given to the subjunctive:

Quan arribarà l'estiu traurem la taula al jardí (also: Quan arribi l'estiu traurem la taula al jardí).
When summer comes, we'll take the table out to the garden.

Quan es trenqui el vidre de l'entrada, ja no en comprarem d'altre (also rephrasable as a conditional: 'Si es romp el vidre de l'entrada . . .').
When the hall window gets broken, we won't buy a new one (If the hall window gets broken . . .).

Concessives show a similar behaviour: the mood selected depends on feasibility. When the facts are potential (normally in the future or in an undetermined time), then the subjunctive is used; when the facts are actual (in past or present time), then the indicative is used:

Encara que em quedi fins a mitja nit, no acabaré la feina.
Even if I stay until midnight, I won't finish my work.

Encara que ahir vaig treballar fins a mitja nit, no vaig acabar la feina.
Although I worked until midnight yesterday, I couldn't finish my work.

Per més que treballo fins a mitja nit, no acabo mai la feina.
However much I work until midnight (everyday), I never finish my work.

As with conditionals, a stronger sense of non-factuality can be expressed by the imperfect subjunctive:

Encara que em quedés fins a mitja nit, no acabaria la feina
Even if I stayed until midnight (and I have no intention of staying), I wouldn't finish my work.

7.1.3.1.3 *Relative clauses*

In relative clauses adjoined to a person, object, place, etc. unknown by the speaker and used in a generalisation, the verb is also in the subjunctive:

L'alumne que copiï suspendrà.
Any student who copies will fail.

Qualsevol persona que hagi vist això se'n deu haver horroritzat.
Anybody who has seen this must have been shocked.

For this reason, any sentence using whenever, whatever, wherever, and so on in English normally requires the subjunctive in Catalan:

Qualsevol cosa que en pensis, serà incorrecta. / En pensis el que en pensis, estarà malament.
Whatever you think about this, it will be wrong.

Escriguis a qui escriguis, no ho entendran.
Whoever you write to, they won't undestand it.

On sigui que vagis, hi trobaràs un metge. / Vagis on vagis, hi trobaràs un metge.
Wherever you go, you'll find a doctor.

7.1.3.1.4 *Agreement between tenses*

The tense of the verb in the subjunctive depending on a main verb in the indicative agrees with it in the following ways. When both perfect and imperfect solutions are allowed, then the completion of state or action determines which to choose:

Main verb (indicative)	Subordinated verb (subjunctive)	
present	present	*T'ordeno que vinguis.* I'm ordering you to come.
	present perfect	*M'agrada que hagis vingut.* I'm glad you've come.
future	present	*Li diré que canti.* I'll tell her to sing.
imperfect	imperfect	*Em feia por que contés aquella història.* I was afraid he would tell that story.

preterite (simple or periphrastic)	imperfect	*Vam desitjar que s'acabés aquell malson.* We wished that nightmare would finish.
	pluperfect	*Van dir que qualsevol viatger que hagués perdut la maleta n'havia d'informar immediatament.* They said that any passenger who had lost their luggage had to let someone know immediately.
pluperfect	pluperfect	*Havien dit que qualsevol passatger que hagués perdut el bitllet ho havia de comunicar immediatament.* They had said that any passenger who had lost their ticket should tell someone immediately.
	imperfect	*Havien prohibit que ens acostéssim a la vorera.* They had forbidden us to approach the verge.

7.1.3.2 Conditional

	Perfect	Imperfect
Conditional	cantaria	hauria cantat

In conditional sentences, the main clause appears in the conditional (indicating that the action of that verb is conditional, or reliant, on something else happening), and the adverbial clause (typically introduced by *si, quan, excepte que*, see p. 148) in the subjunctive:

> **No vindria a aquest restaurant si no m'agradés el menjar que hi fan.**
> I wouldn't come to this restaurant if I didn't like the food they make.

Ens va dir que ens pagaria quan haguéssim acabat la feina.
She told us that she would pay when we had finished the work.

In certain cases the conditional relationship can be established between two subjunctives, but only when the main verb of the relation itself is subordinate to another verb in a relation requiring the subjunctive (see p. 72 above):

Em feia por que els lladres haguessin trobat la clau si l'hagués amagada sota l'estora.
I was afraid the thieves would have found the key if I had hidden it under the mat.

7.1.3.3 Imperative

The imperative has only one tense, and no aspect. Only the *tu* and *vosaltres* forms have a distinct imperative form (see p. 68) – all other forms use the present subjunctive form instead, often preceded by conjunction *que* in for *ell, ella, ells*, and *elles*.

tu	*canta*
ell / ella / vostè	(*que*) *canti*
nosaltres	*cantem*
vosaltres / vós	*canteu* / *cantin*
ells / elles / vostès	(*que*) *cantin*

In pure imperatives, those using a 'you' form, and the 'we' form, any object pronoun must be placed after the verb (just like with infinitives and gerunds):

Canta la cançó → Canta-la.
Sing the song → Sing it.

El dinar, serviu-lo ara.
Lunch? Serve it now.

Si hem d'anar a l'hospital, anem-hi ara.
If we have to go to the hospital, let's go (there) now.

In contrast, the *ell, ella, ells*, and *elles* forms place the clitic before the verb:

La cançó? Que la canti ara.
The song? Let him sing it now.

7.1.3.4 Past participle agreement

In passive structures, past participles agree in gender and number with the subject of that structure:

La beca ha estat adjudicada al millor estudiant.
The scholarship has been granted to the best student.

Les persones grans eren molt ben rebudes en aquella botiga.
The elderly were very welcome in that shop.

Agreement is also usual in compound tenses (with *haver*) between the past participle and the object when the object is represented by any of the clitics *la, els, les*, and *en*:

– Has menjat gaires pomes? – No, només n'he menjades dues.
'Have you eaten many apples?' 'No, I have only eaten two.'

Hauria d'anar a veure la mare perquè fa temps que no l'he visitada.
I should go and see my mother, because I haven't visited her for a long time.

In verbal phrases agreement only occurs when the clitic depends on the compound tense:

– Has vist com esbucaven les cases? – Sí, les he vist esbucar / Sí, he vist esbucar-les.
'Have you seen how they demolished the houses' 'Yes, I have.'

As opposed to:

– Has vist les cases? – Sí, les he vistes.
'Have you seen the houses?' 'Yes, I have.'

In the first example above, *les* depends on *esbucar* and not on the compound tense *has vist*, and therefore there is no agreement, although the clitic (the object pronoun) can also be placed before the main verb by clitic raising (see p. 101). Consider also the following example where *la* depends on *has vist*, and not on *caure*, and agreement can occur:

– Has vist caure la branca? – Sí, l'he vista caure.
'Have you seen the branch falling?' 'Yes, I have.'

7.2 Adverbs

The function of adverbs is adding meaning not just to verbs, but also adjectives, other adverbs or whole sentences for a given circumstance.

Degree or quantity, manner, time, and place are the most typical areas of meaning for adverbs.

7.2.1 *Placing adverbs in the sentence (see p. 133 for general issues on word order)*

Word order in Catalan tends to be freer than in English. Adverbs are most often placed next to the unit they modify. Commonly, verbal adverbs are placed by the verb or at the end of the verb phrase:

Els clients han pagat el compte immediatament.
Els clients han pagat immediatament el compte.
The customers have paid the bill straight away.

It is important to remark that unlike in English, in general adverbs are not placed between the auxiliary and the main verb:

***Els clients han immediatament pagat el compte**

although exceptions can be made with *bé*, turning into *ben* in this position, and *mal*, both not referring to quality (originally meaning 'well' and 'badly'), but to fulfilment or a lack of fulfilment:

Els clients han ben pagat el compte.
The customers have paid the bill in full (and left a tip).

Només havia mal dormit dues hores quan va sonar el telèfon.
I had scarcely slept for two hours when the telephone rang.

Manner and logic adverbs can qualify the whole sentence in order to state the mood of the speaker or to judge the truth value of what is said:

Sincerament, no m'agraden aquestes coses.
Honestly, I don't like these things.

Sa mare li replicà que allò estava mal fet, òbviament.
His mother replied that that was wrong, obviously.

Potser el batlle et perdonarà la multa.
Maybe the mayor will waive your fine.

In such cases the adverbs can be found out of the limits of the verb phrase. Even in the second example above, a comma acts as a border. In these cases the adverb cannot be used in control questions, just as in English *Was it obviously that his mother...? The same can be said about manner adverbs stating not a quality of the action, but, more exactly, a quality of the subject:

Ton pare, ben orgullosament, m'ha mostrat les teves notes.
Your father, full of pride, has shown me your marks (or 'Your very proud father...').

In these cases, the adverb can stand both at the beginning of the sentence or in a parenthetical insert.

7.2.2 *Types*

7.2.2.1 Manner

The most typical manner adverb in Catalan is *així* 'this way / like this', and it can get the opposite, almost ironic form, *això* in explicit confrontations:

– **Ho has fet així?** 'Have you done it like this?'
– **No ho he fet ni així ni això** 'I haven't done it like this or like that.'

Most commonly, however, adverbs of manner are created by adding the suffix *–ment* to the feminine singular form of an adjective. This suffix parallels the English form *–ly*. It is useful to remember that a written stress on a vowel in the feminine form of the adjective is maintained when *–ment* is added, together with the quality of the vowel when pronounced (and so these words get two stresses in pronunciation):

ple – plena – plenament fully
cortès – cortesa – cortesament politely
fàcil – fàcil – fàcilment easily

When two or more adverbs ending in *–ment* are used together (a technique called **coordination**), the suffix in the second (or last) case can be elided:

alegrement i confiadament or **alegrement i confiada** happily and trustfully
fàcilment i ràpidament or **fàcilment i ràpida** easily and quickly

Among manner adverbs special attention must be paid to *bé* / *ben* 'well': when its meaning is absolute *bé* is chosen, and *ben* when it precedes an adjective or another adverb and functions as a degree adverb:

El violoncel·lista ha interpretat molt bé la peça.
The celloist has performed the piece very well.

Avui estic ben cansat.
Today I am so tired.

There is also the adverb *bonament*, regularly constructed on the feminine form of *bo* – *bona*: 'effortlessly, voluntarily'. The opposite of *bé* is not made after *dolenta*, in spite of *dolent* being the opposite of *bo*, but after *mal* – *mala*: *malament* (see p. 25 on *mal*).

Adjectives as *ràpid, lent, tort, dret, fort, fluix, confús, clar, diferent, millor, pitjor* are used as manner adverbs with no need for the suffix *–ment* when describing the action of the subject of verbs of movement, diction, and sense:

Aquest cotxe va molt ràpid.
This car goes very fast.

El pagès volia llaurar dret, però llaurava tort.
The farmer wanted to plough straight, but he ploughed askew.

No ho veig clar.
I'm not sure about this (lit. I don't see it clearly).

However, when a succession of events is described, *lentament* and *ràpidament* are preferred to their simple counterparts:

Els dies passaven molt lentament.
The days passed by very slowly.

Adjectives can also be used with a meaning close to that of adverbs when appearing in a verbal predicate, qualifying a nominal element. In some cases, the noun can be elided, and the adjective stands alone in an adverbial function, as in the second sentence below:

Et vull contar una cosa: no m'ho posis difícil.
I want to tell you something: don't make it difficult for me.

Tot ho cuina molt salat → Cuina molt salat.
He puts too much salt in his cooking (more closely in terms of structure, 'He cooks very saltily').

7.2.2.2 Quantity and degree

so as much	very	too much too little	enough	(a) little	at all	almost more or less	only
tan, *tant*	*molt,* *gaire,* *ben,* *força*	*massa,* *massa poc*	*prou,* *suficient-* *ment,* *a basta-* *ment*	*(un) poc*	*gens*	*gairebé,* *quasi,* *més o* *menys,* *més aviat*	*només,* *just,* *solament*

Some of the words above have already been explained on p. 27. Bear in mind that in the present section we analyse them as adverbs, i.e. qualifying verbs, adjectives, and other adverbs.

- *Tan, tant*

'So', 'so much'. *Tan* introduces an adjective or an adverb, while *tant* stays alone, modifying the verb (see p. 182 on comparing, and p. 154 on consecutive clauses):

És tan alta!
She is so tall!

L'odio tant!
I hate him so much!

- *Molt, gaire, ben, força*

Molt admits the superlative *moltíssim*. *Gaire* can appear instead of *molt* in non-affirmative contexts (negation, question and doubt):

Aquest pa m'agrada moltíssim, però aquest vi no m'agrada gaire.
I like this bread a lot, but I don't like this wine very much.

Que treballes gaire?
Do you work a lot?

No sé si costa gaire.
I don't know if it is very expensive.

When the focus is on the whole sentence and not on the degree of what the verb means, then *gaire* is blocked and *molt* is used:

Aquest vi no m'agrada molt, m'agrada moltíssim.
It's not that I like this wine (I don't just like this wine . . .), I like it a lot.

Ben, meaning 'fully' qualifies only adjectives and adverbs, but not verbs, except for the cases (seen above, on p. 82) of insertion between auxiliary and verb:

Avui estic ben cansat.
I'm exhausted today.

Ben obertament li va dir la seva opinió.
She openly told him her opinion.

Força parallels *molt*, except for the superlative. However, *força* is not widely used:

Aquest pa m'agrada força.
I like this bread a lot.

- *Massa*

'Too', 'too much':

El teu cotxe corre massa.
Your car goes too fast (lit. runs too much).

Aquesta sopa és massa salada.
This soup is too salty.

Viu massa ostentosament.
He lives too ostentatiously.

The opposite of *massa* is *massa poc*. In this adverbial function, *poc* is invariable and so does not agree with the adjective it qualifies:

Els estudiants estaven massa poc preparats.
The students were too poorly prepared.

El teu cotxe corre massa poc.
Your car is too slow (lit. runs too little).

- *Prou, suficientment, a bastament*

When qualifying adjectives or adverbs, *a bastament* is placed after them:

Aquest llistó és llarg a bastament.
This stick is long enough.

L'aire bufa fort a bastament.
The wind is blowing strongly enough.

Aquest noi és prou gran per entendre-ho.
This boy is old enough to understand.

La casa és suficientment gran per a tots.
The house is big enough for everyone.

- *(Un) poc, una mica*

Working alone as an adverb, *poc* translates as 'not too (much)'; introduced by *un* (as its synonym *una mica*), it means 'a bit':

– Saps ballar? – Un poc / Una mica.
'Can you dance?' 'A little.'

– Saps ballar? – Poc.
'Can you dance?' 'Not too much.'

- *Gens*

Meaning 'at all', 'any'. It appears in negative, interrogative, and dubitative sentences. It can be reinforced by *ni mica* (*gens ni mica*).

Que us heu mullat gens?
Have you gotten wet at all?

D'ençà que està malalt no ha sortit gens ni mica.
Since he has been ill, he hasn't gone out at all.

- *Gairebé, quasi*

'Almost', 'nearly'.

Gairebé he caigut de la cadira.
I have almost fallen off my chair.

El llibre està quasi acabat.
The book is nearly finished.

- *Més o menys*

'More or less'.

A quina hora començarà, més o menys?
When will it start, more or less?

- *Només / just*

'Only'

L'entrada només / just costa deu euros.
The ticket only costs ten euros.

Només / just (with an optional preposition *de* or *en* before infinitives) can introduce an infinitive or clause sentence, meaning immediateness or completion:

Només d'entrar-hi ja vaig veure què passava.
As soon as I went in I saw what was going on.

Només que et prenguis una pastilla ja et trobaràs més bé.
After just one pill you'll feel better.

7.2.2.3 Place

7.2.2.3.1 *Deictic adverbs*

Ací, aquí, allí, allà are deictic adverbs in the same way demonstratives *aquest*, *aquell* are used to point at something, a place in the case of the adverbs. In present day Catalan, only two terms of distance remain:

ací / aquí – here
allí / allà – there

In medieval Catalan, and still in certain dialects, three terms of deixis, as in stressed pronouns (I / you / (s)he) is seen under the threefold set *ací* ('close to me') / *aquí* ('close to you') / *allí* or *allà* ('close to them'). The difference between *ací* / *aquí* can (somewhat artificially) appear in letters, especially in commercial and legal ones.

- *Pertot arreu, arreu, pertot* 'everywhere'

As in English, these indicate no single position.

Tenia papers escampats pertot arreu.
He had papers scattered everywhere.

- *Onsevulla* 'wherever'

Onsevulla is rare, with the periphrasis *on sigui* often preferred:

Onsevulla / On sigui que vagis trobaràs una sucursal d'aquest banc.
Wherever you go you'll find a branch of this bank.

- *Enlloc* 'nowhere', or 'anywhere' (in non-affirmative contexts)

  Viatjaràs enlloc aquest estiu?
  Will you travel anywhere this summer?

  – On es venen aquestes sabates? – Enlloc.
  'Where do they sell these shoes?' 'Nowhere.'

7.2.2.3.2 *Position and direction*

The following can appear alone or be preceded by contraction *al*, with no difference in meaning:

davant – in front, opposite

darrere – behind

damunt – above, on (top)

davall – below, underneath

devora – beside

dedins – inside

defora – outside

Davant hi havia un bar / Al davant hi havia un bar.
There was a bar in front (or opposite).

El cotxe duia un cofre damunt / El cotxe duia un cofre al damunt.
The car had a box on top.

The following prepositions cannot be preceded by *al*:

dins / dedins / dintre

enmig – in the middle

(*a*) *baix* – below, downstairs

(*a*) *dalt* – above, upstairs

enfora, (*al*) *lluny* – far

(*a*) *prop* – near

endavant – ahead

enrere, endarrere, arrere – backwards

amunt – upwards

avall – downwards

endins, endintre – inwards

enfora – outwards, far away

7.2.2.3.3 *Time*

- Relative times:

  ara – now
  abans – before
  després – after
  tard – late
  prest / *aviat* – soon (*aviat* also meaning 'quickly')

- Absolute times:

  sempre (rare: *tothora*) – always

  mai – never, (ever in non affirmative sentences: see p. 162 on negation):

  – Has vist mai una balena? 'Have you ever seen a whale?'
  – Mai 'Never.'

  mai més – never again

- Frequence:

  sovint – often
  a vegades / *de vegades* – sometimes
  de tant en tant / *adesiara* – now and then

- Conjoining events:

  llavors / *aleshores* – then

- Simultaneity:

  mentrestant – meanwhile

- Days:

  avui – today
  ahir – yesterday
  abans-d'ahir / *despús-ahir* – the day before yesterday
  demà – tomorrow
  demà passat / *despús-demà* – the day after tomorrow

demà passat l'altre – two days after tomorrow
anit – tonight
anit passada – last night

- Years:

enguany – this year

7.2.2.3.4 *Logic*

The negation adverb is *no* (see p. 163 on its relation with other negative words and the way it works to negate the verb). Also the probability or the logical relation between two sentences can be expressed by means of adverbs:

- Possibility

potser / tal vegada / tal volta – perhaps

- Logical continuity and discontinuity

conseqüentment / per conseqüent – for this reason
tanmateix / nogensmenys (rare) – however

- Addition

també – also
tampoc – neither
a més a més – moreover
fins i tot – even

7.3 Unstressed pronouns

7.3.1 Forms

Unstressed pronouns are a frequent area of difficulty for learners of Catalan. Unstressed pronouns can refer to grammatical persons used as object (what is called the **accusative**), a noun to which something is done or given (called the **dative**), to circumstances (adverbial pronouns *en* and *hi*), as an indication of partition (*en*), or as substitutions for certain verb complements. These pronouns usually precede the verb, except with infinitives, gerunds, and imperatives, when they tend to follow the verb. The exact shape of unstressed pronouns can differ according to their exact position in the sentence and the type of sound (vowel or consonant) they adhere to (last/first sound of the verb or another weak pronoun in a compound). Let us see those shapes by means of these tables:

Personal pronoun (stressed)	Before consonant	Before vowel (or h)	After consonant	After vowel
jo	em	m'	-me	'm
tu	et	t'	-te	't
vostè (m) / ell (acc)	el	l'	-lo	'l
vostè (f) / ella (acc)	la	l'/la	-la	-la
vostè / ell / ella (dat)	li	li	-li	-li
(neuter, acc)	ho	ho	-ho	-ho
nosaltres	ens	ens	-nos	'ns
vós / vosaltres	us	us	-vos	-us
vostès (m) / ells (acc)	els	els	-los	'ls
vostès (f) / elles (acc)	les	les	-les	-les
vostès / ells / elles (dat)	els	els	-los	'ls
3rd pers reflexive	es	s'	-se	's

As with the article *la*, the accusative third person feminine pronoun remains *la* before an unstressed *i* or *u*, even when preceded by (always unpronounced) *h*: *Gutenberg inventà la impremta* 'Gutenberg invented the printing press' → *Gutenberg la inventà* 'Gutenberg invented it'.

Adverbial and partitive pronouns	Before consonant	Before vowel	After consonant	After vowel
	en	n'	-ne	'n
	hi	hi	-hi	-hi

See the combination table on p. 104–5 for the exact shape of the resulting sets when weak pronouns appear in pairs.

7.3.2 *Basic usage*

Except for third persons, accusative and dative pronouns do not differ. Let us see first some examples of accusative in all possible positions:

La meva filla m'estima – My daughter loves me.

Estima'm, filla meva – Love me, my daughter.

No és fàcil estimar-me – It is not easy to love me.

No em pots estimar – You cannot love me.

La teva filla l'estima – Your daughter loves him/her.

Estima'l, filla meva – Love him, my daughter. (Note that 'Love her' would have to be *Estima-la.*)

No és fàcil estimar-lo – It is not easy to love him.

No el puc estimar – I cannot love him.

The same weak forms from the above examples appear when the pronoun is in dative. Differences only arise in the third person. We can check it with examples with the verb *contestar* 'to answer', requiring dative for the person who receives the answer, and accusative for the answer itself:

La meva filla m'ha contestat – My daughter has answered me.

Contesta'm, filla meva – Answer me, my daughter.

No és fàcil contestar-me – It is not easy to answer me.

No em pots contestar – You cannot answer me.

La teva filla li ha contestat – Your daughter has answered her/him.

Contesta-li, filla meva – Answer her/him, my daughter.

No és fàcil contestar-li – It is not easy to answer her/him.

No li puc contestar – I cannot answer her/him.

The basic function of adverbial pronouns *hi* and *en* is substituting for adverbial clauses. *Hi* can appear instead of any adverbial clause, except for those introduced by preposition *de*, in the which case *en* is selected when a substitution is needed:

– Has anat al mercat? 'Have you been to the market?'

–Ara hi vaig 'I'm going (there) now'.

– Has anat al mercat? 'Have you been to the market?'

–Ara en vinc 'I'm coming back (from there) now'.

(Other uses and refinements of *hi* (p. 97) and *en* (p. 95) are explained below.)

Ho is the third-person neuter pronoun. It is never used in functions other than objects and copular predicates. Not appearing as a subject, it cannot translate the whole set of the functions of English 'it'. Its referent can be a neuter demonstrative pronoun (*això* 'this', *allò* 'that') or a whole predicate:

No sé fer el que em demanes perquè el que em demanes és molt difícil. → No ho sé fer perquè (això) és molt difícil.
I do not know how to do what you ask me because what you ask me is very difficult.

No sé que és això, però deixa-ho damunt la taula.
I do not know what this is, but leave it on the table.

7.3.3 *Further refinements*

7.3.3.1 Pronominalising copular predicative expressions

Copulae are verbs with a weak, almost voided meaning, just connecting the subject and predicate, as in English 'to be'. In fact, since the verb is actually part of the predicate, the remainder is called the **predicative expression.** Omitted predicative expressions reappear under the form of an unstressed pronoun. This is an important difference with English, where complements can be omitted leaving no trace (leaving just the verb as a tag, or even just a single word).

a. With *ser* (not locative, i.e. not expressing a place), *semblar*, and *parèixer*, the selected pronoun is *ho*:

   Ell era amic meu, però ja no ho és.
   He was a friend of mine, but he is not anymore.

   Aquest imprès és per sol·licitar la beca o no ho és?
   Is this form for applying for the scholarship or isn't it?

   És un afinador de guitarres? No, no ho és.
   Is it a guitar-tuner? No, it is not.

   Aquest exercici és difícil, no t'ho pareix?
   This exercise is difficult, don't you think?

   La frase és d'en Miquel, però no ho sembla.
   This sentence is Miquel's, but it doesn't sound like it.

   If the predicative expression is a definite noun phrase, also *el / la / els / les* can do the work. However, it seems rather affected and is not used as much anymore:

   – Aquella senyora és la metgessa? – No, no l'és.
   – Is that lady the doctor? – No, she is not.

   The more common answer here is '*No, no ho és*'.

b. With *estar* both *ho* and *hi* can appear in the place of the predicative expression:

   – Estàs cansada? 'Are you tired?'

   – No, no hi estic / – No, no ho estic. 'No, I am not.'

   but phrases depending on **estar** introduced by a preposition are only replaced by **hi:**

   Fa tres dies que estem sense telèfon We have not had a phone line for three days → **Fa tres dies que** hi **estem**

   – Ja esteu de tornada? 'Are you already on your way back?'
   – Sí, ja hi estem 'Yes, we are.'

   Adjective complements introduced by **de** (see p. 31) are pronominalised with **en**:

   Estic fart de veure aquestes coses I'm sick of seeing such things → **N'estic fart** I'm sick of it.

c. With resultative verbs:

c1. Nominal predicates depending on verbs *tornar(-se)* 'to turn', *quedar(-se)*, *parar* and *acabar* 'to end up', substitution is performed by *hi*:

El pare s'ha tornat boig – Dad has gone crazy → **El pare s'hi ha tornat.**

Pararàs malalt si continues així – You'll get ill if you go on like this→ **Hi pararàs si continues així**

c2. *Esdevenir* 'to become' and *resultar* 'to result' require *ho*:

Volíem que fos una bona mestra i ho ha esdevingut.
We wanted her to be a good teacher and she has become one.

No volíem que hi hagués morts, però quatre víctimes ho han resultat.
We did not want anybody to die, but four people have (lit. . . . have resulted (dead)).

c3. With *fer–se* 'to turn up by their own means or effort' both *en* and *hi* can be used:

Metge? El meu fill vols fer-se'n / fer-s'hi.
A doctor? My son wants to become one.

d. Replacing verbs and/or objects moved for emphasis (topicalised predicates):

When a predicate is put under focus and therefore moved often towards the beginning of the sentence, the preposition *de* optionally introduces it. When this occurs, the trace left at its original place in the sentence is *en*; otherwise (when no *de* introduces it), the trace can be either *hi* or *ho* according to what has been said above:

De car no n'era, aquell hotel. / Car no ho era, aquell hotel.
Expensive? That hotel was not expensive.

Segur no hi estic, però em sembla que ell tampoc no hi està.
Sure? I'm not sure, but I don't think he is either.

e. With exclamations:

When the predicative expression with *ser* or *estar* is part of an exclamation, and especially when degree or quantity are underlined, *en* or *ho* can also be the replacing pronoun:

Que és de gran aquesta casa! → Que n'és aquesta casa!
How big this house is!

Que lluny que és això! → Que ho és això!
How far away it is!

f. Predicatives:

When a nominal complement in the predicate – other than the predicative expressions listed above – refers to the subject, the object or any other predicative expression, it is replaceable usually by *hi*:

Va arribar ben tranquil → Hi va arribar
He was calm when he arrived (lit. He arrived very calm).

'He', the subject, both did the arriving, and was calm, although in the Catalan structure 'tranquil' is a complement of the verb.

Va ser consagrat bisbe el 1898 → Hi va ser consagrat el 1898.
He was consecrated bishop in 1898.

Fer when meaning 'to reckon' or 'to consider' takes *hi*:

M'han dit que ja és emèrit, però jo no l'hi feia.
I have been told that he already has emeritus status, but I didn't think he did.

Dir-se ('to be called') can select either *ho* or *en*:

Aquest restaurant es diu L'olivera? No, no s'ho diu / No, no se'n diu.
Is this restaurant called L'olivera? No, it is not.

7.3.3.2 Uses of *en*

7.3.3.2.1 Main function

The main function of *en* is to replace phrases beginning with the preposition *de*. This applies to adverbials, but also to other verb and noun phrases:

Aquestes fruites vénen de Sud-amèrica → Aquestes fruites en vénen.
This fruit comes from South America. (Note that fruit is a mass noun in English, but can be a count noun in Catalan.)

Parlen de política → En parlen.
They are talking about politics.

Ha presentat el ministre i ha defensat el punt de vista del ministre → Ha presentat el ministre i n'ha defensat el punt de vista.
She has introduced the minister and she has defended his point of view.

If the sentence in the last example was *Ha presentat el ministre i ha defensat el seu punt de vista*, then it would imply that the subject defended her own point of view, not the minister's. The original example cannot imply the same because *en* cannot be used in a reflexive way.

7.3.3.2.2 En *with quantifiers and undetermined nouns*

En is used in sentences where a quantified noun functioning as a subject or an object disappears, leaving the quantifiers. In such cases, *en* replaces the noun:

Han vingut tres nois → N'han vingut tres.
Three boys have come → Three have come.

Vull algunes roses → En vull algunes.
I want some roses → I want some.

–Vas agafar un taxi? 'Did you take a taxi?'
– No, no en passava cap. 'No, none came by.'

When a quantified noun is modified by an adjective or an adjectival phrase and the adjective remains in the phrase after the omission of the noun (replaced by *en*), then the preposition *de* is compulsory:

Hi havia quatre cotxes mal aparcats → N'hi havia quatre or **N'hi havia quatre de mal aparcats.**
There were four cars parked badly → There were four.

–Tens una brusa vermella? 'Have you got a red blouse?'
– Sí, en tinc una de vermella i dues de vermelles amb dibuixos blancs. 'Yes, I've got one red one and two red ones with white pictures.'

En is also the pronoun used to replace the object when this is an undetermined noun:

Vols caramels? → En vols?
Would you like some sweets? → Would you like some?

Tenim poca carn? No n'he comprada.
Are we running out of meat? I haven't bought any.

7.3.3.2.3 *Void en*

When *anar* is used in absolute sense, meaning 'to go away', it is pronominal and in addition it requires *en*, even if the place being left (the **procedence complement** introduced by *de*) or intended to be reached (and the introduced by a preposition of direction) is made explicit:

Va acabar la festa i tothom se'n va anar (cap) a casa.
The party finished and everybody went home.

Era tard i me'n vaig anar de la festa.
It was late and I left the party.

There are some other void uses of *en*, giving a verb a special meaning:

Sortir-se'n 'to succeed, to overcome a difficult situation': *Amb aquests polítics, el país no se'n sortirà* 'With politicians like these, the country will not get out of trouble'.

estar-ne (*de*) 'to appreciate', 'to dote on someone': *L'avi n'està molt dels seus nets* 'The grandfather loves his grandchildren very much'.

Observe the redundant use of *en* in respect of the phrase introduced by *de* in the last example. In the following four examples, redundance is avoided in formal language, but usual in colloquial speech:

adonar-se'n 'to realise': *No se n'adona de la realitat* (colloquial) / *No s'adona de la realitat* (formal) 'He doesn't take reality into account'.

riure-se'n 'to laugh at, to ignore': *Se'n riurà del que li diguis* / *Es riurà del que li diguis* 'She will ignore whatever you tell her'.

fotre-se'n (same meaning as *riure-se'n*, but vulgar): *Se'n fotrà del que li diguis* / *Es fotrà del que li diguis* 'She will stick two fingers up at whatever you tell her'.

penedir-se'n 'to regret': *Me'n penedeixo d'haver signat el contracte* / *Em pendeixo d'haver signat el contracte*, 'I regret having signed the contract'.

7.3.3.3 Uses of *hi*

7.3.3.3.1 Main function

The main function of *hi* is replacing any type of complement introduced by a preposition other than *de*:

He anat a Roma cinc vegades → Hi he anat cinc vegades.
I have been to Rome five times → I've been there five times.

El mestre s'interessa per l'aprenentatge dels nens → El mestre s'hi interessa.
The teacher is interested in the children's learning → The teacher is interested (in it).

Estic acostumat a aquestes coses → Hi estic acostumat.
I am used to these things → I am used to it.

With relational prepositions indicating a location (especially *sobre*, *sota*, *damunt*, *davall*, *davant*, *darrere*, and optionally with *dins* / *dintre*, *fora*) *hi* can substitute the place introduced by the preposition. Optionally the relational preposition can be preceded by the weak preposition *a*, which can be turned into the contraction *al* with *davant*, *darrere*, *damunt*, *davall:* but in all cases the relational preposition remains in the sentence as an adverb:

Deixa els llibres damunt de la taula → Veus la taula? Deixa-hi els llibres (a / al) damunt
Leave the books on the table → Can you see the table? Leave the books on it.

S'ha cremat la botiga. Jo hi era (a / al) davant quan van arribar els bombers.
The shop has burnt down. I was in front of it when the fire brigade arrived.

La teva germana és dins de la casa? La hi / L'esperàvem (a) fora.
Is your sister inside the house? We were waiting for her outside.

7.3.3.3.2 *Haver-hi*

A lexicalised use of *hi* is found in the existential verb *haver-hi* ('there is, are, etc.'), where *hi* is compulsory regardless of substitutions:

A la platja hi ha massa gent.
There are too many people on the beach.

No hi haurà clemència per als infractors.
There will be no mercy for offenders.

7.3.3.3.3 *Void uses and meaning nuances of hi*

With the verbs of sense: *veure* ('to see') and *sentir* ('to hear'), *hi* is compulsory when the meaning is absolute and there is no object, i.e. when the verb refers to the capability of seeing or hearing:

Les pedres no hi veuen ni hi senten.
Stones cannot see or hear.

El meu gat s'ha fet vell i ja no hi sent.
My cat has grown old and it cannot hear (but *El meu gat s'ha fet vell i ja no sent els ratolins* – My cat has grown old and it cannot hear the mice).

Tocar-hi (after *tocar*, 'to touch') has a different sense: it is only used in the idiom *no tocar-hi*, meaning 'to be insane, not to understand something' or *tocar-hi*, 'to understand something':

> **Apujar els impostos ara? Aquest ministre no hi toca!**
> Rasing taxes now? This minister is out of touch with reality!

It is also used with the following verbs:

> **Jugar-s'hi** 'to bet', **Què us hi jugueu que el Barça guanyarà la lliga** How much do you bet on the Barça winning the league?
>
> **mirar-s'hi** ' to be careful', **Quan ho contis als nins, mira-t'hi una mica i no els espantis** When you tell it to the children, be a little careful and do not scare them.
>
> **dir-hi** 'to match', **Aquestes sabates no hi diuen amb aquests pantalons** These shoes do not match these trousers.
>
> **pintar-hi** '(colloquially) to pertain, to be pertinent', **En aquella festa jo no hi pintava res** I had nothing to do with that party.
>
> **tornar-s'hi** 'to strike back', **Et digui el que et digui el director, no t'hi tornis** Whatever the director says you, do not answer back.

7.3.3.3.4 *Hi and li*

Hi and *li* overlap in two areas. Firstly, when the indirect object is not a person, *hi* is normally preferred over *li:*

> **Telefonava al director de l'institut → Li telefonava.**
> I was calling the headmaster of the high school → I was calling him.
>
> **Telefonava a l'institut → Hi telefonava.**
> I was calling the high school → I was calling them.
>
> **Pegava cops al seu veí → Li pegava cops.**
> He was hitting his neighbour → He was hitting him.
>
> **Pegava cops a la paret → Hi pegava cops.**
> He was hitting the wall → He was hitting it.

Secondly, the pronoun *li* turns into *hi* when combined with pronouns *el, la, els, les*. In any case, *li* can be maintained, as was usual in classical Catalan and still is in Valencian dialects:

> **Dóna les joguines a la nena → Dóna-les-hi** (and also **Dóna-li-les).**
> Give the toys to the girl → Give her them / Give them to her.

Avui mostraré la ciutat al nostre convidat → Avui la hi mostraré (and also **Avui li la mostraré).**
Today I'll show the city to our guest (Better, 'I'll show our guest around the city') → Today I'll show him it / Today I'll show it to him.

In colloquial Catalan this conversion spreads also to the combination *li* + *en* and to the combinations of *els* (dative) with *el, la, els, les, en.* This over-application of the rule should not affect formal language:

L'avi conta històries al seu net → (formal) **L'avi li'n conta** → (informal) **L'avi n'hi conta.**
The grandfather tells tales to his grandson.

El meu pare escrivia aquestes cartes als seus amics → (formal) **El meu pare els les escrivia** → (informal) **El meu pare les hi escrivia.**
My father used to write these letters to his friends.

7.3.3.3.5 *Combining hi and ho*

When pronouns *hi* and *ho* meet together, the resulting combination is *l'hi*:

He enganxat això a la porta → Ho he enganxat a la porta + Hi he enganxat això → L'hi he enganxat.
I have stuck this on the door.

7.3.3.4 Special uses of dative pronouns

7.3.3.4.1 *Ethic dative*

Dative pronouns can be used to stress the effects of actions on other people:

El nen m'ha suspès tres assignatures.
The boy has failed three subjects (implying that this has an effect on me) (lit., when talking about one's son: 'The boy has failed three subjects for me').

Si no corres, et tancaran la farmàcia.
If you do not rush, you will find the chemist's closed (lit., 'If you do not run, they will close the chemist's on you').

7.3.3.4.2 *Possessive dative*

A certain reluctance experienced in Catalan against overusing possessives favours this construction with datives, normally translatable into English by means of possessives (see p. 43):

Li han pintat la casa.
He has got his house painted (lit. 'They have painted the house for him').

Ens han robat el cotxe.
Our car has been stolen (lit. 'They have stolen the car from us').

7.3.3.4.3 *Redundant use of pronoun*

With certain verbs the use of the dative pronoun is redundant, especially with verbs of (dis)like or interest, occurence, and also in possessive dative constructions (see p. 100 above).

i. Like, dislike, and interest

   Al teu germà li agrada molt discutir.
   Your brother loves arguing (lit. Arguing is very pleasing to your brother).

   Als meus fills les llenties els fan fàstic.
   My children hate lentils.

   Als jugadors no els importava el resultat del partit.
   The players did not care about the result of the match.

ii. Occurence

   Aquestes coses sempre li ocorren a en Pere.
   These things always happen to Pere.

iii. Possessive dative constructions
   The dative is more easily duplicated when the 'possessed' thing is subject of the sentence:

   Als excursionistes els peus els feien mal.
   The hikers' feet hurt.

   A qui li cauen els cabells és al teu amic.
   The person losing his hair is your friend.

   When the thing under possession is not the subject, then duplication becomes optional and clearly colloquial:

   (Li) rentava el cap a sa mare.
   He washed his mother's hair (literally, 'head').

7.3.3.5 Weak pronouns in verbal compounds and clitic raising

As already said, clitics follow the verb when it is an infinitive, a gerund or an imperative. Yet infinitives and gerunds often occur in verbal compounds and modal verb phrases. In such cases, clitics can 'climb' and appear before the main verb, normally inflected as a personal form:

Vaig fer-me gran molt aviat → Em vaig fer gran molt aviat.
I grew up very quickly.

Hauran de pagar amb targeta de crèdit → Hauran de pagar-hi / Hi hauran de pagar.
You (polite, plural) will have to pay by credit card.

No van saber educar-te → No et van saber educar and also **No van saber-te educar.**
They didn't know how to bring you up.

Attention must be paid not to place a clitic by a verb that cannot take a given complement. This occurs with intransitive verbs depending on a verb of sense. In these cases, the clitic acting as an object must be attached to the main verb:

He vist venir els nois → Els he vistos venir (and not ***He vist venir-los,** because *venir* cannot take an object).
I've seen the boys arrive → I've seen them arrive.

(See p. 79 for the usage of past participle and gender and noun agreement.)

Along the same lines, note the following:

Vaig veure venir els nois →	**Els vaig veure venir**
	Vaig veure'ls venir
	***Vaig veure venir-los**
I saw the boys arrive →	I saw them arrive.

7.3.3.6 Combining two or more weak pronouns

When two or more pronouns are to be attached to the same verb, the basic pattern is as follows:

se – dative – accusative – *en* – *hi*

Em dóna la bossa → Me la dóna.
She is giving me the bag → She's giving it to me.

Et poso sal a la sopa → Te n'hi poso.
I'll put salt in your soup → I'll put some in.

However, some exceptions to this basic rule exist:

a. When, as seen above, *li* turns into *hi* in a combination with *el* / *la* / *els* / *les*. In such cases, the order becomes accusative-dative:

   He comprat el cotxe al meu veí → L'hi he comprat (L' for **el cotxe,** accusative, and **hi** for **al meu veí,** dative**).**
   I've bought the car from my neighbour → I've bought it from him.

b. In the compound *se n'ho*, possible when combining *ho* with a transitive verb of movement, as *portar-se'n* or *dur-se'n*:

   Si ho deixes al portal, algú se n'ho durà.
   If you leave it at the main door, someone will take it away.

   Certainly, the synthetic forms *endur* and *emportar* exist, where the pronoun has been absorbed by the verb. At present, the sentence in the example would more commonly be generated as *'Si ho deixes al portal, algú s'ho emportarà'*, where the order inversion does not occur.

   The actual shape of pronouns when combined respect what is said in section 7.3.1 above about their relation to the verb:

   a. *hi* is unstressed, and therefore combinations *la hi* and *-la-hi* produce unapostrophised *la*.
   b. *li* is never reduced to *l'*, and therefore *l'hi* is never a contraction of *li+hi*, but a contraction of *el+hi*.
   c. where verbs begin with vowels, it is the last pronoun in a combination before the verb that is apostrophised, and the apostrophe is between the pronoun and the verb: *me n'he anat* 'I have gone away', and not **me'n he anat*.
   d. inside a pronoun combination, when two solutions seem possible, the winner is the one showing an apostrophe at the rightmost position: *se'n va* 'she goes away', and not **s'en va*; *dur-la'n* 'to bring it (fem)' and not **dur-l'en*. The only exception to this rules is the form *-l'en* (with a masculine object), preferred to *-lo'n*.

The following shows the resulting form when object pronouns are combined. The four forms are for: 1) before a verb beginning with a consonant; 2) before a verb beginning with a vowel; 3) after a verb ending in a consonant; 4) after a verb ending in a vowel.

		Object (and reflexive)											Complement[1] (and other uses)
		el	la	els	les	ho	en	em	et	es	ens	us	hi
Complement (and other uses)	em	me'l	me la	me'ls	me les	m'ho	me'n		te'm	se'm		us em[2]	m'hi
		me l'	me l'	me'ls	me les	m'ho	me n'		te m'	se m'		us m'	m'hi
		-me'l	-me-la	-me'ls	-me-les	-m'ho	-me'n		-te'm	-se'm		-vos-me	-m'hi
		-me'l	-me-la	-me'ls	-me-les	-m'ho	-me'n		-te'm	-se'm		-us-me	-m'hi
	et	te'l	te la	te'ls	te les	t'ho	te'n			se't			t'hi
		te l'	te l'	te'ls	te les	t'ho	te n'			se t'			t'hi
		-te'l	-te-la	-te'ls	-te-les	-t'ho	-te'n			-se't			-t'hi
		-te'l	-te-la	-te'ls	-te-les	-t'ho	-te'n			-se't			-t'hi
	es	se'l	se la	se'ls	se les	s'ho	se'n						s'hi
		se l'	se l'	se'ls	se les	s'ho	se n'						s'hi
		-se'l	-se-la	-se'ls	-se-les	-s'ho	-se'n						-s'hi
		-se'l	-se-la	-se'ls	-se-les	-s'ho	-se'n						-s'hi
	li	li'l	li la	li'ls	li les	li ho	li'n	me li	te li	se li	ens li	us li	li hi
		li l'	li l'	li'ls	li les	li ho	li n'	me li	te li	se li	ens li	us li	li hi
		-li'l	-li-la	-li'ls	-li-les	-li-ho	-li'n	-me-li	-te-li	-se-li	-nos-li	-vos-li	-li-hi
		-li'l	-li-la	-li'ls	-li-les	-li-ho	-li'n	me-li	te-li	se-li	'ns-li	-us-li	-li-hi

	ens	ens el ens l' -nos-el 'ns-el	ens la ens l' -nos-la 'ns-la	ens els ens els -nos-els 'ns-els	ens les ens les -nos-les 'ns-les	ens ho ens ho -nos-ho 'ns-ho	ens en ens n' -nos-en 'ns-en		te'ns te'ns -te'ns -te'ns	se'ns se'ns -se'ns -se'ns		us ens us ens -vos-ens -us-ens	ens hi ens hi -nos-hi 'ns-hi
	us	us el us l' -vos-el -us-el	us la us l' -vos-la -us-la	us els us els -vos-els -us-els	us les us les -vos-les -us-les	us ho us ho -vos-ho -us-ho	us en us n' -vos-en -us-en	me us me us -me-us -me-us		se us se us -se-us -se-us			s'hi s'hi -s'hi -s'hi
	els	els el els l' -los-el 'ls-el	els la els l' -los-la 'ls-la	els els -los-els 'ls-els	els les els les -los-les 'ls-les	els ho els ho -los-ho 'ls-ho	els en els n' -los-en 'ls-en	me'ls me'ls -me'ls -me'ls	te'ls te'ls -te'ls -te'ls			us els us els -vos-els -us-els	els hi els hi -los-hi 'ls-hi
	hi	l'hi l'hi -l'hi -l'hi	la hi la hi -la-hi -la-hi	els hi els hi -los-hi 'ls-hi	les hi les hi -les-hi -les-hi	l'hi l'hi -l'hi -l'hi	n'hi n'hi -n'hi -n'hi	m'hi m'hi -m'hi -m'hi	t'hi t'hi -t'hi -t'hi	s'hi s'hi -s'hi -s'hi	ens hi ens hi -nos-hi 'ns-hi	us hi us hi -vos-hi -us-hi	
	en	l'en el n' -l'en -l'en	la'n la n' -la'n -la'n	els en els n' -los-en 'ls-en	les en les n' -les-en -les-en	n'ho n'ho -n'ho -n'ho		me'n me n' -me'n -me'n	te'n te n' -te'n -te'n	se'n se n' -se'n -se'n	ens en ens n' -nos-en 'ns-en	us en us n' -vos-en -us-en	

Notes

1. For intransitive verbs (non allowing object) with complement as *pegar, telefonar*: *telefoneu als vostres amics a l'hotel → telefoneu-los-hi.*
2. As in *Si us em poseu al davant, no puc passar.*

Chapter 8

Prepositions

Prepositions are part of the syntax of a language and are what is known as a 'closed set'; whereas we can create new nouns, adjectives, and verbs with ease, it is very difficult to introduce new prepositions. This is mainly because of what they do: prepositions indicate a relationship between two parts of a sentence. Prepositions enable us to talk about relationships in space and time – where things are in relation to other things (and this includes how things move in relation to others), and whether events happen before, during, or after other events. There are single-word (simple) and multi-word (complex) prepositions, and they can also be unstressed (atonic) and stressed (tonic).

8.1 Unstressed (atonic) prepositions

There are five simple unstressed prepositions in Catalan (*a*, *en*, *amb*, *de*, and *per*) and one compound preposition (*per a*). Since these are all unstressed, they are subject to vocalic reduction, and so *a* is pronounced [ə], *en* is pronounced [ən], and so on. They are also elided in some situations, as shown in the following, with examples where usage does not correspond to English.

Preposition	Usage	English equivalent	Example
a (a + el = al, a + els = als)	Introducing indirect objects	to	*Escric una carta al meu amic.* I'm writing a letter to my friend.
	location	in, at	*Sóc a casa.* I am at home.

	direction	to	*Vas al supermercat?* Are you going to the supermarket?
en	location	in (See p. 148 on temporal *en*)	*Això només passa en aquest país.* That only happens in this country.
amb		with	
de (d') (de + el = del, de + els = dels)	origin	of, from	
	separation	from	
	cause	of	
	means	on	
	agent	by	
per (per + el = pel, per + els = pels)	location	through, by, over, about	
	temporal manner / cause	during by, through	
	agent (of passive constructions)	by	
	distribution	per	
	substitution	for, on someone's behalf	
	predicative	as, for	
	consideration	for, for the sake of	

	motive destination or purpose	because of for	(see p. 150–2 on *per* and *per a*)
per a (per a + el = per al, per a + els = per als)	beneficiary	for	
	destination or purpose	for	(see p. 150–2 on *per* and *per a*)

It is important to note that prepositions are normally dropped before relative 'que' – see p. 143 on subordinate clauses and p. 206 for common mistakes.

The difference between the usage of *a* and *en* is difficult for English speakers, since these do not fully overlap with the English prepositions 'to' and 'in'. This is particularly the case with expressions of place (**location** and **direction**), where both are used, and there can even be variation across speakers and regions. The rule of thumb is that *a* tends to be used for both location and direction when physical location is being referred to, and when introducing the definite article. In addition, *en* tends to be used before the indefinite article, *algun* and demonstrative adjectives.

In **time expressions,** *a* generally means 'the time at which' something takes place, whereas *en* means an extent of time over which something takes place.

A la tarda et vindré a veure.
I'll come to see you in the afternoon.

En dos dies va tenir la feina acabada.
In two days he had the job completed.

8.2 Simple and compound stressed (tonic) prepositions

Simple (single-word) stressed prepositions in Catalan are as follows:

contra – against

durant – during

entre – between, among

excepte – except

fins – up to, until

malgrat – despite

mitjançant – by means of

no obstant – despite (meaning the same as *malgrat*)

pro – in favour of (somebody or something), on behalf of

salvant, salvat – except for

segons – according to

sobre – on, above, about

ultra – beyond, over and above (this is rarely used)

vers / devers / envers – towards (in terms of motion) (this is rarely used in this sense, and often *cap a* is used instead)

vers / envers – in relation to / towards. This has the same meaning as *de cara a.*

vers / devers – approximately

en vist – in comparison with (this is rarely used)

Contra can be used alone or in the compound *en contra de*, but the latter only when the opposition meant is moral, not physical:

> **va col·locar la cadira contra la paret**
> ***va col·locar la cadira en contra de la paret**
> s/he placed the chair against the wall

> **ha posat la nena contra la mare**
> **✓ha posat la nena en contra de la mare**
> She set the girl against her mother.

There are a set of prepositions that have both simple and compound forms, and the latter is normally formed with *de*. The compound form is compulsory when the preposition is separated from the complement in some way as with an adverb in a parenthetic insertion:

> **Els diners són sota, potser, del matalàs.**
> The money is, perhaps, under the mattress.

Here is a list of compound prepositions:

a part (de) – apart from

(de) cap (a) – towards

dalt (de) – on

damunt (de) – on, over

darrere (de) – behind

davall (de) – under

davant (de) – in front of

deça (de) – this side of

dellà (de) – the far side of

devora (de) – beside

dins (de), dedins (de), dintre (de) – inside

fins (a / en) – up to, until

llevat (de) – except

sobre (de), dessobre (de) – on, above

sota (de), dessota (de) – under

tocant (a) – with respect to

vora (de) – near, beside, almost

Place prepositions (*dalt, damunt, darrere, davall, davant, deçà, dellà, dins, dedins, dintre, devora, sota, dessota, sobre, dessobre*) can be used with or without a following *de*. When a following *de* introduces a personal pronoun, the phrase *de* + pronoun can turn into a possessive:

> **Va caure damunt nosaltres / Va caure damunt de nosaltres / Va caure damunt nostre.**
> It fell on top of us.

The same place prepositions can be preceded by preposition *a*. Except for *dalt, dins, dintre, sobre*, and *sota*, the contracted form of preposition + article *al* can also appear before the main preposition if this is followed by *de*. The meaning does not change and the variation is purely stylistic when not depending on the specific dialect. The same conversion of *de* + pronoun into a possessive can also apply here:

> **Va caure a damunt nosaltres / Va caure a damunt de nosaltres / Va caure a damunt nostre / Va caure al damunt de nosaltres / Va caure al damunt nostre**

Also *fora* can be used alone or preceded by *a*, but when this occurs, a following *de* is compulsory:

Fora (de) la casa fa fred
A fora de la casa fa fred.
It is cold out of the house.

Vora is perceived as feminine, and thus a *la* and not *al* is used to precede it:

Seia vora del foc / Seia vora el foc / Seia a la vora del foc.
S/he was sitting by the fire.

Lluny always requires a following *de* and never admits a preceding *a* or *al*:

La casa era lluny de la carretera.
The house was far from the road.

With *fins* the unstressed prepositions *a* or *en* can be selected or omitted following their individual uses in place and time expressions:

Anirem d'excursió a la muntanya → Anirem d'excursió fins a la muntanya.
We shall go on an excursion to the mountain → We shall go on an excursion up to the mountain.

La setmana que ve farem obres → Fins la setmana que ve farem obres.
We shall do (building) works next week → We shall do (building) works up to next week.

En aquesta hora encara treballeu? → Fins en aquesta hora encara treballeu?
Are you still working at this time? → Have you been working up to now?

The same applies to the presence or omission of *a* in *cap a*:

Vaig cap a la universitat.
I'm heading to the university.

Vaig cap allà.
I going in that direction.

No sé cap (a) on vaig.
I do not know where I'm going.

There are also a set of compound prepositions that do not have alternate forms:

abans de – before (in terms of time)

a menys de – except

arran de – level with, straight after (cause)

a través de – across

com a – as, in one's role as

des de – from, since

després de – after

(de) dret a – towards

enfront de – facing, opposite

enmig de – among

entorn de – around

entremig de – among

fora de, defora de, enfora de – outside, except

llevat de – apart from

lluny de – far from

(a) prop de – near

quant a, pel que fa a, respecte a – with respect to, as regards

tret de – except

Just as when they are standing alone, when unstressed prepositions belong to a compound, they are dropped before a following conjunction *que* (see p. 143 on preposition dropping):

> **Des que el van elegir no s'ha aprovat cap llei.**
> Since he was elected, no laws have been passed.
>
> **Arran que van atacar l'ambaixada, les relacions es refredaren.**
> After the embassy was attacked, relations cooled off.

Com a is normally used to insert a nominal predicate referring to the subject or to a nominal complement in the predicate, and even to an adverb or an adverbial, to draw attention to a quality applied to the referred element. It is translatable as '(acting) as, in the role of':

> **Jo això t'ho explico com a amic.**
> I tell you this as a friend.
>
> **Admiro molt la teva germana com a metgessa.**
> I admire your sister as a doctor (she is a doctor).

The sense of an implicit copula is felt in such usage, and it can turn explicit for emphasis or disambiguation as seen here:

Jo això t'ho explico com a amic que sóc.
Admiro molt la teva germana com a metgessa que és.

In certain dialects *com a* can be used instead of comparative *com* before undetermined nouns:

Els soldats van arribar bruts com a xinxes.
The soldiers arrived as dirty as pigs (lit.: 'as bedbugs').

Prepositional phrases built with prepositions combined with adverbs or adverbials are very common, and the list seems to be open. See some of the most usual here:

Place: *a l'entorn de*, *al voltant de* 'around'; *al capdamunt de* 'on top of'; *al capdavall de* 'at the bottom of'; *al nivell de* 'at the level of'; *a tocar de*, *a frec de* 'close to'; *a l'abast de* 'in reach of'; *a la cara de* 'in front of, opposite'; *de camí (cap) a* 'on the way to'

Time: *al llarg de* 'during'; *a punt de*, *a les portes de* 'about to'; *al cap de*, 'after'; *a partir de* 'since, after'

Intention: *per tal de*, *a fi de* 'for'; *a favor de* 'in favour of'; *de cara a*, *en vista a* 'in order to'

Cause: *gràcies a* 'thanks to'; *a causa de*, *per mor de* 'because of'; *amb motiu de* 'on the occasion of'

Agent: *per part de*, *a càrrec de* 'by' (in passives or noun constructions); *a costa de* 'at the expense of'

Condition: *a condició de* 'on condition that'; *en virtut de* 'by virtue of'

Exception: *a excepció de* 'except'; *a pesar de* 'despite'

Relation: *pel que fa a*, *a propòsit de*, *pel que respecta a*, *respecte a*, *respecte de* 'about'; *d'acord amb* 'according to' (see p. 176 on copulative sentences)

Chapter 9

Derivation: Creating words from other words

Prefixes and suffixes are used to create new words from already existing ones. In many cases, their use is already fixed and the new word appears in the dictionary, even with speakers being unaware of the relationship with the original word. This process is called **lexicalisation**. In other cases, the use of affixes is productive, open to speakers' creativity. Some of these affixes are qualifying: they introduce aspects such as size, attitude, place, time, quantity, or relation. Other affixes create new words for new concepts, usually changing grammatical categories, as in English *special* (adj.) → *specialist* (noun). This section focuses on such operations, namely converting words into other words.

9.1 Qualifying affixes

Suffixes are added to stems, not to fully inflected words. Therefore the resulting order of components is: stem, suffixes, verbal/nominal inflection morphemes. For example:

pot – potet (pot – small pot)

pot-s – potet-s (pots – small pots)

cas-a – caset-a (house – small house, especially one in the countryside)

Even when a feminine does not show an explicit mark for gender in its basic form (see p. 22), it takes one when a suffix is added:

carn – carneta (e.g. a bit of meat)

por – poreta (fear – a bit of fear)

Remember that most of the nouns ending in a stressed vowel are the result of an omitted final *–n* that reappears in plurals and before a suffix:

mà – maneta (hand – small hand)

perdó – perdonar (pardon – to pardon)

ple – emplenar (full – to fill)

camí – caminal (path – dirt track / animal track)

9.1.1 *Augmentatives and diminutives*

It is impossible to distinguish between augmentatives (making something larger), amelioratives (indicating approval from the speaker), and pejoratives (indicating disapproval from the speaker), for augmentatives always include a notion of like or dislike:

a. Augmentative + ameliorative: *–às/–assa*
   cavall – cavallàs (horse – great big horse)
   casa – casassa (house – massive house)
   cotxes – cotxassos (cars – huge (and impressive) cars)
   olles – ollasses (saucepans – great big saucepans)

Some words have already been lexicalised with such suffixes and appear in the dictionary with their own meaning, often independent of the nominal meaning of the suffix, for instance: *bordegàs* 'lad', *barcassa* 'barge', *carassa* 'grimace, gargoyle', *gallinassa* 'hen droppings', *maregassa* 'heavy sea', *vinassa* 'wine dregs'.

b. Augmentative + pejorative: *–ot/–ota*, *–arro/–arra*
   llibre – llibrot – llibrarro (book – long (boring) book)
   cova – covota – covarra (cave – big (dark and scary) cave)
   troncs – troncots – troncarros (trunks – big (ugly) trunks)
   gàbies – gabiotes – gabiarres (cages – large (and unpleasant) cages)

Some words already lexicalised with such suffixes include: *bassiot* 'puddle', *clatellot* 'slap on the back of the neck' (equivalent to a 'clip around the ear'), *illot* 'small island', *mastegot* 'blow, slap', *xicot* 'boy, boyfriend', *carota* 'grimace', *paraulota* 'swearword', *pigota* 'smallpox', *riota* 'guffaw, mockery', *cagarro* 'turd', *llobarro* 'sea bass'.

c. Diminutive + ameliorative: *–et/–eta*, *–ó/–ona*
   animal – animalet – animaló (animal – little animal)
   mare – mareta – marona (mum – mummy)
   petits – petitons – petitones (small – tiny)
   mans – manetes – manones (hands – little hands)

Some lexicalised words with these suffixes include: *arquet* '(violin) bow', *cavallet* 'easel', *coloret* 'rouge', *cotxet* 'pram', *curset* '(learning) workshop', *disquet* 'diskette', *fullet* 'leaflet', *llibret* 'booklet', *pitet* 'bib', *tamboret* 'stool', (*fer l'*) *ullet* 'to wink', *xiulet* 'whistle'; *avioneta* '(small) plane', 'light aircraft', *banqueta* '(small) bench', *barbeta* 'chin', *bombeta* 'light bulb', *burleta* 'ridiculer', *camioneta* 'van', *camiseta* 't-shirt', *careta* 'mask', *carreta* 'low cart', *cullereta* 'tea spoon', *cometes* 'inverted commas', *horeta* 'nap', *llengüeta* 'tab', *mamballeta* 'clap', *maneta* 'door handle', *metralleta* 'machine gun', *nineta* '(eye) pupil', *proveta* 'tube flask', *samarreta* 't-shirt', *tereseta* 'puppet', *vinagreta* 'vinaigrette', *xancleta* 'slipper', *xinxeta* 'pin'; *aleró* 'spoiler, wing flap', *balenó* 'baby whale', *barbó* 'chin, chin beard', *barreró* 'post', *calderó* 'small stew pot', *canaló* 'guttering (on a roof)', *carabassó* 'courgette', *carreró* 'lane', *cordó* 'string', *escaló* 'step', *espatlló* 'shoulder blade', *paretó* 'roadside parapet', *regiró* 'scare', *tovalló* 'napkin'; *carona* 'delicate face', *rodona* 'circle; whole note'.

Other suffixes for size and quality exist, but are less used except for some already lexicalised concepts: *–í/–ina, –ol/–ola, –ell/–ella, –ic, –im* as in *corbatí, barretina; ventijol, banderola; cordill, forquilla; altell, portella; carric; plugim.*

9.1.2 Superlatives

Adjectives and adverbs can appear under the highest degree of comparison, the superlative (see p. 183 for more on how to use these). This can be achieved by suffixation (*–íssim/–íssima/–íssims/–íssimes*) or by using the definite article and the adverb *més*:

> *Una nena alta* – A tall girl > *una nena altíssima* a very tall girl (i.e. the tallest you could imagine).
>
> *La nena més alta* (*de totes*) – The tallest girl (of all).

Two notes on word formation: (a) adjectives ending in *–ble* (see p. 126 below) turn into *–bilíssim* in the superlative degree: *amable* > *amabilíssim*. (b) A short list of adjectives prefer *–èrrim/–èrrima/–èrrims/–èrrimes* instead of forms of *–íssim*: *cèlebre* > *celebèrrim, íntegre* > *integèrrim, míser* > *misèrrim, pobre* > *paupèrrim, pulcre* > *pulquèrrim, salubre* > *salubèrrim*, although regular counterparts with *–íssim* are also possible.

As in the example above, superlatives with *–íssim* are always absolute and they do not stand comparison (**la nena altíssima de totes*), although a prepositional complement introduced by (*d'*) *entre* ('among') can be added:

> **Una nena altíssima (entre totes les de la classe).**
> A very tall girl among those in the class.

9.1.3 *Other quality-changing suffixes*

Suffixes *–enc/–enca, –ós/–osa, –ís/–issa* add a nuance of approximation to adjectives (like in the English '–ish'): *vermellós* ('reddish' < *vermell*), *groguenc* ('yellowish' < *groc*), *malaltís* ('sickly' < *malalt*). There is a difference in use, though – whereas in English *–ish* is rather colloquial, in Catalan these can be used in all registers.

9.1.4 *Qualifying prefixes*

Beyond those prefixes listed below (see p. 121) that turn nouns, adjectives, or adverbs into verbs, other prefixes are used to add a given nuance to the word meaning. We offer here a list of them with indication of their general meaning and examples. These prefixes refer to four types of information: place, time, quantity, and relation, and occasionally some combination of them.

PLACE (physical or metaphorical, such as for rank):

amfi- both sides: **amfiteatre** amphitheatre

circum- around: **circumval·lació** ring road

cis- this side: **cisalpí** Cisalpine

infra- of a lower category: **infrahumà** subhuman

juxta- beside: **juxtaposició** juxtaposition

sobre- above, higher, in excess: **sobrealimentació** overfeeding

sota- below: **sotasignat** undersigned

sots-/sub- lower in rank, below: **subaquàtic** underwater

super- higher, abundant: **superdotat** exceptionally gifted

supra- above: **suprarenal** above the kidneys

trans- across: **transfronterer** cross-border

ultra- beyond, excessive: **ultramarí** overseas

vice- lower in rank, deputy: **vicepresident** vice-president

TIME:

ex- former: **exdona** ex-wife

post- after: **postguerra** post-war period

pre- previous: **prefabricat** prefabricated

neo- new: **neogòtic** neogothic

QUANTITY:

arxi- superlative: a

con-/com-/col-/cor- in common: **coautor** coauthor **col·lateral** collateral

hiper- hyper: **hipercorrecció** hypercorrection, overcorrection

mono- one: **monolingüe** monolingual

multi- many: **multilingüe** multilingual

pan- all: **panamericà** Pan-American

pluri- several: **plurianual** lasting for several years

poli- many: **poliesportiu** sports complex

semi- half, incomplete: **semiautomàtic** semiautomatic

uni- one: **unicolor** all one colour

RELATION:

a-/an- opposite: **asimètric** asymmetric

anti- opposition, protection: **vacuna antigripal** flu vaccine

contra- opposition, reciprocity: **contraexemple** counter-example

de(s)- reversal, negation: **decréixer** to decrease

no- no: **no-intervenció** non-intervention

pro- pro, in favour of: **proavortista** pro-choice (in abortion rights)

PLACE & QUANTITY:

extra- outside, extra: **extraescolar** out-of-school

PLACE & TIME:

ante- previous: **antepenúltim** antepenultimate, third from last

avant- previous: **avantsala** entrance hall

entre- between: **entreacte** interval

PLACE & RELATION:

para- beside, not exactly: **paramilitar** paramilitary

TIME & QUANTITY:

bes-/bi(s)- twice: **besavi** great-grandfather

di- twice: **diòxid** dioxide

re- repetition: **readmissió** readmission

sesqui- one and a half: **sesquicentenari** 150th anniversary

tri- three: **tripartit** three-party coalition

TIME & RELATION:

per- insistently, completely: **perfer** to finish completely

9.2 Category changing affixes

New verbs, nouns, adjectives, and adverbs can be created from different word classes by affixation, too. Articles, pronouns, demonstratives, quantifiers, prepositions, and conjunctions are what are called **closed sets**, so new examples of them cannot be created from other words.

9.2.1 *Creating new verbs*

Verbs are derived from other words by adding a verb ending (*–ar* or *–ir*, see p. 58, *–er/–re* do not produce new verbs), by a prefix and a verb ending, or by a suffix and a verb ending. There are no clear rules on verb creation, though. Many derived verbs have been lexicalised and are listed in the dictionary, such as *golejar*, formed from the noun *gol* + the verb ending *ejar*, meaning to score lots of goals.

In many cases the only difference between the noun and verb form of a word is the verb ending: *bany–banyar; barra–barrar; corda–cordar; gir–girar; bes–besar; falca–falcar; moc–mocar; pas–passar; rem–remar; so–sonar; tap–tapar; vot–votar; xap–xapar*, etc. In some of these cases and others, the verb seems to have come first, and then the noun is created by taking away the verb ending (making the noun **deverbal**).

9.2.1.1 Verbal derivation by suffixation

Verbal derivation by suffixation makes use of *–ejar, –itzar, –inar, –egar, –ificar, –itar.* Of these, *–esar, –ificar*, and *–itzar* are the most used.

–ejar: This suffix shows (iterative) movement, tendence, frequency or cause. Movement: *bracejar, pernejar, ditejar, balancejar, boquejar, butxaquejar, collejar, cuejar, falcejar, furetejar, bufetejar, glopejar, golejar, grapejar, papallonejar, pipellejar, sabatejar, sacsejar;* tendence, imposture, approximation, i.e. 'to be like' or 'to show like'. In this sense, it can also be used to indicate what the weather is like, and also with some transitive verbs meaning 'to cause something to be like': *doctorejar, golafrejar, grandejar, grisejar, groguexar, guerxejar, justejar, malaltejar, mandrejar, mestrejar, padrinejar, poquejar, rarejar, sordejar, terrejar, vermellejar, vesprejar, verdejar*.

–itzar: When added to a noun means 'to turn something into', and with a reflexive weak pronoun means 'to become (something)', 'to do something related to' (such as in the English '*–ise*'): *aguditzar, alcoholitzar, autoritzar, caracteritzar, castellanitzar, centralitzar, climatitzar, colonitzar, democratitzar, esclavitzar, familiaritzar, globalitzar, humanitzar, independitzar, normalitzar, organitzar, professionalitzar, realitzar, sensibilitzar, simbolitzar, tranquil·litzar, utilitzar*, etc.

–ificar: Means 'to convert (something)', 'to turn into (something)'. The verb is normally transitive or pronominal intransitive (except for *nidificar, mel·lificar, fructificar* and some partial meanings of *prosificar* and *versificar*, which can be fully intransitive): *amplificar, autentificar, certificar, clarificar* (*aclarir* also exists), *codificar, crucificar, dosificar, exemplificar, identificar, justificar, modificar, personificar, pacificar, planificar, qualificar, rectificar, simplificar, unificar, verificar*.

–egar: The use of this suffix implies co-occurrence of one of the prefixes *a–, des–, en–/em–, es–, re–*. It is not a productive suffix anymore. The meaning of the resulting verb mainly depends on the stem and the prefix: *abonyegar, afamegar, amuntegar, apedregar, assedegar, despredregar, empolsegar, empudegar, enllitegar, esdentegar, revessegar.*

–itar: This is used to derive verbs from adjectives. It is not productive, and so does not create new forms. It means 'to turn' or 'to convert': *agilitar, (in)capacitar, debilitar, facilitar, felicitar* ('to wish happyness', not 'to make happy'), *(in)habilitar, (im)possibilitar*.

–inar: This is not productive, and is rare. It means 'to cover with', 'to attack with', 'to do something to somebody', '(certain animals) to give birth': *aporrinar, burxinar, clenxinar, (des)encalcinar, emblanquinar, gatinar, talpinar, torpedinar*.

9.2.1.2 Verbal derivation by prefixation

Forming verbs from other categories by prefixation requires in any case the addition of a verbal ending. Prefixes used for such purpose are *a–, con–, de–/des–, en–/em–, es–, in–/im–, re–*. Other prefixes appear in verbs, but they do not function as verbalisers. For instance, *contraatacar* 'to counter-attack' exists, but it relates to the noun *contraatac*. Compare it to *ciment* > *encimentar* 'to cover with cement' (*en-ciment–ar*, **enciment*), *pell* > *espellar* 'to flay' (*es-pell–ar*, **espell*). Examples are: *abaratir* ('to make cheaper' < *barat*), *acomodar* ('to accomodate' < *còmode*), *apropar* ('to bring nearer' < *prop*); *concentrar* ('to concentrate' < *centre*), *condensar* ('to condense' < *dens*), *congelar* ('to freeze' < *gel*); *deformar* ('to deform' < *forma*), *descarnar* ('to remove flesh from' < *carn*), *desgelar* ('to thaw' < *gel*); *enamorar* ('to inspire love' < *amor*), *embarcar* ('to embark' < *barca*), *entonar* ('to intone' < *to*); *esbrancar* ('to lop branches' < *branca*), *esparracar* ('to tear' < *parrac*), *esventrar* ('to disembowel' < *ventre*); *incomodar* ('to inconvenience' < *còmode*), *impugnar* ('to contest' < *pugna*), *intoxicar* ('to poison' < *tòxic*); *recolzar* ('to lean' < *colze*), *refredar* ('to cool' < *fred*), *retardar* ('to delay' < *tard*).

9.2.2 *Creating new nouns*

9.2.2.1 Creating nouns from verbs

The following suffixes make nouns from verb stems:

a. Meaning 'action or effect of such an action': *–ment, –ció, –nça, –dera, –dura, –dures, –all, –alla, –alles, –or, –atge, –dissa, –im, –era, –et, –ància, –ència, –ió: aclariment* ('explanation' < *aclarir*), *assoliment* ('achievement' < *assolir*), *cobrament* ('earnings' < *cobrar*); *concepció* ('conception' < *concebre*), *abolició* ('abolition' < *abolir*), *complicació* ('complication' < *complicar*); *confiança* ('trust' < *confiar*), *prometença* ('engagement' < *prometre*), *alabança* ('praise' < *alabar*); *xiuladera* ('whistling' < xiular), *llampegadera* ('lightning' < *llampegar*), *bullidera* ('boiling' < *bullir*); *banyadura* ('action of getting wet' < *banyar*), *investidura* ('investiture' < *investir*), *llimadura* ('filing' < *llimar*); *agranadures* ('sweepings' < *agranar*), *peladures* ('peelings' < *pelar*), *afalagadures* ('flatteries' < *afalagar*); *degotall* ('leak' < *degotar*), *començall* ('beginning' – rarer than *començament-* < *començar*); *contalla* ('story, tale' < *contar*), *deixalla* ('left-over' < *deixar*), *ploralla* ('crying' < *plorar*); *acaballes* ('ending' < acabar), *sobralles* ('left-overs' < *sobrar*); *abundor* ('abundance' < *abundar*), *bullor* ('boiling' < *bullir*), *inflor* ('swelling' < *inflar*); *reciclatge* ('recycling' < *reciclar*), *tatuatge* ('tattoo' < *tatuar*), *rodatge* ('film shooting' < *rodar*); *xiuladissa* ('whistling' < *xiular*), *trencadissa* ('breakage' < *trencar*), *cremadissa* ('burning' < *cremar*); *degotim* ('leak' < *degotar*), *ventim* ('beating' < *ventar*), *xerrim* ('chatter' < *xerrar*); *cacera* ('hunting' < *caçar*), *voltera* ('detour' < *voltar*); *refilet* ('trill' < *refilar*), *xuclet* ('mark on skin made by suckling' < *xuclar*); *abundància* ('abundant' < *abundar*), *extravagància* (rare – 'extravagance' < *extravagar*), *ressonància* ('resonance' < *ressonar*); *assistència* ('attendance' < *assistir*), *existència* ('existence' < *existir*), *excel·lència* ('excellence' < *excel·lir*); *admissió* ('admission' < *admetre*), *emissió* ('emission, broadcast' < *emetre*); *dispersió* ('dispersion' < *dispersar*), *reunió* ('meeting' < *reunir*).

b. Meaning 'object, instrument used in a given action': *–dor/a, –all, –et: rentadora* ('washing machine' < *rentar*), *aspirador* ('vacuum cleaner' < *aspirar*), *espolsador* ('duster' < *espolsar*); *abrigall* ('over coat' – anything used to protect oneself against the cold: *abric* is 'coat' as a specific garment < *abrigar*), *aturall* (< 'obstacle' *aturar*), *ventall* ('fan' < *ventar*); *rodet* ('bobbin' < *rodar*), *bolquet* ('dumper truck' < *bolcar*), *trinxet* ('curved knife' < *trinxar*).
c. Meaning 'place for a given action': *–dor, –tori, –all*: *menjador* ('dining room' < *menjar*), *rebedor* ('vestibule' < *rebre*), *estenedor* ('drying rack' < *estendre*); *dormitori* ('bedroom' < *dormir*), *oratori* ('chapel' < *orar*), *observatori* ('observatory' < *observar*); *amagatall* ('hiding place' < *amagar*), *estimball* ('cliff' < *estimbar*), *llenegall* ('slippery place' < *llenegar*).
d. Meaning 'person who performs a given action or profession': *–dor, –or, –(c)tor, –aire, –er*: *empaperador* ('paperhanger' < *empaperar*), *administrador* ('administrator' < *administrar*), *traïdor* ('traitor' < *trair*); *cantor* (old fashioned for 'singer' -more usual *cantant* < *cantar*), *editor* ('editor' < *editar*), *pintor* ('painter' < *pintar*); *conductor* ('driver' < *conduir*), *traductor* ('translator' < *traduir*), *dissector* ('dissector' < *dissecar*); *cantaire* ('choir singer' < *cantar*), *captaire* ('beggar' < *captar*), *rifaire* ('person in charge of a raffle' < *rifar*); *cuiner* ('cook' < *cuinar*), *arxiver* ('archivist' < *arxivar*), *viatger* ('traveller' < *viatjar*).

9.2.2.2 Creating nouns from adjectives

Adjectives can be turned into nouns by using a preceding article or, when in the plural, as undefined nouns. In the first case, the structure can be understood as a noun elision – when the noun can be recovered from the context, or as a nominalisation of the adjective, i.e. as the name of a quality. English can rarely do this, since it normally needs to use a noun empty of meaning such as 'one' or 'thing':

M'agraden els teus vestits excepte el verd. El verd no m'agrada.
I like your dresses except the green one. I don't like the green one (*verd* as a nominalised adjective) / I don't like the colour green (*verd* as a noun).

Many adjectives show the same form as related nouns:

Quin fred (noun) que fa!
My, it's cold!

Avui el dia és fred (adj.).
The day is cold today.

Menges massa dolços.
You eat too many sweets / sweet things.

Els caramels eren massa dolços.
The sweets were too sweet.

In some cases a nominalised adjective can bear a specialised meaning, already lexicalised in the dictionary with a specific sense:

Avui hi ha hagut ple a l'ajuntament.
The town council board has met today.

Crec que demà farà bo.
I think the weather will be good tomorrow.

El baix està desafinat.
The bass is out of tune.

Nominalisation can also be obtained by using suffixes as the following: *–or, –(e)dat, –(e)tat, –itat, –esa, –ia, –eria, –ària, –ada, –ura, –úria, –itud, –ió, –isme*. They all convert an adjective into a feminine noun, except for *–isme*, which produces masculine nouns: *grogor* ('yellowness' < *groc*), *fredor* ('coldness' < *fred*), *dolçor* ('sweetness' < *dolç*); *bondat* ('goodness' < *bo*), *claredat* ('clearness' < *clar*), *soledat* ('loneliness' < *sol*); *brevetat* ('briefness' < *breu*), *igualtat* ('equality' < *igual*), *novetat* ('novelty', 'newness' < *nou*); *actualitat* ('currentness', 'current time' < *actual*), *sinceritat* ('sincerity' < *sincer*), *respectabilitat* ('respectability' < *respectable*); *petitesa* ('smallness' < *petit*), *bellesa* ('beauty' < *bell*), *pobresa* ('poverty' < *pobre*); *malaltia* ('illness' < *malalt*), *cortesia* ('politeness' < *cortès*), *covardia* ('cowardliness' < *covard*); *beneiteria* ('stupidity' < *beneit*), *murrieria* ('flattery' < *murri*), *badoqueria* ('bewilderness' < *badoc*); *amplària* ('width' < *ample*), *curtària* ('shortness' < *curt*); *llargada* ('length' < *llarg*), *pagesada* ('farmer-like action' < *pagès*); *blancúria* ('whiteness' – rarer than *blancor* < *blanc*), *foscúria* ('darkness' – rarer than *foscor, fosca-* < *fosc*), *vellúria* ('oldness' < *vell*); *quietud* ('quietness' < *quiet*), *verosimilitud* ('verisimilitude' < *verosímil*), *laxitud* ('slackness' < *lax*); *tensió* ('tension' < *tens*), *precisió* ('accuracy' < *precís*), *concisió* ('succintness' < *concís*); *cristianisme* ('Christianism' < *cristià*), *realisme* ('realism' < *real*).

9.2.2.3 Using adverbs and conjunctions as nouns

Some adverbs and conjunctions can be used as nouns, with a similar meaning to their original meaning or function:

Dóna'm un **sí** *i seré feliç.*
Give me a yes and I'll be happy.

Ja compto més **ahirs** *que* **demàs.**
I already count more yesterdays than tomorrows.

Estic cansat dels teus **peròs.**
I'm tired of your buts.

Deixa de posar-me **emperons.**
Stop finding buts (i.e. arguments against).

Except for *emperò*, when adverbs and conjunctions ending in a stressed vowel are treated as nouns, they do not add *–n* before *–s* in the plural.

9.2.3 *Creating new adjectives*

9.2.3.1 Creating adjectives from nouns

Most of the suffixes in the list below share the general meaning 'related to' the noun in question, which on some occasions can be divided between 'similar to', 'produced by', or 'coming from'. When such senses are clear, we indicate them. Two notes on word formation:

a. In general, word stress falls on the suffixes themselves, except for those called 'preaccented', which require stress to fall on the previous syllable in the word.

b. When no alternation is indicated in the list below, the suffix creates invariable adjectives for gender. The gender of adjectives depends on the gender of the ruling noun, and not from the gender of the primitive noun from which the adjective is derived.

Adjectival suffixes: *–à/–ana, –al, –ani/–ània, –aqüi/–àqüia, –ar, –ari/–ària, –enc/–enca, –eny/–enya, –er/–era, –erol/–erola, –estre, –eu/–ea, –èvol/–èvola, –í/–ina, –ià/–iana, –ís/–issa, –ista, –iu/–iva, –ívol/–ívola, –ó/–ona, –ori/–òria, –ós/–osa*, and the preaccented *–ic/–ica, –fil/–fila, –fob–/–foba, –fon/–fona:*

Stressed: *andorrà/andorrana* ('Andorran' < *Andorra*), *ciutadà/ciutadana* ('citizen' < *ciutat*); *ambiental* ('ambient' < *ambient*), *especial* ('especial' < *espècie*); *momentani/momentània* ('instant' < *moment*), *instantani/instantània* ('instantaneous' < *instant*); *terraqüi/terràqüia* ('earthly' – rare except in *globus terraqüi* < *terra*); *cel·lular* ('cellular'< *cèl·lula*), *solar* ('solar' < *sol*); *alimentari/alimentària* ('alimentary' < *aliment*), *bancari/bancària* ('related to banks' < *banc*); *estiuenc/estiuenca* ('summer' < *estiu*), *canadenc/canadenca* ('Canadian' < *Canadà*); *ferreny/ferrenya* ('iron-like' < *ferro*), *caribeny/caribenya* ('Caribbean' < *Carib*); *fruiter/fruitera* ('relating to fruit' < *fruita*), *brasiler/brasilera* ('Brazilian' < *Brasil*); *camperol/camperola* ('coming from the countryside' < *camp*), *bosquerol/bosquerola* ('coming from the woods' < *bosc*); *campestre* ('relating to the countryside' < *camp*), *terrestre* ('relating to the Earth' < *Terra*); *europeu/europea* ('European' < *Europa*), *plebeu/plebea* ('plebian' < *plebs*); *benèvol/benèvola* ('benevolent' < *bé*), *malèvol/malèvola* ('malevolent' < *mal*); *diamantí/diamantina* ('diamantine' < *diamant*), *marroquí/marroquina* ('Moroccan' < *Marroc*); *cristià/cristiana* ('Christian' < *Crist*), *darwinià/darwiniana* ('Darwinian' < *Darwin*); *ferrís/ferrissa* ('made of iron' < *ferro*), *roquís/roquissa* ('abundant in rocks' < *roca*); *classista* ('classist' < *classe*), *capitalista* ('capitalist' < *capital*); *abusiu/abusiva* ('abusive' < *abús*), *significatiu/significativa* ('significative' < *significat*); *senyorívol/senyorívola* ('lordly' < *senyor*), *germanívol* ('brotherly' < *germà*); *setmesó/setmesona* ('born after seven months of pregnancy' < *set mesos*), *rodanxó/rodanxona* ('short and fat' < *rodanxa*); *il·lusori/il·lusòria* ('illusory' < *il·lusió*), *decisori/decisòria* ('decision-making' < *decisió*); *boirós/boirosa* ('foggy' < *boira*), *orgullós/orgullosa* ('proud' < *orgull*).

Pre-accented: *alcohòlic/alcohòlica* ('alcoholic' < *alcohol*), *escultòric/escultòrica* ('relating to sculpture' < *escultura*); *columbòfil/columbòfila* ('relating to dove-breeding' < Lat. *columba*); *membranòfon/membranòfona* ('membranophonic' < *membrana*).

9.2.3.2 Creating adjectives from verbs

Suffixes: *–able* (after transitive verbs of the 1st conjugation), *–ible* (after transitive verbs from the 2nd and 3rd conjugations), *–ant* (after verbs from the 1st conjugation), *–ent* (after verbs from the 2nd and 3rd conjugations), *–int* (rare, after *oir* and *sortir* and derived forms); *–aire, –dís/–dissa, –dor/–dora, –ívol/–ívola, –tori/–tòria.*

Amable ('friendly' < *amar*), *edificable* ('buildable' < *edificar*); *creïble* ('believable' < *creure*), *admissible* ('admissible' < *admetre*); *convertible* ('convertible' < *convertir*), *insubstituïble* ('nonreplaceable' < *substituir*); *triomfant* ('victorious' < *triomfar*), *creixent* ('growing' < *créixer*), *sobresortint* ('protruding' < *sobresortir*); *dansaire* ('dancing' < *dansar*), *ploraire* ('cry-baby' < *plorar*); *aferradís/aferradissa* ('sticky' < *aferrar*), *plegadís/plegadissa* ('foldable' < *plegar*); from *–dor* (relating to the ability to perform the action implied by the verb): *menjador/menjadora* (*la nena no és gaire menjadora* 'the girl is not a good eater' < *menjar*), *prometedor/prometedora* ('promising' < *prometre*); from *–dor* ('worthy of becoming the object of the verb'): *menjador/menjador* ('edible' < *menjar*), *mostrador* ('worthy showing' < *mostrar*); *mengívol/mengívola* ('edible' < *menjar*), *escoltívol/escoltívola* ('worthy a listen heard' < *escoltar*); *inflamatori/inflamatòria* ('inflammatory' < *inflamar*), *classificatori/classificatòria* ('classificatory' < *classificar*).

9.2.4 ***Creating new adverbs***

Adverbs can be created easily from adjectives – see p. 79.

Chapter 10

Compounds

Catalan includes a good deal of **compound words** – words built from two stems and one single word ending, as in English 'bookcase', 'dishwasher' or 'skyscraper'. In general, the main difference with English is that Catalan compounds tend to place the main component on the left and the qualifying component on the right: *rentavaixelles* ('dishwasher'), *bocagròs* ('bigmouth'). Some compounds are written in two separate words, such as nouns followed by another noun acting as an adjective. In this section we revise compounds according to their grammatical structure.

10.1 Verb + noun

These are formed by verbs in third-person singular indicative (with elision of eventual final *–ix* in verbs from the 3rd conjugation, and addition of *–e* to 2nd conjugation verbs) followed by a noun. The meaning of the resulting word, metaphorical or not, relates to a person or a thing carrying out the action conveyed by the verb on the noun, understood as the verb's object (*comptagotes, matamosques, portacigarretes*) or as an adverbial (*correcamins, pixatinters*). So, a *rentaplats* (dishwasher) is a machine that washes dishes (or plates, in Catalan).

10.1.1 With the noun in plural

These compounds have the same ending in both the singular and plural:

> *cagadubtes, cagamiques; cobreobjectes; comptafils, comptagotes, comptapasses, comptaquilòmetres; correcames, correcamins;*

eixugamans, eixugaparabrises, eixugavidres; escurabutxaques, escuradents, escura-xemeneies; estrenyecaps; giracamises, giradiscos, giratroncs; guardaagulles, guardacostes, guardacotxes, guardaespatlles, guardajoies, guardamobles, guardapits; llevataps, llevataques; marcapassos; matasegells, mataespurnes, matamosques, matallums; menjamiques, menjacapellans; obrecartes, obrellaunes, obreampolles; parallamps, paracaigudes, para-xocs; petjapapers; pixatinters, pixa–reixes; ploracossos, ploramiques, ploramorts; portaavions, portabombetes, portacigarretes, portaclips, portadocuments, portafirmes, portalàmpades, portallapis, portamonedes, portamines, portaobjectes, portaviandes; rentamans, rentapeus, rentaplats; tallaungles, tallapapers, tallapins; tapaboques, tapaforats, tapajuntes; tocadiscos; torracollons, torrapipes; trencaclosques, trencacolls, trencanous.

10.1.2 With the noun in singular

Singular and plural alternation of the resulting word is possible:

cagaferro, cagalatxa; cobrellit, cobretaula, cobrecap, correbou; eixugamà; esclata-sang; gira-sol, girapeix; gratacel; guardabarrera, guardafoc, guardafred; torcebraç; matafoc, matafred, matagent; parabrisa, para-sol, paravent; portabandera, portacreu, portaveu; tallacircuit, tallafoc, tallagespa, tallavent; tornaboda, tornaveu.

10.2 Noun + noun

In this combination the second noun acts as an adjective modifying the first one. In general, however, the second noun stays unaltered in the plural (*una festa sorpresa – dues festes sorpresa*), except for some especial cases as *berenar sopar – berenars sopars, jutge àrbitre – jutges àrbitres. Figaflor* admits both *figaflors* and *figues flors.*

berenar sopar, cafè teatre, camió cisterna, ciutat dormitori, cotxe bomba, cuina menjador, falda pantaló, festa sorpresa, figaflor, gos llop, idea força, jutge àrbitre, paper moneda, peix lloro, sobre bossa, sofà llit, vagó restaurant.

The name of a colour can be followed by the name of an object or an animal for precision. These combinations follow the general rule, i.e. the plural affects just the first element: *gris perla, groc canari, verd poma, vermell cirera.*

10.3 Noun (or pronoun) + verb

Syntactic relations between the compound's elements can differ: they can be object + verb as in *capgirar, colltrencar-se, bocabadant*; subject + verb as in *terratrèmol* or *pellobrir-se*; or adverbial + verb as in *collportar, peucalcigar, aiguabatre*, or *manllevar.* Those words appearing as infinitives can be inflected as verbs; those appearing as participles can be inflected as adjectives: *No capgiris el llit. Les teves amigues semblen alacaigudes.*

aiguabarrejar-se, aiguabatre, aireferit, alacaigut, alaestès, alaferit, alalligat, alapintat, alatrencat, bocabadant, capgirar, capllevar, caragirar, casatinent, collportar, corprendre, culcosit, drethavent, esmaperdut, garratibat, esquenaromput, manllevar, palplantar-se, pellobrir-se, peucalcigar, salprendre, sangcremar, terratinent, terratrémer, ullprendre.

With the pronoun *que*, the following nouns can be obtained: *quemenjar, quemullar, queviures* (see below for combinations of two pronouns and a verb).

10.4 Noun + adjective / adjective + noun

Resulting in adjectives, often referring to physical aspect of people or animals. As adjectives, they can be inflected in gender and number: *panxacontent / panxacontenta / panxacontents / panxacontentes.*

alablanc, alablau, alallarg, barbablanc, barbaflorit, barbaclòs, barbafresc, barbafort, barbagrís, barbamec, bectort, bocaestret, bocagròs, bocamoll, bocatort, camacoix, camacurt, camaobert, camaprim, camatort, capblanc, capbuit, capcot, capdret, capgròs (also a noun referring to a processional figure), *capdret, colltort, esquenadret, galtaplè, merdacaner, panxabuit, panxacontent, peuterrós, pocapena, poca-roba, pocatraça, pocavergonya, terraplè* (noun).

PART III

Clauses and sentences

Chapter 11

Word order

11.1 The basics

Word order is part of the syntax of a language, and can be at the core of syntax. English is fairly fixed in its word order, meaning that the grammatical role of an element will often depend on where it occurs in the sentence. So, 'Dog bites man' and 'Man bites dog' mean two very different things, since in English we expect the subject to come before the verb, and the object to come after it. Word order in Catalan is freer than in English; a frequent mistake made by learners of Catalan (and other similar Romance languages) is to look at words and then assume that the syntax is regular. In reality, we need to work out the syntactical role of each part of the sentence, since as we can see from the example above, syntax is part of meaning too.

11.1.1 *Subject – Verb – Object*

The normal and basic word order of Catalan clauses is the same as in English: the subject comes first, then the verb, then the object (this is frequently abbreviated to SVO).

> **La meva tia regala bombons.**
> My aunt gives away chocolates.

However, there is a significant difference between Catalan and English; whereas this order is rarely broken in statements in English, in Catalan you can change the order, particularly to place emphasis on a certain section. This is because in Catalan a main way to focus on information is to place it at the end of the sentence. This is unlike English, which (in speech at least) uses verbal emphasis where the information takes place, such as the difference between 'The *house* over the hill is red,' meaning the house and not another building, as opposed to 'The house *over* the hill is red,' meaning the house over the hill and not the one before it. This is called the **information focus.**

L'home llegeix el diari avui.
The man is reading the newspaper *today*.

Avui llegeix el diari l'home.
The man is reading the newspaper today.

Note that the second option, in not following the normal word order, is much more marked; it makes the listener or reader pay more attention to the structure and the information at the end of the sentence. The trouble for English-language learners in Catalan is in figuring out which is the subject, and which the object, since in English this is clear from the order. For the most part in Catalan, this is calculated based on the meaning of the sentence; in the above example, we expect the verb 'read' to have a human subject, and for the object to be some type of product of written language.

Word order also changes in questions (see below) and subordinated clauses (see p. 136 below).

11.1.2 Adverbials

Unlike in English, Catalan tends to place adverbials immediately before or after the words they relate to.

Va ratificar formalment les funcions del department.
He formally ratified the department's powers / He ratified the department's powers formally.

If the adverb is placed elsewhere, this is marked and is used to focus attention on the content of the adverb itself.

Remember that in most cases adverbs cannot be placed between the auxiliary and the verb, as stated on p. 80.

11.2 Word order in specific contexts

11.2.1 Questions

11.2.1.1 Yes–no questions

Yes–no questions are where the answer is either yes or no. In English, the typical way to construct these is to place the subject after the auxiliary verb:

Do you like that?
Are you hungry?
Can you see me?

In English, particularly in informal contexts, we can also use the normal declarative sentence structure but add rising intonation:

You like that?

You're hungry?

In Catalan, typically the second option is followed for forming yes–no questions: the declarative sentence is said with a different intonation to indicate it is a question. When nothing else is added or changed to indicate it is a question, the intonation is normally rising:

Neva?
Is it snowing? (As opposed to '*Neva*', 'It is snowing.')

T'agrada?
Do you like that? (As opposed to '*T'agrada*', 'You like that.')

Tens gana?
Are you hungry? (As opposed to '*Tens gana*', 'You're hungry.')

Somewhat confusingly for English speakers, questions can (and frequently do) have a falling intonation in Catalan. This is the case when the conjunction '*que*' is used to introduce a yes–no question: all of the above could be expressed as '*Que neva?*', '*Que t'agrada?*', and '*Que tens gana?*', and the meaning wouldn't change. It is important for English speakers not to confuse this structure with the interrogative pronoun '*què*' – both the written accent and the difference in some varieties of the spoken language are important for meaning:

Que t'agrada?	**Què t'agrada?**
Do you like it?	What do you like?

Here 'What do you like?' is what is often referred to as a wh– question in English, and in grammar has the term **partial questions**, where answers are not limited to 'yes' and 'no'.

It is also possible to invert the subject and verb in Catalan to form a question. However unlike English, the subject should go after both the verb and object, rather than straight after a verb:

Ens farà treballar amb ell, el director? (Much rarer: Ens farà el director treballar amb ell?)
Will the boss make us work with him?

This is because the verb and object form the predicate, and this is treated as a separate group to the subject. This is even the case when the subject is a personal pronoun:

Saps qui és, tu?
Do you know who she is?

Although '*Saps tu qui és?*' might be heard from native speakers, it is recommended to avoid this type of construction and stick to the standard structure *Saps qui és?* Also, see p.164 for more on questions.

11.2.1.2 Wh– questions (partial questions)

For partial questions, see p. 166.

11.2.2 Subordinate clauses

In subordinate clauses, Catalan avoids placing anything apart from weak object pronouns between the subordinator (e.g. *que*) and the subordinated verb. This means that frequently word order is verb – object – subject in subordinated clauses.

He llegit el llibre que em va enviar l'editorial.
I've read the book that the publishers sent me.

As seen in the example, this can mean that in English the elements of the sentence need to be reorganised. A way to maintain the order of the elements, if the order is important, is to use a passive structure in English:

I've read the book sent to me by the publishers.

The Catalan word order can lead to ambiguity, which the reader or listener needs to resolve through the context:

És ell, l'home que volia veure l'Ariadna.
It's him, the man who wanted to see Ariadna / It's him, the man (who) Ariadna wanted to see.

See p. 205 for preposition *a* introducing stressed relatives to avoid such ambiguities, as in:

És ell, l'home a qui volia veure l'Ariadna.

11.2.3 Cleft sentences

Cleft sentences are used to highlight a piece of information from a sentence. They get their name from 'cleaving' (that is, splitting) a clause into two parts, each one getting its own verb. The main clause normally has 'it' as the subject and 'be' as the verb in English, and in Catalan the verb '*ésser*' is used. The second clause then begins with a relative pronoun.

Serà la setmana vinent quan arribarà el paquet.
It will be next week when the package arrives (emphasising the time when it will arrive).

Since the second part of the cleft sentence is a subordinate clause, then the word order is the same as with other subordinate clauses: verb – object – subject.

See p. 174 for more information on cleft sentences.

11.2.4 *Current redundant repetitions (pleonasms)*

A pleonasm is where an element of a phrase is repeated, either unnecessarily or for emphasis. In terms of word order, this frequently occurs when the word order is changed to be able to put emphasis on an element at the start or end of the sentence, a phenomenon known as left detachment and right detachment.

11.2.4.1 Left detachment

With left detachment, an element is placed at the start of the sentence, essentially to say what the sentence is about. If the section 'detached' is necessary for the verb, that is, it is a direct or indirect object, or another necessary complement, then it must replaced by a pronoun.

Les tovalloles, les he esteses a la terrassa.
The towels? I've hung them on the terrace.

11.2.4.2 Right detachment

Right detachment places a section at the end of the sentence, almost as an afterthought. Again, those sections that are a necessary for the verb are replaced by a pronoun (see p. 89 on pronominalisation).

Dóna-me'l, el llibre.
Give it to me; just give me the book.

See p. 205 on overuse of pleonasm.

Chapter 12

Relating elements

12.1 Coordination

12.1.1 Concept

Coordination is where conjunctions are used to join two elements in a sense of addition, alternation or opposition. Addition is performed by copulative conjunctions (*i, ni*), alternation by disjunctive conjunctions (*o*), and opposition by adversatives (*però, sinó*). These are dealt with in more detail below, but here are some examples.

Copulative conjunctions:

La meva mare és arquitecta i el meu pare és mestre.
My mother is an architect and my father is a teacher.

No era alt ni gras.
He wasn't tall or fat (= 'he wasn't tall and he was not fat'; not alternatives).

Disjunctive conjunctions:

Què t'agrada més, la carn o el peix?
What do you like best, meat or fish?

No vull sopar a casa ni a fora.
I don't want to have dinner at home or outside (= 'I don't want to have dinner either at home or outside'; strictly alternatives).

Adversative conjunctions:

Han tingut un accident, però no s'han fet mal.
They have had an accident, but they are not injured.

El paquet no era blanc, sinó negre.
The parcel was not white, but black.

12.1.2 *Types*

12.1.2.1 Copulatives

As can be seen in the example above, *i* is the normal link adding two elements in affirmative sentences. The elements can be sentences, phrases, or words. Special attention must be paid to gender agreement in such constructions: when a masculine and a feminine are linked, a postposed adjective referring to both elements will appear in the neutral form, which coincides with the masculine in Catalan:

La casa i el cotxe han resultat massa cars (massa cares*).**
The house and the car turned out too expensive.

In contrast, a determiner common to two coordinated nouns will appear in the gender of the first one:

Aquestes (fem.) vacil·lacions (fem.) i dubtes (masc.) no tenen sentit.
These hesitations and doubts make no sense.

Due to the sense of addition conveyed by the adverb *també*, it can appear accompanying *i*, or, with a more intensive sense, in the copulative phrase *com també*:

Llegesc en català i també en francès.
I read in Catalan and also in French.

Perseguirem el plagi, com també els textos ofensius.
Plagiarism will be prosecuted, as will offensive texts.

Així com can be used with the same sense as *com també*.

Ni has a copulative sense in negative contexts when no exclusion is intended, as in the example above *No era alt ni baix* (= *No era alt i no era baix*). In these cases, duplication is possible:

No era ni alt ni baix.

Other correlative copulatives exist, as *tan*(*t*) . . . *com* . . ., but *i* . . . *i* . . . is not allowed in Catalan:

M'agrada tant la verdura com la carn.
I like both vegetables and meat.

12.1.2.2 Disjunctives

o 'or', and *ni* 'nor' admit a duplicate use, that is they can appear before both members of an opposition, which is their normal usage when they are comparable terms:

O llegeixo o escric, però no puc fer les dues coses alhora.
I read or I write, but I cannot do both things at the same time.

La festa no es farà ni ara ni mai.
The party won't take place neither now nor ever.

This duplicate use is blocked after the conjunction *si* introducing a noun clause (see p. 143) and rare after conjunction *que* in the same function. In this second case, the combined reinforcing formula *o bé . . . o bé . . .* is preferred:

***No sé si o ve o se'n va → No sé si ve o se'n va.**
I don't know whether she is coming or going.

Assegura't que o paga o torna la mercaderia → Assegura't que o bé paga o bé torna la mercaderia.
Make sure that he either pays or returns the goods.

Duplication is not possible with imperatives, which are replaced by the present tense in combined disjunctives:

***O demana perdó o vés-ten → O demanes perdó o te'n vas → Demana perdó o vés-te'n.**
You can either say sorry or leave / Say sorry or leave.

Other coordinated disjunctive formulae have a temporal origin: *adés . . . adés . . ., ara . . . ara . . ., ja . . . ja . . .*

Ja et dóna les gràcies, ja es queixa.
Either he thanks you, or he complains.

Sia . . . sia . . . involves a conditional sense (*whether . . . or. . .*)

Sia molt o sia poc, vull cobrar.
Whether it's a lot or a little, I want to get paid.

12.1.2.3 Adversatives

Both *però* and *sinó / sinó que* translate 'but', however *sinó* should be used when following a negative clause. Furthermore, *sinó que* replaces *sinó* when it introduces a clause with a verb in a personal form:

Vam decidir no anar al cinema, sinó només a sopar.
We decided not to go to the cinema, but rather just have dinner.

L'estiu passat no vaig viatjar, sinó que em vaig quedar a casa treballant.
Last summer I did not travel, (but) rather I stayed at home working.

Sinó can appear even when the first member of the coordination is only implicit:

No parla sinó anglès.
He doesn't speak (any other language) but English.

However, *però* can also appear after a negative clause when both statements involved are combinable, i.e. when no open opposition is intended (when no 'instead' would fit):

Vam decidir no anar al cinema, però no perquè no ens agradi.
We decided not to go to the cinema, but not because we don't like it.

L'estiu passat no vaig viatjar, però en tenia ganes.
Last summer I did not travel, but I wanted to.

There exists an adverbial concessive usage of *però*, not to be confused with this adversative function. When concessive, *però* does not appear at the beginning of the clause, and moreover it often appears between commas:

Estic malalt. La malaltia, però, no és greu.
I'm ill. The illness, however, is not serious.

12.1.3 Elision

Coordination allows elision of an element in order to avoid repetition. Just think about how in English repetition of a noun can be avoided by using 'one(s)' in the second instance, or a verb by using 'do' or any other auxiliary verb involved. In Catalan both cases would be solved by simple elision:

Prefereixes les sabates negres o les vermelles?
Do you prefer the black shoes or the red ones?

El meu pare se n'ha anat d'excursió, però jo no.
My father has gone on a trip, but I haven't.

As observed on p. 28–9, preposition *de* is required when the second, isolated adjective does not refer to a determined noun: *No sé si prefereixes unes sabates negres o unes de vermelles*. However, no preposition is needed when no pronominalisation is intended and the element to be elided is a noun (not a clause) already present in the sentence: *Què prefereixes posar-te, sabates negres o vermelles?* 'Which do you prefer wearing, black or red shoes?'.

When the verb is elided, the weak pronouns and auxiliaries accompanying it disappear too, as in the example above. Modal verbs can appear alone when the main verb has been elided:

El meu amic ja balla, però jo no goso (ballar).
My friend is already dancing, but I don't dare.

12.2 Subordinate clauses

12.2.1 *Infinitive and noun clauses*

A clause with the verb in the infinitive is only possible in Catalan if:

i. the clause acts as the subject of the main sentence:
   Anar al cinema m'agrada molt.
   I love going to the cinema. (Lit. Going to the cinema pleases me a lot.)

   Votar aquest partit és llençar el vot.
   Voting for this party is throwing your vote away.

ii. the infinitive clause and the main clause have the same subject:
   No vull anar al cinema.
   I don't want to go to the cinema.

   Recorda't de preparar el berenar dels nens.
   Remember to prepare the children's lunch.

iii. the subject of the infinitive is not known:
   Prohibit donar menjar als animals.
   (It is) forbidden to feed the animals.

In case (i) when the subject of the infinitive is explicit and this subject appears *after* the verb:

Arribar ell i començar els problemes va ser tot u.
His arriving and the beginning of trouble were instantaneous. (Or better, 'No sooner did he arrive than the problems started.')

In any other case, the preference is for a noun clause introduced by a conjunction (usually *que* or *si*). In such cases the verb is conjugated according to the agreement rules on p. 76:

No vull que vagis al cinema.
I don't want you to go to the cinema.

Ja us vam advertir que no votéssiu aquest partit.
We already told you not to vote for this party.

When the subordinate clause is a request for information or the object of a doubt, the conjunction *si* is used:

Em podria dir si el tren de les 4 arribarà amb retard?
Could you tell me if the 4 o'clock train will be delayed?

No sabien si quedarien a dormir a casa de la seva amiga o si haurien d'anar a un hotel.
They didn't know whether they would sleep at their friend's or go to a hotel.

The verb *dubtar* (to doubt) takes *que* when it is transitive, and *si* when its complement begins with *de*:

Dubto que vingui. / Dubto de si vindrà.
I doubt he is coming.

It is important to note that weak prepositions (*a, de, en, amb*) are dropped before the conjunction *que* (see Prepositions):

No confiava en la teva vinguda → No confiava que vinguessis.
I did not think you would come.

Això depèn de la pujada dels preus → Això depèn que els preus s'apugin.
This depends on the price rise.

En la carta al·ludia al final de la relació → En la carta al·ludia que la relació s'acabava.
In her letter she alluded to the end of their relationship.

Ens amenacen amb l'acomiadament. → Ens amanacen que ens acomiadaran.
They're threatening us with dismissal.

In these cases, and in order to clarify the syntactic structure, a noun can be added:

> **No confiava en** *la possibilitat* **que vinguessis.**
> I didn't believe there was the chance you would come.
>
> **Això depèn** *del fet* **que els preus s'apugin.**
> This depends on the fact that the prices are going up.

Observe that even with these structures, based on noun complements, the preposition *de* has also been elided before conjunction *que*:

> **La possibilitat de la teva vinguda – La possibilitat que vinguessis.**
> **Això depèn del fet de la pujada dels preus – Això depèn del fet que els preus s'apugin.**

12.2.2 *Relative clauses*

Relative clauses can function either as nouns when no precedent is known or it has been elided, or adjectives if they modify a noun.

12.2.2.1 Nominal relative clauses

These are where the whole clause functions as a noun. Those referring to things are introduced by *el que, allò que* ('what'):

> **El que costa de trobar s'aprecia més.**
> What is difficult to find is better appreciated.
>
> **Allò que tothom diu no és necessàriament la veritat.**
> What everybody says is not necessarily the truth.

Note that *allò* here does not refer to a specific object or fact. It has a void referential meaning, just as the article *el* in the first example. It is not replaceable by *això* ('this'). If it were, we would have an adjectival relative clause (see p. 145) modifying the demonstrative pronoun *això*, as in

> **Això d'aquí / Allò d'allà m'agrada ≈ Allò que veig allà m'agrada / Això que veig aquí m'agrada.**
> I like that thing here / there ≈ I like what I see here / there.

Just as how nouns can be elided when they are already known, and their function fulfilled by an accompanying adjective (and 'one(s)' in English), also a noun modified by an adjectival relative clause can disappear:

El cotxe que has comprat és verd, i el que tenies abans era vermell.
The car you have bought is green, and the one you had before was red.

When referring to unknown people, *qui* ('who') is used:

Qui pensi això s'equivocarà.
Who thinks so, will be wrong.

In cases such as this one, *qui* can be preceded by *el(s)*, *tot(s) el(s)* ('all'), *aquell(s)* ('that'/'those'), *tothom* ('everyone') and *qualsevol* ('whoever'). In all these cases *qui* can be replaced by *que*:

Qualsevol qui et veiés ara no et coneixeria.
Whoever saw you now, would not recognise you.

Tothom qui s'esforça venç.
Everyone who strives, succeeds.

12.2.2.2 Adverbial relative clauses

Place, tense, and manner can also be expressed with relative clauses with no antecedent by using *on* ('where'), *quan* ('when'), and *com* ('how'), giving the relative clause an adverbial usage. In such a structure, *on* is often preceded by a place adverb (*allà, allí, aquí*):

On tens el cor tens un tresor.
Where your heart is, you have a treasure too.

No recordava quan el va conèixer.
She did not remember when she met him.

No sé com fer aquest plat.
I do not know how to cook this dish.

12.2.2.3 Adjectival relative clauses

This is where clauses modify an existing noun, and these can be restrictive or non-restrictive:

Restrictive:

Els convidats que menjaren pastís estan malalts.
The guests (and only those guests) who ate a piece of cake are sick.

Non-restrictive:

Els convidats, que menjaren pastís, estan malalts.
The guests, who ate a piece of cake (and all of them did), are sick.

The most frequent relative pronoun for both restrictive (R) and non-restrictive (NR) clauses is *que*, when not preceded by a preposition:

(R) El noi que m'ha saludat és el meu nebot.
The boy who greeted me is my nephew.

(NR) Aquell noi, que m'ha saludat, és el meu nebot.
That boy, who by the way greeted me, is my nephew.

NR relative clauses also use *el qual* (*la qual, els/les quals*) instead of *que*:

Les teves filles, les quals encara no conec, són amigues de la meva.
Your daughters, whom I do not know yet, are friends with mine.

After a preposition, *que* is not used. Rather, the following relatives, depending on whether the antecedent is human or non-human, are selected in both restrictive (examples 1 and 3) and non-restrictive (examples 2 and 4) clauses:

	Restrictive and non-restrictive
Human	*qui / el qual / la qual / els quals / les quals*
Non-human	*què / el qual / la qual / els quals / les quals*

(1) Els amics amb qui soparem portaran el vi – Els amics amb els quals soparem portaran el vi.
The friends we're having dinner with will bring the wine.

(2) El metge nou, a qui ja he fet dues consultes, és molt amable – El metge nou, al qual ja he fet dues consultes, és molt amable.
The new doctor, whom I have been to see twice, is very kind.

(3) La data de què parlem va bé a tothom – La data de la qual parlem va bé a tothom.
The date we're talking about suits everybody.

(4) Aquells paquets, per què estava tan preocupat, ja han arribat – Aquells paquets, pels quals estava tan preocupat, ja han arribat.
Those parcels, which I worried about so much, have now arrived.

When the referent is a whole sentence, it can be replaced by the relative phrases *cosa que* and *la qual cosa*, the latter also taking prepositions before *la* ([prep.] *la qual cosa / cosa* [prep.] *la qual*):

Estava molt preocupada per les eleccions, la qual cosa l'allunyava de l'acció de govern.
She worried about the election, and this kept her away from the job of governing.

Havia après xinès de petit, cosa que el va ajudar en els negocis.
He had learnt Chinese as a child, which helped him in his business.

Van condecorar tres persones, amb la qual cosa (or **cosa amb la qual) va acabar-se la celebració.**
Three people received an award, and with that the celebration came to an end.

Place, time, and manner relative clauses can also have an antecedent:

	Restrictive	Non-restrictive
Time	*en què, en el qual, que* (1)	*quan, en què, en el qual, que* (2)
Place	*on, en què, en el qual* (3)	*(aquí / allà) on, en què, en el qual* (4)
Manner	*com, amb què, amb el qual, que* (5)	*(així) com, amb què, amb el qual* (6)

(1) El dia que tu vas néixer va nevar.
The day you were born it snowed.

(2) L'any 1918, quan va acabar la guerra, fou l'any de la grip.
1918, when the war ended, was the year of the Spanish flu.

(3) L'aula en la qual vam tenir la classe té dues pissarres.
The room where we had the class has two blackboards.

(4) La classe serà a la mateixa aula de l'altre dia, on hi ha dues pissarres.
The class will take place in the same room as the other day, where there are two blackboards.

(5) Amb la manera que fas les coses no et pot sortir res bé mai.
Given the way you do things, you'll never get anything right.

(6) Amb el mètode tradicional, com sempre hem fet les coques, no hi ha perill d'equivocar-se.
With the traditional method, the way we have always baked cakes, there is no risk of making a mistake.

12.2.3 *Adverbial clauses*

12.2.3.1 Temporal

12.2.3.1.1 Non-personal tenses

When two actions share the subject and are temporarily connected, they are typically expressed with a temporal adverbial clause by means of an infinitive, a gerund, or a participle. Participles, gerunds, and infinitives can be used as nuclei of temporal clauses.

The sense of anteriority of the subordinate clause can be translated by a participle or an infinitive. In this latter case, it can only be done when the action is concrete and non-durative (not ongoing), and the infinitive needs to be preceded by preposition '*en*', which is optional before a participle:

Acabada la conferència, van començar les preguntes.
Once the lecture finished, the questions began.

El professor va pronunciar la conferència. En acabat, van començar les preguntes.
The lecturer gave the lecture. Once he finished, the questions began.

En penjar el telèfon va recordar una cosa que li hauria d'haver dit.
After hanging up the phone, she remembered something that she should have said to him.

Simultaneity ('while . . .') is usually expressed by gerunds, alone or preceded by '*tot*', an intensifier. Infinitives preceded by '*en*' also express simultaneity when the verb is durative (ongoing):

(Tot) baixant pel camí he vist un arbre florit.
On my way downhill, I saw a tree in bloom.

No faceu renou en menjar.
Do not make noise while eating.

Posteriority requires using a compound preposition '*després de*', in the same sense as anteriority is also translatable by '*abans de*':

Després de córrer sempre em costa respirar.
After running I find it difficult to breathe.

Abans de deixar la feina, assegura't de tenir-ne una altra.
Before quitting your job, make sure you've got a new one.

12.2.3.1.2 *Personal tenses*

The most common way of introducing temporal clauses is with *quan*. See p. 72 for whether to use the subjunctive or indicative. Note that the verb always appears in a personal form, so *quan* followed by a participle is not possible.

Quan ha vingut el carter, ja no hi eres.
When the postman came, you were not here.

Quan vindrà ta mare, en parlarem.
When your mother arrives, we'll talk about it.

For time comparison, *abans que* and *després que* are used with the same meaning as *abans de* and *després de* (see above) when two diferent subjects are in play. For simultaneity, *mentre* (with no *que*) is used:

Abans que tu hi arribessis, ja t'hi esperaven.
Before you got there, they were already waiting for you.

Després que va passar allò, ningú no se'l podrà creure.
After that happened, no one could believe him.

Mentre deia allò, ja pensava que m'havia equivocat.
While I was saying that, I already thought that I was wrong.

Des que (or *d'ençà que*) and *fins que* imply simultaneity from the beginning or until the end:

Des que (or d'ençà que) ho sé, no puc dormir.
Ever since I've known it, I can't sleep.

Trucaré a la porta fins que m'obrin.
I'll knock at the door [and keep knocking] until they open.

Sempre que with a verb in indicative has a temporal sense ('every time') and a conditional sense when introducing a subjunctive ('whenever, if ever'):

Sempre que em crides, vinc.
Every time you call for me, I come.

Sempre que em cridis, vindré.
Whenever you call for me, I'll come.

12.2.3.2 Causal

Causality, when something causes something else, is expressed by means of prepositional phrases introduced by *per, per causa de, a causa de, per raó de*, and some other rarer ones when no verb is involved:

La votaré per la seva bona feina.
I'll vote for her because of her good work.

Per / A causa de la crisi l'empresa ha tancat.
Due to the crisis the company closed.

Degut ('due') works as an adjective and must agree in gender and number with a noun or a pronoun:

Les destrosses, degudes al temporal, impediren el pas.
The damage, caused by the storm, blocked the way.

A form of uninflected *degut a* can also be used as a causal prepositional compound:

Degut al temporal hi va haver moltes destrosses.
Owing to the storm, there was a lot of damage.

When the main clause asserts the result of an action the latter can be introduced by a compound infinitive (*haver* + past participle):

Van multar-lo per haver conduït begut.
He got a fine for drunk-driving.

Simple infinitives can be read and heard in the same role (especially with copulative or static verbs, which imply continuity), although they are normally avoided in formal language (substituted by a personal verb introduced by *perquè*):

Sempre l'estafen per ser tan confiat → Sempre l'estafen perquè és tan confiat.
They always swindle him because he is too trusting.

Causal phrases with inflected verbs can relate to already known facts or to new information. In the first case, *com que*, *ja que*, and *atès que* (more formal) appear normally at the beginning of the sentence:

Com que tu no venies he dinat tot sol.
As you did not come I have had lunch on my own.

Ja que ells han guanyat, que paguin la festa.
Since they won, let them pay for the party.

When the information introduced by the causal phrase is new, *perquè* is the most frequent option, and it is the normal way to answer a 'why' question (*per què*). Observe the difference between *perquè* and *com que*:

Vaig deixar aquella feina perquè no em pagaven prou, i com que no tenia feina no podia pagar el lloguer.
I quit that job because I wasn't paid enough, and as I had no job I could not pay the rent.

External causal clauses, i.e. clauses not answering 'why?', but 'why do you say so?', especially in sentences expressing order, permission, or recommendation, are introduced by the conjunction *que*:

Posa't l'abric, que fa fred.
Put on your coat, (because) it is cold.

Resultative clauses related to quantity can appear after prepositions *de, amb, després de*:

De tant com he parlat / Amb el que he parlat / Després de parlar tant, tinc la boca seca.
After talking so much, my mouth is dry.

12.2.3.3 Final

Final clauses indicate purpose, and are mainly introduced by the preposition *per a*:

Faig aquest pastís per a la teva festa.
I'm baking this cake for your party.

It can be used also with infinitives sharing a subject with the main clause, although depending on dialects and styles, simple *per* often appears instead (recall p. 150 on causal *per*).

T'escric per (a) comunicar-te la meva adreça.
I'm writing to you to communicate my new address.

Per a is usually preferred when depending on a noun, an adjective, or a non voluntary verb:

És un paper per a inscriure's.
It is a registration form.

Una jove molt preparada per a feines tècniques.
A young woman well prepared for technical work.

Ha estat nomenat per a ocupar el càrrec.
He has been appointed to take on the post.

When a stronger sense of finality is needed (such as in the English 'in order to'), *per tal de, a fi de* are used:

A fi / Per tal d'efectuar el pagament, li agrairé que m'enviï la factura.
In order to complete payment, I would appreciate it if you could send me an invoice.

Clauses with inflected verbs replace the preposition *per* (*a*) with the conjunction *que*, and compound prepositions *per tal de / a fi de* with compound conjunctions *per tal que / a fi que*. It is important to notice that in all these cases, finality requires the subordinate clause to bear a verb in the subjunctive:

Va dir tot allò perquè ens confonguéssim.
He said all that so we would get confused.

Convidarem els millors artistes per tal / a fi que ens ensenyin les seves tècniques.
We shall invite the best artists in order for them to teach us their techniques.

12.2.3.4 Concessive

When concessions are stated with nouns, nominal phrases, adjectives, adverbs, or non personal verb forms, there is a wide range of conjunctons to introduce them: *malgrat, tot i, i tot,* (*per*) *bé que, per més que, encara que, a pesar de / que, a desgrat de*.

Malgrat els nostres esforços, hem perdut el partit.
In spite of our attempts, we have lost the match.

Malalt i tot, encara he arribat dels primers.
Even though I'm sick, I have been one of the first to arrive.

(Per) bé que a poc a poc, el cotxe encara marxa.
Although it's slow, the car still works.

Note that *a pesar que* substitutes *a pesar de* before a gerund, a past participle, or an adverb: *Has guanyat la cursa, a pesar que fent trampa / Has guanyat la cursa, a pesar de les trampes* – You have won the race, although you cheated; *El paquet m'ha arribat, a pesar que tard / trencat* – The parcel has reached me, although it's late / broken.

It is important to distinguish between factual (actually existing) and non-factual (non-existing) concessions. The former are expressed with the indicative mood of the verb and conjunctions *malgrat que, encara que, si bé*, while the latter are the domain of the subjunctive together with conjunctions *encara que* or *ni que*:

Factual:

Malgrat que dormien al ras, tenien calor.
Although they slept outside, they were hot.

Encara que t'hi esforces, no ho fas prou bé.
Although you try hard (and you do try hard), you don't do it well enough.

Non-factual:

Encara que t'hi esforcis, no ho faràs prou bé.
Even if you try hard (and it is not certain that you do), you won't do it well enough.

Ni que treballés molt, no podria guanyar el concurs.
Even if he worked a lot (and it is not certain he does), he wouldn't be able to win the contest.

More rarely, *baldament* (*que*) can be used with the subjunctive for both factual and non-factual meanings:

Baldament ho hagis dit tantes vegades, no et crec.
Although you have said it so many times, I don't believe you.

No ho faria baldament que la terra s'obrís.
I wouldn't do it even if the ground opened up.

Concessive parenthesis ('even so'), are made with *no obstant* accompanying *això* ('this') when the reference is a whole sentence or accompanying any other more specific phrase:

Vaig dir que m'agradava aquella feina, i això no obstant (or **i no obstant això**)**, l'ambient no era bo.**
I said I liked that job, but nevertheless the work atmosphere was not good.

Vaig dir que m'agradava aquella feina, i no obstant el que vaig dir, l'ambient no era bo.
I said I liked that job, but despite what I said, the work atmosphere was not good.

12.2.3.5 Consecutive

The result of what is said in the main clause, especially with a sense of quantity or degree following *tant, tan* ('so (much)'), *tal* ('such'), or *cada* ('each'), can be expressed in a subordinate clause introduced by *que*:

Aquell restaurant em va agradar tant que hi torno sovint.
I liked that restaurant so much that I often go back there.

La meva filla està tan canviada que no la reconeixeries.
My daughter has changed so much (lit. is so changed) that you would not recognise her.

Va presentar unes factures tals, que tothom en va sospitar.
He produced such invoices that everybody suspected them.

Els tècnics et fan cada explicació que cal demanar-los aclariments.
Technicians give you such explanations that you have to ask them to be clear.

Other consecutive expressions link clauses in a cause–consequence relation, such as *així que, de manera que, de forma que, d'aquí que*:

Estic cansat, així que me'n vaig a dormir.
I'm tired, so I'm going to bed.

No respon les meves trucades, de manera que no hi insistiré.
She does not answer my calls, and so I shall not insist.

12.2.3.6 Conditionals

Conditional clauses are typically introduced by the conjunction *si*. Also typically, the distinction observed in concessives applies here: actual possibilities require the indicative, while non-actual need the subjunctive (see p. 72 on verb moods):

Si comença a ploure, farem la festa dins la casa.
If it starts raining, we'll have the party in the house.

Si el teu avi fos viu, avui estaria content.
If your grandfather were alive, he would be happy today.

Condition normally precedes the statement when the information it conveys is something that is already known. Otherwise, it tends to be placed at the end:

Et contaré la història només si em promets discreció.
I'll tell you the story only if you promise to be discreet.

Other ways of introducing condition are by means of *quan, en cas de / que, mentre, sempre que*, the simple use of adjectival clauses or gerunds, or coordinated disjunctive constructions:

Quan els preus caiguin / En cas que els preus caiguin, comprarem accions.
When prices fall, we'll buy shares.

Mentre continuïs / Sempre que continuïs produint beneficis, mantindràs la feina.
As long as you keep on producing profits, you'll keep the job.

Vestit d'aquesta manera / Vestint-te d'aquesta manera ningú no et respectarà.
Dressed like that / If you always dress like that, nobody will respect you.

O arregles el motor o no cobres.
If you don't fix the engine, you won't get paid.

Exceptions are also conditions, and they can be expressed with *excepte* (*que / si*), *fora* (*de / si*), or *llevat de / que* (*llevat* is invariable here) (see section 8.2):

La festa serà al jardí excepte que ploqui / excepte si plou / fora si plou / llevat que plogui.
The party will be in the garden, unless it rains.

Fora de parlar amb els de la teva edat, res no vares aprendre a escola (Raimon).
Except for talking to your peers, you learnt nothing at school.

Llevat del mal de ronyons, estic bé.
Except for my kidneys aching, I'm all right.

PART IV

Doing things and real language

Chapter 13

Intention

13.1 Affirmation

As in any other language, affirmation is the default mode of a sentence in Catalan. Therefore, no special marks are applied to obtain an affirmation. However, in some cases, emphasis is needed to oppose a negative statement or presupposition. There is no mechanism like the usage of the auxiliary verb 'to do' in English in cases like 'I did do that'. Instead, the adverb *sí* 'yes' or the adverbial phrase *i tant* followed by a subordinate *que* clause (also *i tant, com*) can do the job. In explicit oppositions, the *que* clause can be omitted. Since *tant* is a quantifier that can be both an adjective and a pronoun, it can agree in number and gender with a following (normally implicit) noun in this type of constructions. When such agreement is made, the *que* / *com* clause cannot be omitted.

Contràriament al que pensava tothom, sí que vam arribar a temps.
Against all expectations, we arrived on time.

Als gats no els agrada l'aigua, però als gossos, sí (que els agrada).
Cats do not like water, but dogs do (like it).

Què dius, que el grec no és una llengua indoeuropea? I tant, que / com ho és!
What do you mean, that Greek is not an Indo-European language? Of course it is!

Que no hi ha cerveses dintre de la nevera? I tant! / I tantes, com n'hi ha!
There are no beers in the fridge (you say)? Of course there are!

Adverbs *prou* and *bé* (optionally followed by *que*) and *ja* can also be used for emphasis, although they do not oppose a negative statement:

Ella prou (que) havia estudiat quan va fer l'examen.
Of course she had studied when she took the exam.

S'ha suspès la reunió? Ja m'ho pensava.
Has the meeting been cancelled? I thought so (*or colloquially* I didn't see that one coming).

Bé (que) serà cuit el sopar quan els convidats arribaran.
Of course dinner will be ready when the guests will arrive.

Other ways for focusing sentence elements can be seen on p. 170.

13.2 Negation

13.2.1 *Negating sentences*

The simplest way of negating a sentence is by adding *no* before the verb:

En Miquel ve → En Miquel no ve.
Miquel comes → Miquel doesn't come.

In contrast with 'not' in English, compound verbs receive this *no* before the auxiliary (and any subject pronouns), and not before the full verb:

Jo no havia dit res, i ara tampoc no ho diré.
I had not said anything, and neither will I say anything now.

However, modal phrases admit *no* between the modal verb and the infinitive. In these cases, what is negated is not the whole sentence, but the verb immediately following *no*, giving a different meaning:

No li ho he pogut dir.
I could not tell him.

He pogut no dir-li-ho.
I could avoid telling him.

No cal prendre aquest camí.
There's no need to take this path.

Cal no prendre aquest camí.
This path should not be taken.

However, *deure* (with a probabilistic meaning, i.e. 'maybe') and *haver de* do not admit this distinction. As a result, some ambiguities are possible:

No surtis, que ara deu ploure.
Don't go out, it's probably raining now.

Surt, que ara no deu ploure. (*Surt, que ara deu no ploure.)
Go out, it's probably not raining now.

No heu de llegir aquest llibre.
You mustn't read this book (*but also*, You don't have to read this book).

Also aspectual verbal phrases (those denoting the duration or type of activity) place negation before the personal verb form and not by the infinitive or gerund:

Comença a llegir el llibre. → No comencis a llegir el llibre.
Start reading the book. → Don't start reading the book.

Ha continuat fent aquestes coses. → No ha continuat fent aquestes coses.
She has kept on doing such things. → She hasn't kept on doing such things.

In the last example, if you want to negate the action implied by the infinitive or gerund you need to replace the aspectual, inflected verb:

Ha deixat de fer aquestes coses.
She has stopped doing such things.

13.2.2 *Negating single elements*

Negation can focus on specific elements, rather than just verbs and sentences. This is normally accompanied by an adversative statement with *sinó*, and it can generate a cleft sentence (see p. 174):

Ho he dit no a en Miquel, sinó a la Maria.
I've said it not to Miquel, but to Maria.

No és a en Miquel, a qui ho he dit, sinó a la Maria.
It's not Miquel, to whom I've said it, but Maria.

Both emphatic formulae depart from the neutral *No ho he dit a en Miquel, sinó a la Maria* which does not convey special emphasis.

A quite common specific additive construction takes advantage of this possibility: *no només . . . sinó també . . .* – 'not only . . . but also . . .'

M'han robat no només la cartera, sinó també les claus.
Not only have they stolen my wallet, but also my keys.

When talking about a verb complement, *no només* can also be placed before the verb with the same meaning. However, when the element under scope is the whole sentence, the second element requires *que també*:

No només m'han robat la cartera, sinó també les claus.
Not only have they stolen my wallet, but also my keys.

but:

No només m'han robat la cartera, sinó que també m'han pegat.
Not only have they stolen my wallet, but they have also hit me.

13.2.3 *Pas*

Catalan can make use of the negative adverb *pas*, placed after the verb, but it is used only to reinforce prohibitions with a sense of strictness or urgence, or to cancel presuppositions:

No diguis pas això!
Don't you say that!

Llegíem moltes novel·les, però no en compràvem pas gaires.
We used to read many novels, but we didn't buy many of them at all.

The use of *pas* is not compulsory, and it does not appear in dialects other than central and northern Catalan.

13.2.4 *Negative polarity words*

These pronouns and adverbs denote negation by themselves:

res ('nothing') – **Què has menjat? – Res**
'What have you eaten?' 'Nothing.'

ningú ('nobody') – **Qui ha vingut? – Ningú**
'Who has come?' 'Nobody.'

cap ('none') – **Quants llibres has llegit? – Cap**
'How many books have you read?' 'None.'

mai ('never') – **Quan aprendràs a conduir? – Mai**
'When will you learn how to drive?' 'Never.'

enlloc ('nowhere') **– On venen aquests quadres? – Enlloc**
'Where do they sell these paintings?' 'Nowhere.'

(no) gens ('at all') **– T'agrada aquest ballet? – (No) gens**
'Do you like this ballet?' 'Not at all.'

tampoc ('neither') **– Jo no he votat aquest partit – Jo tampoc**
'I haven't voted for this party' 'Neither have I.'

These words all express negation when appearing alone, as seen above. However, they cannot negate a whole sentence; to do that, *no* is required (as with *gaire*, 'not many / much', seen below):

Avui no he menjat res.
I've eaten nothing today.

No ha vingut ningú.
Nobody has come.

No he llegit cap llibre.
I haven't read any books. / I haven't read a single book.

Mai no va aprendre a conduir.
He never learned to drive.

Aquests quadres no els venen enlloc.
These paintings are not sold anywhere.

No tinc gaires diners.
I don't have much money.

Aquest ballet no m'agrada gens.
I don't like this ballet at all.

Jo tampoc no he votat aquest partit.
I haven't voted for this party either.

When the negative word is placed after the verb, the presence of *no* is compulsory to the extent that a native speaker would not understand a sentence such as *Has menjat res avui*, or would simply interpret it as a question meaning 'Have you eaten anything today?' (see below). On the other hand, when the word appears before the verb, many speakers dispense with the requirement for *no*:

Ningú no diu això. = Ningú diu això.
Nobody says this.

When expressing doubt or when questioning, the negative polarity words are used in an affirmative sense as in English *anything, anybody, any, ever*, or *anywhere*:

Vols res?
Do you want anything?

Que ha vingut ningú quan jo no hi era?
Has anybody come while I was away?

Ell et dirá si hi ha cap client a la botiga.
He'll tell you whether there are any customers at the shop.

Dubto que hagi llegit cap llibre mai.
I doubt he has ever read a single book.

13.3 Questions

13.3.1 *Full questions*

Full or yes–no questions are easy to formulate, as any asseverative sentence can turn into a question just by changing intonation (see p. 134):

Plou → Plou?
It rains – Does it rain / Is it raining?

Demà s'acaba el termini per pagar l'impost de la renda → Demà s'acaba el termini per pagar l'impost de la renda?
The deadline for paying income tax is tomorrow – Is it tomorrow the deadline for paying income tax?

However, the elements' order can change due to focusing by using a cleft sentence (see p. 174), or by placing the main source of interest at the end of the sentence:

La Isabel ha trucat.
Isabel has phoned.

No focusing:

La Isabel ha trucat?
Has Isabel phoned?

Cleft sentence:

És la Isabel, qui ha trucat?
Is it Isabel who has phoned?

Focusing on the subject:

Ha trucat la Isabel?
Isabel, has she phoned?

When the element under focus is not the subject, that element can move forwards or backwards, leaving a pronominal trace in its original place:

A la platja, hi vindreu?
Will you come *to the beach*? (The same effect comes from leaving the place adverbial at the end, after a pause, and announcing it with the adverbial pronoun *hi*: *Hi vindreu, a la platja?*)

El pa, l'has deixat damunt de la taula?
The bread: have you left it on the table?

Això a l'Ignasi no li ho has dit?
Haven't you said *this? To Ignasi*? (with both object and complement under focus)

Full questions can be introduced by *que*, which is just a question marker with no meaning, usually appears when a certain content or attitude is implied, such as surprise, when the speaker is being polite. In any case, this particle must be followed by a verb:

Que has llegit el diari?
Have you read the newspaper? (T Because there's something in it you should know.)

Que et sabria greu tancar la porta?
Would you mind closing the door? (I want it closed.)

Que plou?
Is it raining? (It doesn't look like it.)

Que estàs embarassada?
Are you pregnant? (I'd never have guessed!)

In the last two cases, implying surprise, *que* can be replaced by conjunction *o* ('or') with the same effect. With this formula the need for a verb to follow immediately the question marker *o* disappears:

O plou? O ara plou?
Is it really raining? Is it really raining now?

O estàs embarassada? O la teva parella està embarassada?
Are you pregnant? Is your partner pregnant?

13.3.2 *Partial questions*

Partial questions, which allow a reply from a wide range of possibilities, use the following interrogative words:

què ('what') **Què has menjat avui?** What have you eaten today?
qui ('who') **Qui és aquest senyor?** Who is this gentleman?

quin ('which, what') (adj.) **Quin color t'agrada més?** What colour do you like best?

quant (de) / ('how much / many') (adj.) **Quanta (de) gent ha vingut?** How many people have come?

quan ('when') **Quan has arribat?** When did you arrive?

on ('where') **On he deixat les claus?** Where have I left my keys?

com ('how') **Com estàs?** How are you?

per què ('why') **Per què no et poses tranquil?** Why don't you relax?

Question words (except *com* and *per què*) can be preceded by a preposition:

Per a què serveix aquest aparell?
What is this device for?

Contra qui clama aquest article?
Who is this article against?

De quin color és la falda que t'has comprat?
What colour is the skirt you have bought?

Sense quantes dents va sobreviure a l'accident?
How many teeth did he lose in the accident?

Des de quan prens aquesta medecina?
How long have you been taking this medicine for?

Cap a on vas?
Where are you heading to?

In colloquial speech, and especially when seeking clarification on what has been said, the question word can take the place of the information being asked:

I dius que vindràs quan?
And you say you'll come when? (Formally) *Quan dius que vindràs?* When do you say you will come?

Et va dir què?
He told you what? (Formally) *Què et va dir?* What did he tell you?

13.3.3 *Tag questions*

In order to obtain the confirmation of the person being spoken to, it is common to use *oi?*, *o no?*, or *no?* after an assertion. Other longer formulae are also available, such as *oi que sí/no?*, *veritat?*, *no és així?*, *no és ver?* This is normally done in English using an auxiliary verb:

Els coberts són a la taula, oi?
The cutlery is on the table, isn't it?

Tu parles bé l'anglès, o no?
You speak English well, don't you?

Demà és 30, veritat?
Tomorrow is the 30th, isn't it?

13.4 Exclamation

Apart from the emphasis that can normally be attached to any assertion (see p. 159), specific exclamations can be built by adding qualifiers or quantifiers at the beginning of the sentence, depending on whether the fact to stress is a quantity or a quality.

que is used in both cases, followed either by an adjective or an adverb, expressing quality or quantity:

Que simpàtica que és la teva mare!
How nice your mother is!

Que poca gent que ha vingut a la festa, però que molta que n'hem convidada!
How few people have come to the party, but how many we invited!

Que lluny que viuen els nostres amics!
How far away our friends live!

In all the cases above, a whole sentence is attached to the exclamation by means of a relative (*que*). A simpler way to achieve the emphasis required for an exclamation is by use of 'si que' at the beginning of a sentence. In this case only one 'que' is needed, but the subject must be placed at the end:

Si que és simpàtica la teva mare!
Si que ha vingut poca gent a la festa!
Si que viuen lluny els nostres amics!

This *si que* (with no stress on *si*) must not be confused with *sí que* seen on p. 159 and used for opposing negations.

When the object of exclamation is a noun, it appears after the adjective *quin/quina* ('what'), and, if there is a quality as well, it appears after *més* ('more'), *més poc* ('so little') *tan* ('so'), or *tan poc* ('so little'):

Quina veu!
What a voice!

Quina manera més rara d'anar-se'n!
What a strange way to leave!

Quin llibre més bo! Quin llibre tan bo!
What a good book!

Quines maneres més poc / tan poc agradoses!
What unpleasent manners!

The way to do something can be underlined by *com* ('how') or, as above, by *quina manera de* ('what a way to') preceding the verb. In these cases, the subject appears at the end of the sentence. If an adverb is to be added to the verb, then the preposition *de* must intervene:

Com canta la teva germana! →Com canta de fort la teva germana!
Your sister is quite the singer! →Your sister sings loudly!

13.5 Giving orders

The imperative is the mood for giving orders (see p. 78). However, requirements are often formulated in a more polite form, addressing the interlocutor's collaboration by means of questions or conditions:

Tanca la porta.
Close the door.

Que pots tancar la porta?
Can you close the door?

Que podries tancar la porta?
Could you close the door?

(Que) et sap greu tancar la porta?
Do you mind closing the door?

Si no et sap greu, podries tancar la porta?
If you don't mind, could you close the door?

When *per favor* or *si us plau* ('please') are used, they appear as a sentence satellite, not in the middle of the verb phrase:

Per favor, que em pots passar el diari?
Can you please pass me the newspaper?

Em deixeu cinc euros, si us plau?
Would you please lend me five euros?

Orders, prohibitions, and petitions embedded in a sentence and depending on verbs such as *dir* ('say, tell'), *ordenar* ('order'), *demanar* ('ask'), *suplicar* ('beg') are normally presented as subordinate clauses in the subjunctive. An infinitive is also possible instead of a verb inflected in the subjunctive. In this case, the infinitive must be introduced by the preposition *de*:

He dit al cambrer que ens porti el compte.
I've told the waiter to bring us the bill.

Em va suplicar que no ho digués a ningú.
He begged me not to tell anybody.

La mare em va demanar d'acompanyar-la al metge.
My mother asked me to accompany her to the doctor.

Orders and prohibitions in public notices are usually written as addressed to *vós*, the second person polite form conjugated the same as the second person plural:

Valideu el bitllet abans d'entrar al tren.
Please validate your ticket before boarding the train.

No doneu menjar als animals.
Please do not feed the animals.

Chapter 14

Focusing

14.1 Passive

The most usual sentence in Catalan, as in English, is an active sentence with a subject carrying out the action of the verb. However, when the focus of interest is placed on the object, a passive sentence can be built up in a similar manner as in English: the direct object takes the place of the subject and then a passive verb is created by using *ésser* and a past participle, agreeing in gender and number with the subject. The agent (who or what carries out the action) can be introduced by means of preposition *per* (or *de*):

Les autoritats lliuren els premis als estudiants més destacats. → Els premis són lliurats per les autoritats als estudiants més destacats.
The authorities hand out the prizes to the best students. → The prizes are handed out by the authorities to the best students.

La junta d'accionistes pren aquestes decisions. → Aquestes decisions són preses per la junta d'accionistes.
The shareholders' board takes these decisions. → These decisions are taken by the shareholders' board.

However, although possible, these types of passive constructions are not as common in Catalan as they are in English. Furthermore, there are some restrictions:

i The indirect object cannot become the subject of a passive:
I've been given a present → ***He estat donat un regal.**
In this case, if you wanted to emphasise 'I' other means are necessary, such as pleonasm (see p. 137).
M'han donat un regal a mi.

ii. An object or a verb complement under focus is usually placed at the beginning of the sentence, and its function is repeated by a weak pronoun closer to the verb (see p. 137):

Els premis, els lliuren les autoritats a les persones més destacades (accusative plural pronoun **els** referring to **els premis**).
A la persona més destacada, les autoritats **li** lliuren un premi (dative singular pronoun **li** referring to **a la persona més destacada**).

iii. Undefined passive subjects are extremely rare, even in newspaper headlines:

***Bancs són arrossegats per la crisi financera → Els bancs són arrossegats per la crisi financera.**
Banks are swept along by financial crisis.

?Nous ministres seran nomenats demà → Els nous ministres seran nomenats demà
New ministers will be named tomorrow.

iv. Some verbs like *tenir, saber, posseir, costar, mesurar* (static: 'to be of a certain measure'), *pesar* (static: 'to be a certain weight') cannot be formed in the passive: 'the house was owned by my father' **la casa era posseïda pel meu pare.*

Sharing a subject with an active sentence can support the appearance of an otherwise avoidable passive:

Els treballadors no volien planificar la feina ni ser controlats.
The workers did not want to plan the work nor be supervised.

Tu has suspès perquè no has estat ben aconsellat pel teu tutor.
You have failed because you haven't been given good advice by your tutor.

When the agent is to be expressed, the preposition *per* plays the role of English 'by', although verbs of knowledge or feeling, or creation, can introduce the agent by *de*:

L'accident és investigat per l'autoritat aeroportuària.
The accident is being investigated by the airport authority.

Els bombers són admirats per/de tothom.
Firemen are admired by everybody.

Aquest plat no és fet meu.
This dish has not been cooked by me.

In the last example, '*meu*' stands for '*de mi*'. It is remarkable that this type of construction an agent introduced by '*de*' in passive sentences, becomes attributive and aspect is blurred: *Aquest plat no* és *fet meu* is preferred to *Aquest plat no* ha estat *fet meu*, and covers its meaning.

14.2 Impersonal sentences and pronominal passive

Impersonal sentences can be purely impersonal, with no subject at all, mostly relating to atmospheric circumstances or similar, or they can include an impersonal subject, or be built as a pronominal passive.

Plou / Neva / Fa fred / Fa sol.
It rains / It snows / It is cold / It is sunny (or 'It is raining', etc.).

Es fa fosc / Es fa tard.
It is getting dark / It is getting late.

The impersonal pronoun *hom* can appear in very formal texts. It agrees with the verb as a third person singular, and has no referential meaning at all:

En alguns països hom no vota el cap de l'estat.
In some countries the head of state is not elected.

Hom diu aquestes coses per espantar els nens.
These things are said to scare children.

Hom can be preceded by *un* to stress singularity or to reference oneself, but it cannot take any adjectives. Also *un / una* can be used with this self-referential sense:

De vegades un hom parla sense pensar / De vegades un parla sense pensar.
One speaks thoughtlessly sometimes.

The third person plural is a good solution when no definite subject is known. When the pronoun has no referential meaning, then the sentence is understood as impersonal:

Diuen que no plourà en tota la setmana.
They say that it won't rain all week.

Quan tornen vells, perden moltes habilitats.
When people get old, they lose many abilities.

More informally, the second person singular can have a non-referential, impersonal meaning, especially in conditions:

Quan tornes vell, perds moltes habilitats.
When you get old, you lose many abilities.

Llegeixes aquest llibre i tens ganes de visitar Irlanda.
You read this book and you feel like visiting Ireland.

In normal speech *hom* is not used, and its role is performed by the impersonal third person pronoun *es*. Notice that this is only possible when no direct object is involved:

Es viu molt bé, en aquesta terra.
One lives very comfortably in this land.

No es pot ser més idiota.
It is not possible to be more idiotic.

En aquesta carrera es llegeix molt.
One reads a lot in this course.

With *es* playing the role of indefinite subject it can only occur before the verb, and never after it, even when the verb is an infinitive:

No es pot ser sincer i esperar que no passi res (*No pot ser-se sincer . . .)
One cannot be honest and expect nothing to happen.

Impersonal *es* cannot coexist with reflexive, reciprocal *es* or with pronominal verbs already holding *es*:

***Es es renta dins aquesta habitació → Hom es renta dins aquesta habitació** (or 3rd person plural impersonal: **Es renten dins aquesta habitació)**
One washes oneself in this room.

***Quan es es casa, se s'engreixa → Quan hom es casa, s'engreixa / Quan es casen, s'engreixen**
One puts on weight when one gets married.

When the verb has an object, an impersonal construction is possible via converting the object to a subject and placing the weak pronoun *es* as an object. As a result, a type of reflexive construction is created, a pronominal passive sentence, which is much more frequent than the standard passive with *ésser* + past participle:

Hom prohibeix això → Això és prohibit → Es prohibeix això
This is forbidden.

Hom llegeix pocs llibres actualment → Pocs llibres són llegits actualment → Es llegeixen pocs llibres actualment
People read few books nowadays.

Hom ven taronges → *Taronges són venudes (see above about undefined passive subjects) **→ Es venen taronges**
Oranges for sale (lit. Oranges are sold).

14.3 Cleft sentences

An important device used to focus on a part of the sentence is splitting the sentence by means of a cleft structure, which we met on p. 136 when discussing word order. These are combinations of copulae and relative phrases, as followings, with the unmarked affirmative sentence first:

En Miquel ha telefonat.
Miquel has phoned.

És en Miquel (el) qui ha telefonat.
It is Miquel who has phoned.

(El) qui ha telefonat és en Miquel.
The one who has phoned is Miquel.

When the copula (a form of *ser* 'to be') appears at the beginning of the sentence, we call it a cleft sentence, as in the first example above; conversely, when the relative phrase comes first, the structure is called a pseudo-cleft sentence.

There are two main differences with English parallels to keep in mind:

i. The copula in a cleft sentence must agree in person and number with the subject:

És en Miquel (el) qui ha telefonat – It is Miquel who has phoned.
but
Som nosaltres els qui hem telefonat – It is us who have phoned.

The tendency is the reverse in pseudo-cleft sentences, where agreement is far more difficult:

Qui ha **telefonat** hem **estat nosaltres**

It is also possible to make *ésser* agree in tense with the following verb, but not compulsory:

Ha estat en Miquel qui ha telefonat (also **És en Miquel qui ha telefonat)**
Hem estat nosaltres els qui hem telefonat (also **Som nosaltres els qui hem telefonat)**

and, in pseudo-cleft sentences whole agreement is preferred when the order has been swapped, so that the relative phrase appears after the copula, and the copula after the focused phrase (sharing with normal pseudo-cleft sentences the fact that the copula is not at the beginning of the sentence):

Nosaltres hem estat els qui hem telefonat (more common than **Nosaltres som els qui hem telefonat)**

ii. Prepositions are repeated both in the copulative phrase and in the relative and cannot be left alone at the end of the sentence:

És amb nosaltres amb qui has de parlar.
It is us you must talk to.

With stressed prepositions the simple relative *que* is preferred:

És contra vosaltres que diuen aquestes coses (also És contra vosaltres contra qui diuen aquestes coses).
It is against you that they say such things.

És de mi que parlen (also **És de mi de qui parlen).**
It is me that they talk about.

Conversely, pseudo-cleft sentences always require the preposition to be repeated:

Contra qui parlen és contra vosaltres.
The one they talk against is you.

Sense qui faran la festa serà sense vosaltres.
The one they'll have the party without is you.

Chapter 15

Defining

15.1 The article

Defining is the main function of articles, already explained earlier in Section 6.3.

15.2 Copulative sentences: Linking subjects and predicates

15.2.1 *Pure copulative sentences*

Pure copulative sentences link a subject and a **predicative expression** as though in an equation:

El doctor Mas és el nostre metge de capçalera.
Doctor Mas is our GP.

La meva germana és la teva directora.
My sister is your manager.

Aquell edifici d'allà és la biblioteca.
That building there is the library.

In this type of sentence, with both the subject and the predicate being determined nouns or noun phrases, the verb number tends to be plural when one of the two elements is a noun in plural:

El millor de la vida són els amics. (*El millor de la vida és els amics.)
The best thing in life is friends.

(See p. 174 for agreement of copulae in cleft sentences as in *Som nosaltres qui hem telefonat* / *Qui ha telefonat hem estat nosaltres*.)

15.2.2 *Descriptive copulae: ser vs estar*

Other constructions do not establish an equation between two noun phrases, but they describe a subject. Adjectives, undetermined nouns and prepositional phrases can appear as predicative expressions:

Aquesta casa és lletja.
This house is ugly.

Els funerals són esdeveniments poc agradables.
Funerals are unpleasent events.

La teva ajuda és molt d'agrair.
Your help is very much appreciated.

A difficulty for non-native speakers is selecting the right verb for a describing copula, as *ser* (*ésser* is just another form of the verb) competes for this position with *estar*. Ideally, *ser* is used to connect the subject with a permanent quality describing it, and *estar* for temporal qualities, as in:

El meu pare és un malalt del cor.
My father has a poorly heart.

Avui no hi haurà classe perquè la professora està malalta.
There will no be class today because the lecturer is poorly.

Aquesta biga és torta.
This beam is crooked.

Ha vingut el paleta i ha tocat la biga. Ara està torta.
The builder has come and he has hit the beam. It is crooked now.

Que cansat que és el teu cosí: sempre conta les mateixes coses!
How tiresome your cousin is: he always tells the same stories!

Els excursionistes estan molt cansats: han caminat tota la nit.
The walkers are very tired: they have walked all night long.

With marital statuses such as *solter* 'single', *fadrí* 'single', *casat* 'married', *separat* 'separated', and *divorciat* 'divorced', the verb traditionally used is *ser*, although *estar* is also now used; with *vidu* only *ser* is used.

Mort 'dead' is normally used with *ser*, although e*star mort* can be used with a sense of recent discovery: *Vaig trobar estrany que l'ocell no piulés, i quan vaig acostar-me a la gàbia vaig descobrir que* era/estava *mort* 'I found it strange that the bird wasn't chirping, and when I approached the cage I discovered that it was dead.'

Estar is used with the following predicative expressions:

a. a manner adverb or an expression of time: *avui estic bé, però ahir estava ben* malament 'I am well today, but I was really bad yesterday', *estaràs tres anys abans de poder caminar bé* 'It will be three years before you can walk well'.
b. most participles (working as adjectives), especially those meaning the final state of a process: *encantat* 'delighted', *admirat* 'delighted', *enfadat* 'upset', *preocupat* 'worried', *esperançat* 'hopeful', *il·lusionat* 'excited', *emcionat* 'excited', *acabat* 'finished', *començat* 'started', *trencat* 'broken', *romput* 'broken', *arreglat* 'repaired', etc. Also, other adjectives, not participles, sharing the same idea, as *llest* 'ready' or *conclús* (rare) 'finished' use *estar*.
c. prepositional phrases implying a state: *de festa* 'celebrating', *de celebració* 'celebrating', *de dol* 'mourning', *d'enhorabona* 'in luck', *en coma* 'in coma', *de baixa* 'on sick leave', *d'alta* 'being a member; in hospital leave', *de vacances* 'on holiday', *de tornada* 'back', *de partida* 'leaving', *de pega* 'redundant', *de sort* 'in luck', *de part* 'in labour, giving birth'.

   Also *estar* is used with *a punt* 'ready', *a la venda* 'for sale', *a l'abast* 'at reach', although *ser* is often overused in such cases at present.

   Estar per means 'to be about to', 'to feel like', and also (esp. in negative usage and followed by an infinitive) 'to afford' and (esp. in negative usage and followed by a noun or noun phrase) 'to be in need of'. *Estava per marxar quan va sonar el telèfon* 'I was about to leave when the telephone rang', *Jo no estic per votar aquest partit* 'I do not feel like voting for this party', *Ara no estic per comprar un cotxe* 'I cannot afford to buy a new car now', *No estava per unes sabates noves* 'He was not in need of a pair of new shoes'. *Estar en* means 'to lie, to consist of'. *La solució està en no amoïnar-s'hi* 'The solution lies in not worrying about it.'

   Opinions can be expressed by the following phrases following *estar: d'acord* 'to agree', *en contra de* 'to be against of', *a favor de* 'to be in favour of', but *ser de l'opinió de, ser partidari de* (see section 8.2 on prepositional phrases).

orgullós 'proud', *gelós* 'jealous' and *envejós* 'envious' are used with *ser* if their meaning is absolute: *No et demanarà perdó; és massa orgullós* 'He will not apologise; he is too arrogant', but *Estem molt orgullosos dels nostres fills* 'We are very proud of our children'; *Era tan gelós que ningú no es podia acostar a la seva parella* 'He was so jealous that nobody could get close to his partner', but *No està gens gelosa del seu germà* 'She is not jealous at all of her brother'; *Sou uns envejosos* 'You are so envious', but *No estigueu envejosos de mi* 'Do not envy me.'

Some adjectives admit either *ser* or *estar* when the function is strictly descriptive, the choice depending mainly on dialect or style: *brut* 'dirty', *net* 'clean', *fred* 'cold', *calent* 'hot', *fort* 'strong, hard', *fluix* 'weak', *flonjo* 'soft', *buit* 'empty', *ple* 'full', *fosc* 'dark', *clar* 'clear', *banyat* 'wet', *humit* 'humid', *eixut* 'dry', etc.

15.2.3 Placing

The place of a subject is expressed with *ser* as default:

Les claus són damunt de la taula.
The keys are on the table.

Ara sóc dins del tren i no puc parlar. Et trucaré quan seré a casa.
I am on the train and I cannot talk. I shall call you when I get home.

However, in certain cases, *estar* is used:

- when the place is where one lives or works, implying permanence:

  La meva germana ja no està a Igualada, ara està a Vilafranca.
  My sister does not live (or work) in Igualada, she is now living (or working) in Vilafranca.

  La veïna de dalt ara està a la residència, però avui és a casa seva.
  Our upstairs neighbour is now living in the nursing home, but today she is at home.

The pronominal *estar-se* means 'to stay':

Ens estarem a l'hospital fins que la metgessa digui que tot va bé.
We shall stay at hospital until the doctor says everything is all right.

- when the place is a point on a scale:

  Les accions estan a vuit euros. Espera que estiguin a nou, i ven-les.
  The shares are now at eight euros. Wait until they are at nine, and sell them.

  El nen està a trenta-vuit de febre.
  The child has a temperature of thirty-eight degrees.

- when the place is metaphoric:
  Després d'una bona dormida estic al cel.
  After a good sleep I am in heaven.

  Es pensa que està per damunt el bé i el mal.
  He thinks he is above good and evil.

Some constructions admit both verbs, for example when a participle such as *situat* 'situated' can be inferred between the subject and place:

Barcelona és / està (situada) entre el Llobregat i el Besòs.
Barcelona lies between the river Llobregat and the river Besòs.

The main existential construction (stating that something exists) in Catalan is *haver-hi* 'there is, are, etc.', used impersonally with an object:

Hi ha dues persones a la platja.
There are two people on the beach.

Hi havia una finestra aquí on ara hi ha la porta.
There used to be a window where there is now a door.

With definite people *haver-hi* can also be used. Only when such an object is placed before the verb as a result of focusing, it turns into a subject and *haver-hi* switches to *ser-hi*:

– Bon dia, que hi hauria en Miquel? 'Good morning, is Miquel there?'
– No, en Miquel ara no hi és 'No, Miquel is not in now.'
– A la sala hi ha en Miquel, però no hi serà tota la tarda 'Miquel is in the room, but he will not be there all afternoon.

15.2.4 *Timing*

Ser is used with times and dates:

Avui és dilluns.
Today is Monday.

Ara són dos quarts de dues.
It's half past one.

Days and dates can take the place of the predicate, and a personal subject can appear: (implicit) *nosaltres* 'we'. In this case, *ser* is used if the predicate is not introduced by a preposition, and *estar* when a preposition opens the predicate, but the meaning is the same:

Avui som dilluns / Avui estem a dilluns.
It's Monday.

Avui som 24 d'abril / Avui estem a 24 d'abril.
It's April 24th.

15.2.5 *Semicopulae*

Parèixer 'to look like', *semblar* 'to look like', *continuar* 'to go on', *tornar* 'to become', *quedar(-se)* 'to remain', *romandre* 'to remain', *tornar(–se)* 'to become', *esdevenir* 'to become', *parar* 'to end up', *acabar* 'to end up' are semicopulative verbs, connecting subject and predicative expression in the same way that pure copulative verbs do, although adding some differential meaning as of seemingness, continuity, conversion, or result (see section 8.1 on selecting the right pronoun to replace complements).

Parèixer and *semblar* are synonyms, but *parèixer* is rarer with adjectives implying non permanent qualities:

El teu oncle pareix enfadat.
El teu oncle sembla enfadat.
Your uncle seems angry.

El teu oncle pareix que està enfadat.
Your uncle seems to be angry.

The last sentence shows a subject extracted from the subordinate clause:

Pareix que el teu oncle està enfadat It seems that your uncle is angry → **El teu oncle pareix que està enfadat** Your uncle seems to be angry.

Both verbs can use a dative, with a sense of opinion:

Al dentista li sembla / pareix que t'haurà d'arrabassar un queixal.
The dentist thinks he will have to pull out one of your back teeth.

With this type of construction only adjectives expressing a permanent quality can appear as predicative expressions; otherwise, the predicate is rephrased with a subordinate clause:

La mar li semblava gran.
She thought the sea was huge.

?La mar li semblava agitada → Li semblava que la mar estava agitada
She thought the sea was rough.

Chapter 16

Comparing

16.1 Comparing single elements

16.1.1 *Comparing adjectives and adverbs*

The simplest way to compare objects, states, and actions is by means of adjectives and adverbs accompanied by the degree adverbs *tan* 'as', *més* 'more', *menys* 'less' and conjunctions *que* 'than' / *com* 'as', as in the following table:

First term	Verb	Degree	Adjective / adverb	Conjunction	Second term
la sopa the soup	és is	tan as	dolenta bad	com as	la carn the meat
aquella casa that house	és is	més bigger	gran	que than	la nostra ours
aquest negoci this business	és is	menys less	lucratiu profitable	que than	l'altre the other
aquest metge this doctor	treballa works	més more	intensament intensely	que than	el seu company his colleague
la moto motorbikes	corre are (lit. runs)	més faster	aviat	que than	el cotxe cars

As we can see in the table above, the basic structures are:

tan ____ *com*

més ____ *que*

menys ____ *que*

It is not unusual to see *més poc* ___ *que* instead of *menys* ___ *que*: *aquest noi és més poc intel·ligent que son pare* 'This boy is less intelligent than his father'.

Some adjectives and adverbs have synthetic comparatives, that is, they have forms where whole words replace the phrase formed by degree adverb and adjective / adverb (just as in English 'better', 'worse'. etc.):

bo/bona/bons/bones / bé 'good / well' → **millor/millors** 'better'

dolent/dolenta/dolents/dolentes / malament 'bad / badly' → **pitjor/pitjors** 'worse'

gran/grans 'big, great, aged' → **major/majors** 'bigger, greater, elder'

petit/petita/petits/petites 'small' → **menor/menors** 'smaller'

However, unlike in many English cases, the usage of synthetic forms of comparison is not compulsory:

Aquest seient és pitjor que l'altre, però per sort aquesta pantalla és major que la de l'altra sala.
Aquest seient és més dolent que l'altre, però per sort aquesta pantalla és més gran que la de l'altra sala.
This seat is worse than the other one, but luckily this screen is bigger than the one in the other room.

In comparisons of inferiority and superiority (i.e. comparisons of more or less), the conjunction *que* can be optionally followed by *no (pas)*. This does not add new meaning to the sentence, but only emphasis:

Aquest noi és més alt que l'altre.
Aquest noi és més alt que no l'altre.
Aquest noi és més alt que no pas l'altre.
This boy is taller than the other one.

16.1.2 *Superlatives*

The superlative identifies the most outstanding element out of a given set when it is **relative**, or the highest degree of a quality when it is **absolute**.

Relative superlatives are constructed as follows:

el/els/la/les

+

més, menys or *més poc*

+

adjective (i.e. the quality that is the base of the comparison)

+

noun being compared (which can be omitted if it is clear from the context)

+

de

+

the set against which the noun is being compared:

La teva germana és la més alta de la seva classe.
Your sister is the tallest in her class.

Note that you could also say *la noia més alta* and 'the tallest girl/child' in the example above, but the noun is omitted because it is clear from context.

La cicuta és la planta més verinosa de totes.
Poison hemlock is the most poisonous plant of all.

Relation to the element's set can also be made as follows:

un/una/uns/unes (this is optional)

+

dels / de les

+

noun in the plural (which can be omitted when it is clear from the context)

+

més, menys or *més poc*

+

adjective (i.e. the quality that is the base of the comparison)

+

de

+

the set

La planta cicuta és (una) de les (plantes) més verinoses.
The plant poison hemlock is one of the most poisonous (plants).

Absolute superlatives just state that a given quality is possessed in an utmost degree, and there are several ways of doing this:

i. degree adverbs: *molt, ben, tan* (with no second term to which to compare), *absolutament*, *completament*, etc.:

   D'ençà que m'he jubilat sóc completament feliç.
   Since I retired I am utterly happy.

   Les relacions humanes són tan difícils!
   Human relationships are so difficult!

   Aquesta fruita és ben dolça.
   This fruit is very sweet.

ii. by repeating the adjective or adverb:

   Aquests pisos són lletjos lletjos.
   These apartments are very ugly.

   Avui estic cansat cansat.
   Today I'm so tired.

iii. by adding the suffix *–íssim/–íssima/–íssims/–íssimes* to the adjective or adding it as an infix to the (feminine) adjectival stem of an adverb of manner:

   Aquest llibre és interessantíssim.
   This book is very interesting.

   He fet aquest pastís especialíssimament per a tu.
   I have baked this cake especially for you.

A small set of adjectives produce irregular superlatives, which can equally be replaced by their regular forms:

bo/bona/bons/bones good	*òptim/òptima/òptims/òptimes*
dolent/dolenta/dolents/dolentes bad	*pèssim/pèssima/pèssims/pèssimes*
cèlebre/cèlebres famous	*celebèrrim/celebèrrima/celebèrrims/ celebèrrimes*

íntegre/integra/íntegres complete, integer	*integèrrim/integèrrima/integèrrims/integèrrimes*
lliure/lliures free	*libèrrim/libèrrima/libèrrims/libèrrimes*
míser/mísera/mísers/míseres miserable	*misèrrim/misèrrima/misèrrims/misèrrimes*
pobre/pobra/pobres poor	*paupèrrim/paupèrrima/paupèrrims/paupèrrimes*
pulcre/pulcra/pulcres nice, clean	*pulquèrrim/pulquèrrima/pulquèrrims/pulquèrrimes*
salubre/salubres healthy	*salubèrrim/salubèrrima/salubèrrims/salubèrrimes*

It is worth remembering that as in other areas of inflected words spelling can change in order to preserve the pronunciation dictated by the stem, normally visible in the feminine form:

cec/cega – seguíssim/ceguíssima (remember that <u> is unpronounced in <gu> followed by a front vowel ('i' and 'e')

mut/muda – mudíssim/mudíssima

bla/blana – blaníssim/blaníssima

An exception to this rule is *antic/antiga – antiquíssim*, and *greu – gravíssim* is also an exception due to the change of the stem vowel.

16.2 Clauses

Structures used in comparing clauses are:

superiority	*més que* – more than
inferiority	*menys que / més poc que* – less than
equality (quantity)	*tant com* – as much as
(un-)equality (quality)	*(talment) com* – like *igual(ment) que* – equally *diferent(ment) de* – different(ly) from *semblant(ment) / similar a* – similar(ly) to

El cafè m'agrada més que el te.
I like coffee more than tea.

A l'agost fa menys calor que al juliol.
August is less hot than July.

Escric tant com llegeixo.
I write as much as I read.

La teva filla parla (talment) com la seva àvia.
Your daughter speaks (just) like her grandmother.

Les males notícies arriben igual que les cireres: de dues en dues.
(Lit.) Bad news comes along like cherries: two by two.

Nosaltres hem d'actuar diferentment de com actuen els nostres rivals.
We must act in a different way from our rivals.

La fàbrica de paper ha tancat i, semblantment, la distribuïdora.
The paper factory has shut down and, likewise, the distributor.

When comparing clauses in terms of an unequal comparison and there are two verbs, *del que* is used to introduce the second term of comparison, and the unmarked article *el* can be inflected for gender and number when comparison is established between objects depending on a verb:

El mestre en sap més del que et penses.
The teacher knows more than what you think.

El mestre sap menys coses de les que et penses.
The teacher knows fewer things than what you think.

Instead of *del que*, *que no* can be used:

El mestre en sap més que no et penses.
The teacher knows more than what you think.

El mestre sap menys coses que no et penses.
The teacher knows fewer things than what you think.

The use of *que no* (*pas*) is compulsory for comparing clauses when the second term of comparison is a clause introduced by *que*, in order to avoid a clash of two uses of *que*:

M'estimo més que em caigui la casa a sobre que no (pas) que la venguis tan barata.
***. . . a sobre que que la venguis tan barata**
I would rather the house fell down on my head than you sell it so cheap.

Also clauses can be turned into superlatives by adding a degree adverb (see above):

Llegir és el que més m'agrada.
Reading is what I like best.

Córrer és el que faig més malament.
Running is what I do worst.

Aquella nedadora és la que neda més ràpid de totes.
That swimmer is the one who swims fastest of all.

Enguany és quan ha plogut més.
This year is when it has rained the most.

Chapter 17

Treatments

17.1 Degrees of politeness

There are three levels of politeness when speaking to someone in Catalan, as visible in the stressed singular pronouns *tu* / *vostè* / *vós*. *Tu* is used in conversations with known equals; *vostè* is the most polite form used to address superiors in a non-familiar relation; *vós* is a polite form used to show respect to superiors (normally in age) without completely breaking familiarity. In fact, most speakers stick to a two-member system, in which *tu* is opposed to a polite form of address, this being either *vós* or *vostè*, the connotations being more rural and traditional for *vós*, and more urban for *vostè*. In any case, *vós* is preferred for public notices aimed at an unknown audience, such as *Cediu el pas* 'Give way' or *No fumeu* 'No smoking'. The latter convention is helped by the fact that *vós* has no plural other than *vosaltres*, showing that this degree of politeness is neutralised in the plural.

17.2 Grammatical relations of polite pronouns

It is important to notice that even if the referred person is the addressee, and therefore a second person according to pragmatics, the grammatical relations of *tu*, *vós*, and *vostè* are not the same, as in the following table:

Stressed	Unstressed (accusative)	Unstressed (dative)	Verbal person	Possessive
tu	*et*	*et*	2nd sg	el teu (etc.)
vós	*us*	*us*	2nd pl	el vostre
vostè	*el*	*li*	3rd sg	el seu
vosaltres	*us*	*us*	2nd pl	el vostre
vostès	*els*	*els*	3rd pl	el seu

Examples:

Si ens ho demaneu vós, aleshores us enviarem el paquet a casa vostra.
If it is you who orders it, then we shall send you the parcel to (your) home.

Quan vostè ha arribat, el seu net li ha dit bon dia.
When you arrived, your grandson said good morning to you.

Al seu fill li importa el que els pugui passar a les seves vacances.
Your son cares about what may happen to you on your holidays.

In spite of *vós* being conjugated in the plural, as the referent is singular, it agrees with adjectives in the singular:

Esteu cansat?
Are you tired? (vs *Esteu cansats?* Are you (all) tired?)

Sou soltera o casada?
Are you single or married?

17.3 Honorifics

Honorific titles introduced with a possessive (as in the English 'Your Majesty'), are simple in Catalan as the possessive depends only on the possession and not on the possessing person. In all cases, the possessive appearing in an honorific form of appeal is the unstressed feminine *sa*: *Sa Majestat* 'Your Majesty', *Sa Il·lustríssima*, *Sa Excel·lència* 'Your Excellency', *Sa Santedat* 'Your Holiness', *Sa Eminència* 'Your Eminence'. Treatments of this type take verbs in the third person singular, and possession is also indicated in the third person singular (*el seu*, etc.). Any agreeing adjective must appear in the singular and in the correct gender according to whether the addressee is a woman or a man:

For a Pope: **Sa Santedat ha de ser consultat.**
His Holiness must be consulted.

For a queen: **Sa Majestat ha de ser consultada.**
Her Majesty must be consulted.

Nós is the majestic form for the first person. It requires verbs and possessives in the first person plural, but adjectives should appear in the singular and in the correct gender according to the person:

Nós, Jaume de Barcelona, prometem guardar els furs i les constitucions del nostre regne.
I, Jaume de Barcelona, promise to warrant the rights and constitutions of our kingdom.

17.4 Titles before surnames

Regarding titles preceding surnames, there is an important difference compared to English: the definite article is compulsory in Catalan, except when the person is being addressed directly (what is called vocative usage):

La doctora Mas ha participat en un congrés molt important.
Doctor Mas has attended a very important conference.

El senyor Reig ha reservat taula per a les dues.
Mister Reig has booked a table for two o'clock.

A quina hora creu que arribarà, pare Bonet?
At what time do you think you will arrive, Father Bonet?

Chapter 18

Emphasizers

18.1 Emphasizing single elements

Emphasizing single elements is possible by adding degree adverbs such as those in on p. 83. Other emphasizing systems are by means of (a) adjectives and adverbs, (b) subcategorizing the emphasized element to a noun expressing quantity or degree, (c) an affix, and (d) adding an interjection to a question or exclamative word.

18.1.1 *Adjectives and adverbs as emphasizers*

Mateix, meaning 'same', acts as an intensifier, sometimes with the sense of 'oneself' added to a proper name, a noun, or a pronoun. When appearing before a name it stresses identity, thus the meaning is plainly 'same'. However, when it appears after an element, it just emphasizes it. In this latter position, *mateix* can operate either as an adjective, and therefore agreeing in gender and noun with a previous noun, or as an adverb, remaining invariable:

Ella mateixa ens va dir que no havia fet les coses bé.
She herself told us that she had not behaved properly.

Ens van convidar a la festa les nostres amigues mateix.
It was our friends who invited us to the party.

L'estanc encara és allà mateix.
The tobacconist's is still at the same place.

Propi is an adjective meaning 'own'. It emphasizes the meaning of the possessive.

Ho he vist amb els meus propis ulls.
I have seen it with my own eyes.

Cèsar fou traït pel seu propi fill.
Caesar was betrayed by his own son.

Using *propi* with the same emphatic, although only adjectival and preposed, use of *mateix*, is deemed incorrect, although is frequently heard.

Tot is invariable when emphasising a gerund, stressing the simultaneity of actions between the gerund and the main verb:

Repassava el discurs tot dinant.
She revised her speech while having lunch.

Tot baixant per la drecera he vist un arbre rosat (Maragall).
While walking down the shortcut, I saw a pink tree (Maragall).

Fins i tot is an adverbial compound translating English 'even'. It can emphasize a verb, a noun, an adjective, or an adverb. In all cases, *fins i tot* can be reduced to *i tot* when following the emphasized element:

Ha vingut tothom, fins i tot la Isabel / Ha vingut tothom, la Isabel i tot.
Everybody has come, even Isabel.

Ja es troba millor: fins i tot menja / Ja es troba millor: menja i tot.
She feels better: she even eats.

Ho feia bé, fins i tot a consciència / Ho feia bé, a consciència i tot.
He did it well, even thoroughly.

18.1.2 *Subcategorization to a phrase expressing quantity or degree*

Phrases as *un munt de*, *un bé de Déu de*, *la mar de* emphasize quantity or degree by replacing a noun, or in some cases an adjective or an adverb, and converting it into a noun complement, in a similar way to how 'a lot of', 'tons of', or any partitive works in English:

Hi havia molts cotxes → Hi havia un munt de cotxes.
There were many cars → There were a load of cars.

Sap moltes coses → Sap un bé de Déu de coses.
He knows many things → He knows a good amount of things.

Tinc molts amics → Tinc la mar d'amics.
I have many friends. → I have loads of friends.

Out of these elements, only *la mar de* can modify adjectives and adverbs as well as nouns:

Quan va sentir allò va posar-se la mar de vermell.
When he heard that, he got very red.

Ha arribat la mar de lluny.
It has gone very far.

The construction *qui-sap-lo* deserves special attention. This is an emphasizer acting either as an adverb or an adjective, and in the latter case, agreeing in gender and number with the noun:

Ahir vam pescar qui-sap-los calamars.
Yesterday we fished so many squid / who knows how many squid.

Estic qui-sap-lo cansat.
I'm so tired.

18.1.3 By means of a prefix

Qualifying affixes have already been analysed on p. 114. He, we shall look at a particular qualifying prefix, used colloquially with adjectives, adverbs, and even verbs: *rede–*. It can appear modifying one of these elements, although it is usually found coordinated with the same element before prefixation:

Aquest camí és redellarg.
This way is very long.

Estic farta i redefarta de sentir aquestes coses.
I'm utterly fed up of hearing such things.

He llegit i redellegit aquesta novel·la i no hi trob res d'interessant.
I've read this novel time and again and I can't find anything interesting in it.

18.1.4 Adding an interjection to exclamative words

Exclamative and interrogative words can receive emphasis from a postposed taboo word. This belongs to a vulgar, rude register of language, although euphemistic words are often used. With exclamation words, a similar syntactic movement as on p. 193 above occurs.

No sé què dimonis passa dins l'altre vagó.
I do not know what the hell is happening in the other coach.

Com diantre entraràs a la casa si no en tens la clau.
How the devil will you enter into the house if you don't have the key?

Quin coi d'home, que és! No hi ha qui l'aguanti!
What a tosser of a man, he is! Nobody can stand him!

18.2 Emphasizing whole phrases

18.2.1 *Emphasizing assertions*

An assertion can be emphasized by using *és clar que*, *i tant que*, or *i tant com* before it:

Que si he llegit el teu informe? És clar que l'he llegit.
If I have read your report? Of course I have read it.

I tant com els habitants de Venècia estan cansats del turisme invasiu.
Of course the inhabitants of Venice are tired of invasive tourism.

I tant que aniré a queixar-me a l'Ajuntament.
I shall certainly go to report at the Town Hall.

Segur que and *per descomptat* also work as emphasisers:

Segur que en arribar voldràs descansar.
For sure you will want to rest after arriving.

Per descomptat els diputats del seu partit la votaran.
No doubt that her party's MPs will vote for her.

18.2.2 *Emphasizing exceptions*

Rai, following an element, even a phrase, minimises for that element the effect of what is said in the sentence (to emphasise something else):

Que haguéssim de caminar rai, el pitjor va ser haver de transportar l'equipatge.
Having to walk was nothing; the worst was having to carry our baggage.

La Maria rai, que sap nedar, els nens em feien patir.
Maria's fine, she can swim; it's the kids I was worried about.

Si ens porten el material a temps rai; el problema serà que no arribi.
No problem if they bring us the material on time, but we shall be in trouble if they don't.

Chapter 19

Interjections and ideophones

Partially as a complement to word formation seen in Part II, we offer here a list of interjections: and ideophones (both imitative and non-imitative).

Surprise	*ah, alça, àngela maria, carall, caram* (euphemic for '*carall*', as are '*carat, caratxos, cavall*'), *cony, coi* (euphemic for '*cony*'), *com, collons, eu, fotre, fosca* (euphemic for '*fotre*'), *ha, hola, hòstia, jesús, renoi, oh, oi, òndia* (euphemic for '*hòstia*'), *renoi, ui, xe*
Agreement, approval	*amén, bé, bo, conforme, ja, natural, oi* (used in tag questions as in '*oi que sí?*'), *i tant, és clar* (see p. 195 for the usage of these units with as emphasizers of sentences), *fort* ('well-deserved!', especially facing someone else's punishment or misfortune)
Disapproval	*ca, ca barret* ('no way!'), *jas, per aquí* ('take this', ironic)
Dislike, disagreement	*aire* ('go away', 'far from me'), *apa* (ironic), *bah, bo* (ironic), *bufa, ca, coi* (euphemism for '*cony*'), *com, collons, fotre, fosca* (euphemism for '*fotre*'), *hòstia, malviatge, merda, oh, òndia* (euphemism for '*hòstia*'), *punyeta, redeu, uf, vaja, vatua, vatualmon, vatuadell, xe*
Achievement, success	*bingo, pataplaf, eureka* (after finding a solution)
Failure	*tururut*
Doubt, distrust	*hem, hum, pse*

Pain	*ai, ui*
Disgust	*ecs, ec, uf, uix*
Happinness, satisfaction	*al·leluia, bravo, hurra, millor, visca*
Cheering	*amunt, apa, au, avant, som-hi, vinga, hala* ('come on'), *up* (when lifting an object), *upa* (same as 'up'),
Taunting	*ela, elis* (normally in pairs as in ela-ela, elis-elis)
Prohibition	*alto* ('halt'), *basta, prou* ('enough')
Orders	*ferms* (military command: attention!, shun!), *foc* (fire!), *mutis* (silence!)
Amount, sequence	*vinga* (as in sequences '*i vinga guanyar diners, i vinga guanyar diners*')
Warning	*alerta, atenció, compte*
Calling attention	*eh, ehem, ei, ep*
Sounds for addressing animals	*arri* ('move'), *xo, arruix* ('go away'), *oixque* ('turn left'; also 'hurry up'), *ollaó* ('turn right'), *ou* ('stop'), *tites* (used to call chickens)
Greetings	*adeu, adeu-siau, vinga* ('goodbye'), *ei, hola* ('hello'), *jesús* ('bless you' after someone sneezes), *perdó* ('sorry')
'Here you are'	*jas* (sg), *jau* (pl), *té* (sg), *teniu* (pl)

The following are ideophones:

Animal ideophones	*bub-bub* (dog), *cloc-cloc* (hen), *piu-piu* (birds), *quiquiriquic* (cock), *ric-ric* (cricket), *meu* (cat), *roc-roc* (frog), *xut* (owl), *be* (sheep, goat), *mu* (cow), *xau-xau* (partridge and quail)

Other ideophones	*atxim* (sneeze), *crec* (breaking), *crac* (breaking), *catacrac* (breaking), *catric-catrac* (machine working), *cric-crac* (machine working), *clac* (clash), *dring* (metal or glass clash), *flist-flast* (hitting), *fru-fru* (clothes, especially silk, moving and grazing), *gloc-gloc* (a liquid through a bottle-neck or a drain), *ha! ha! ha!* (laugh), *ning-nang* (bell), *ning-ning* (handbell), *nyac* (catching), *nyam-nyam* (eating), *nyec-nyec* (arguing), *nyeu-nyeu* (hypocritical speaking), *nyic* (chirp), *nyic-nyic* (talking over-insistently), *nyigo-nyigo* (untuned violin), *paf* (falling, crashing), *pam* (hit, shoot), *patapam* (falling and hitting the floor or an object), *patatx-ap* (splash), *pif-paf* (sequence of hits in a fight), *pim-pam* (shooting), *plof* (falling on a soft surface), *pum* (explosion), *ric-rac* (grazing, rubbing), *rum-rum* (confused noise, clamour), *taf-taf* (an engine), *tampatantam* (a drum), *taral·larà* (singing), *tararà* (a trumpet), *tararí* (a bugle), *tic-tac* (a watch), *trip-trap* (heart beats), *tris-tras* (walking), *xap* (splash), *xep-a-xep* (whispering), *xiu-xiu* (whispering), *xip-xap* (splash), *xup-xup* (boiling), *zas* (quick movement in the air), *zim-zam* (swing), *zum-zum* (confused noise, clamour), *xim-xim* (fanfare)

A list of sound expressive words, although non-imitative, formed in the same way of certain ideophones above, by repetition or quase–repetition, are listed below according to their grammatical category and meaning:

Adverbs

Moving disorderedly or from one side to the other	*balandrim-balandram, banzim-banzam, barrim-barram, pengim-penjam*
Continuously, especially for walking	*daixo-daixo, xano-xano, xino-xano, tira-tira, tris-tras*
Limping	*coixim-coixam*

By the coast (sailing)	*terrús-terrús*
In cash	*bitllo-bitllo, trinco-trinco*
Neither well nor badly	*així-aixà, tal·là-tal·lera, tau-tau, xau-xau*
About to happen	*leri-leri*

Nouns

Unreliable person	*baliga-balaga* (m/f), *barliqui-barloqui* (m/f), *tarit-tarot* (m/f)
A jumble	*barrija-barreja* (f), *farri-go-farrago* (m), *poti-poti* (m)
Noise-making tools	*xerric-xerrac* (m) 'ratchet', *zing-zing* 'rattle'
Sounds	*gori-gori* (m) '(colloquially), funeral chant', *tol·le-tol·le* 'uproar'
Drizzle	*xim-xim* (m) (see 'other ideophones', above)
'To keep body and soul together'	*viu-viu* (f) (in the idiom *fer la viu-viu*)
Zigzag	*zig-zag* (m), *ziga-zaga* (f)
Throbbing	*zub-zub* (m)

Adjective

Of a poor quality	de nyigui-nyogui

Chapter 20

Frequent native-speaker mistakes (solecisms)

As any other living language, Catalan evolves and some uses are deemed wrong by the official grammar – go to any internet forum in English and you'll find somebody writing 'I could have done it.' This phenomenon may be stronger in a language where there are no monolingual speakers, and where switching between languages is a fact of life. Although Catalan is the first language for a good amount of the population in Catalan-speaking areas, laws such as the Spanish constitution, and the availability of public services and the media mean that in reality there are no monolingual Catalan speakers – depending on the territory, speakers also need to know Spanish, French, or Italian. The point of this section is not to analyse lexical interference among these languages, but rather point out some common errors. Not all of these are due to language interference either; some are self-generated by the Catalan-speaking communities.

20.1 Morphology

20.1.1 Gender

Hesitations in the usage of gender for inanimate objects are visible in words where traditional gender assignation differs in Catalan and Spanish, or where the word ending challenges the customary forms for masculine or feminine. Incorrect usage can lead to transformation of the ending in order to adapt it to what is more common in the wrong gender, as in *empara* → **empar*, or *espinacs* → **espinaques*. The following list includes many of those problematic nouns with the correct gender in Catalan:

Masculine: *afores* 'suburbs', *aroma* 'aroma', *avantatge* 'advantage', *bacteri* 'bacterium', *compte* 'bill, care', *corrent* 'flow', *costum* 'custom, habit', *deute* 'debt', *dot* 'dowry', *dubte* 'doubt', *escafandre* 'diving suit', *espinacs* 'spinach', *estratagema* 'stratagem', *front* 'forehead', *full* 'sheet of paper or any other material', *llegum* 'legume', *pendent* 'slope', *senyal* 'signal'.

Feminine: *alicates* 'pliers', *allau* 'avalanche', *anàlisi* 'analysis', *dent* 'tooth', *destrossa* 'destruction, ruin', *disfressa* 'fancy dress', *empara* 'protection', *esplendor* 'splendour', *flaire* 'smell', *olor* 'smell', *resta* 'rest', *síncope* 'syncope', *síndrome* 'syndrome', *suor* 'sweat'.

It is also worth noting that adjectives with masculine and feminine forms are sometimes made invariable for gender, also often owing to Spanish influence. The following have separate masculine and feminine forms in Catalan but are sometimes (wrongly) used invariably:

calent/calenta 'hot', *comú/comuna* 'common', *covard/covarda* 'coward', *cortès/cortesa* 'polite', *ferm/ferma* 'firm', *fort/forta* 'strong' (usually misused in **caixa fort* instead of *caixa forta* 'safe box'), *gris/grisa* 'grey', *límitrof/limítrofa* 'bordering', *pobre/pobra* 'poor', *trist/trista* 'sad', *valent/valenta* 'courageous', *verd/verda* 'green'.

Traditionally, as in the other Romance languages, the masculine has been used also as the neutral gender or the unmarked when talking about gender-mixed sets of individuals, so that *els alumnes* 'the pupils' means 'the male and the female pupils'. An intense debate is taking place at the moment in Catalan-speaking society on this topic, with linguists arguing in favour of maintaining grammatical correctness, as gender segregation in speech and writing leads to unwieldy expression at times, and can even make it difficult to understand since it is not easy to separate genders throughout a long text. The main point here is not to forget that grammatical gender is a different concept from biological gender, as attested with object's names, or with words as *persona* 'person' (f) / *ésser humà* 'human being' (m), both of them suitable for individuals of either (biological) gender. Elsewhere, nowadays the official dictionary includes dimorphic profession names, such as *arquitecte/arquitecta*, *metge/metgessa*, *jutge/jutgessa*, *advocat/advocada*, *mestre/mestra*, *psiquiatre/psiquiatra*, etc.

20.1.2 Number

You will often hear the non-standard plurals *masses, prous, qualques*, but *massa*, *prou* and *qualque* should be always kept in the singular, even when, due to their meaning, they refer to a plurality of objects:

***Hi ha *masses* estudiants dintre d'aquesta aula → ✓Hi ha *massa* estudiants dintre d'aquesta aula.**
There are too many students in this classroom.

***No hi ha *prous* cadires per a tothom → ✓No hi ha *prou* cadires per a tothom.**
There are not enough chairs for everyone.

***He llegit *qualques* llibres d'aquest autor → ✓He llegit *qualque* llibre d'aquest autor.**
I've read the odd book by this author.

Weekdays remain in the singular with the article preceding them when speaking about an action that takes place that day every week. The plural (only affecting the article or *dissabte* and *diumenge*) is only used when speaking about specific days:

Dissabte aniré a visitar la teva germana / El dissabte visito la teva germana / Els dos primers dissabtes del mes que ve visitaré la teva germana.
Next Saturday I'll visit your sister / Every Saturday I visit your sister / The first two Saturdays of July I'll visit your sister.

Apart from *dissabte* and *diumenge*, names of the days of the week are invariable: **dillunsos, *dimartsos, *dijousos.*

The word *esquena* 'back' is erroneoulsy heard sometimes in the plural when referring to one person, due to interference with *espatlles* 'shoulders' and the existence of the Spanish idiom *a espaldas de*. The latter has the Catalan parallel *per darrere de*.

20.1.3 Verbs

Some verbs, such as *parèixer, conèixer*, and derived verbs as *comparèixer, desaparèixer, desconèixer, reconèixer*, etc., belong to the second conjugation and end in *–éixer/–èixer*, are incorrectly treated like inceptive -ir verbs (p. 58), and thus erroneous forms can be generated as in **pareixo, *coneixo, *compareixo, *desapareixo*, etc. instead of *parec, conec, comparec, desaparec*, etc.

Also some other verbs from the second conjugation and from the pure (non-inceptive) model of the third conjugation are also wrongly treated as inceptive. Some of them are *ressentir-se, bullir, concebre, debatre, inscriure, transcriure, recloure, excloure, infondre, transfondre*, erroneously conjugated as **ressenteixo, *bulleixo, *concibeixo, *debateixo, *inscribeixo, *transcribeixo, *reclueixo, *exclueixo, *infundeixo, *transfundeixo*, formed as though the infinitives were **concebir, *debatir, *infundir, *inscribir, *transcribir, *recluir, *excluir, *infundir.*

As Catalan students know full well, gerunds cannot end in *–guent* and *–quent*. However, mistakes are common and you can hear the following: **capiguent*, **sapiguent*, **coneguent*, **correguent*, **poguent*, **apareguent*, **meresquent*, **rebiguent*, **escriguent*. These should correctly be *cabent*, *sabent*, *coneixent*, *corrent*, *podent*, *apareixent*, *mereixent*, *rebent*, *escrivint*.

20.1.4 Unstressed pronouns (coneixe'ns, lis)

The unstressed pronouns, their combination, and the form in which they attach to verbs are important sources of variation.

The pronoun *li* should be *els* / *-los* in plural. This lack of balance leads some speakers to the analogy **lis*, especially in postpositions: **Hem vingut a donar*-lis *la benvinguda* 'We have come to welcome them' instead of ✓*Hem vingut a donar*-los *la benvinguda*.

The 3rd person dative pl pronoun *els* appears sometimes combined with an unnecessary *hi*, used to reinforce the sense of dative, but not replacing in fact any complement: **Els hi telefonareu?* 'Will you phone them?' instead of ✓*Els telefonareu?* The combination is acceptable only if *hi* replaces an adverbial, as in *Telefonareu als vostres cosins a casa?*

Colloquially, any accusative pronoun combining with dative *els* can turn to *hi*, and the combination *els* (dat.) *en* (acc.) can turn to *els n'hi*:

Portaràs la fruita als pares? Will you take the fruit to my parents?

→ (Colloquial) **Els hi portaràs?**; (Formal) **Els la portaràs?** Will you take it to them?

Portaràs fruita als pares? Will you take fruit to my parents?

→ (Colloquial) **Els n'hi portaràs?**; (Formal) **Els en portaràs?**

Attaching unstressed pronouns to infinitives is another common mistake. Combinations such as *coneixe'ns*, *mereixe-us*, *porteu-se*, and *menjà'l* are the result of simplifying the infinitive or imperative ending and processing them as if they ended in a vowel. These forms are colloquial and must be avoided in writing and formal speech:

***coneixe'ns** → ✓**conèixer-nos** to know each other
***mereixe-us** → ✓**merèixer-vos** to deserve you

***comporteu-se bé** → ✓**comporteu-vos bé** behave
***menjà'l** → ✓**menjar-lo** to eat it

20.2 Verb usage

20.2.1 *Gerunds*

Especially in journalistic writing, it is common to find gerunds indicating a state or action in fact posterior to that of the main verb. They are normally replaceable by a personal form of the verb linked by a copulative conjunction:

> ***Va caure per la finestra, morint al cap de pocs minuts → ✓Va caure per la finestra, i va morir al cap de pocs minuts.**
> He fell out of the window and he died a few minutes later.

> ***Les noces seran a la capella, traslladant-se els convidats a un restaurant proper per al dinar → ✓Les noces seran a la capella, i els convidats es traslladaran a un restaurant proper per al dinar.**
> The wedding will be at the chapel, and the guests will move to a nearby restaurant for lunch.

20.2.2 *Conditional sentences with a compound tense*

The main clause in a conditional sentence with a compound tense should be built up with a conditional compound, and not, as usual in careless speech, with a plusquamperfect subjunctive:

> ***Si m'haguessis escoltat, no t'**haguessis equivocat → ✓**Si m'haguessis escoltat, no t'**hauries equivocat – Had you listened to me, you wouldn't have made that mistake.

20.2.3 *Expressing obligation*

There is the rather usual mistake in native speech of the obligation formula *tenir que*. This is a clear and unnecessary borrowing from Spanish. The Catalan traditional expression of obligation is *haver de*:

> ***Em molesta que tinguem que anar mudats a la recepció → ✓Em moltesta que haguem d'anar mudats a la recepció** – It bothers me having to attend the reception in formal dress.

20.3 Syntax

20.3.1 *Object with 'a'*

A direct object does not require a preposition in Catalan. However, especially when the object is a person, sentences like **He vist a la Maria* (instead of ✓*He vist la Maria*) 'I have seen Maria' **No voteu a polítics corruptes* (for ✓*No voteu partits corruptes*) can be heard and read. The preposition must be omitted in all cases, except in the following, where it is allowed:

i. When the object is a quantifying pronoun referring to persons (*algú*, *qualcú*, *cadascú*, *qualsevol*, *ningú*, etc): *No insultis* (*a*) *ningú d'aquesta família* 'Do not insult anybody.' It is rarer to find the preposition when the object is not restricted to a given set of candidates: ?*No insultis a ningú*. Observe that *molts*, *pocs*, and such phrases as *més de* + a number can become pronominalised, and adopt the preposition *a* when in a direct object, especially when their ruling verb is a causative (i.e. noting causation: an effect cast on the object): *Això espantarà a molts* shows a pronominalised *molts* in an absolute sense, meaning 'many people', with no referent taken out of a given set, but *Això n'espantarà molts*, which is also possible and correct only without the preposition, inserts a partitive *n'* pronoun which indicates that there must be a *de* phrase replaced by it (i.e. a particular group), such as in *Això espantarà molts dels nostres amics*.
ii. When the object is *qui* (either interrogative or relative), *quin*, *quants*, or *el qual*, especially if the preposition resolves confusion regarding who is the subject and who is the object: *A qui mira en Miquel* 'Who is Miquel looking at?' shows unambiguously that *en Miquel* is the subject and *qui*, the object. *A quants nois han convidat els teus germans?* 'How many (people) have your brothers invited?' *Ta mare ha escrit a la senyora a la qual va atropellar el teu germà*. 'Your mother has written to the lady that was knocked down by your brother.'
iii. *A* can also introduce the object when it has been moved right- or left-wards and replaced in its original place by an unstressed pronoun (see p. 137): *A les regles, has de seguir-les totes* (also *Les regles has de seguir-les totes*) 'The rules, you must follow all of them', *Ja les has exposades, a les teves objeccions* (also *Ja les has exposades, les teves objeccions*) 'You have already stated them, your objections'.
iv. Whenever ambiguity is possible, normally by the fact that subject and object appear next to each other, it is advisable to mark the object with the preposition *a*: *Els gossos empaiten els gats, i els gats als ratolins* 'Dogs chase cats, and cats, mice'.

20.3.2 *Pleonasms with unstressed pronouns*

Unstressed pronouns are abused on certain occasions when the complement they could replace is explicit. This occurs particularly with dative *li*/*els*, as in **Li diràs a la Margarida que passarem a saludar-la?*, **Els hem regalat un llibre a les teves germanes*. There is no need in these sentences to repeat the complement by means of a pronoun: *Diràs a la Margarida que passarem a saludar-la?* 'Will you tell Margarida that we shall go to see her' and *Hem regalat un llibre a les teves germanes* 'We have given a book to your sisters' are well-formed sentences without the redundant pronouns.

However, as already pointed out on p. 101 above, with verbs of (dis)like or interest, occurence, and also in possessive dative construction, the redundancy is allowed, as in *Al teu amic no li agrada la música* 'Your friend does not like music', *Aquestes coses sempre li passen a en Pere* 'These things always happen to Pere', *Als excursionistes els feien mal els peus* 'The hikers had foot ache'.

20.3.3 Conjunctions preceded by a preposition

Prepositions *a, de, en, amb* are avoided before the conjunction *que* in writing and formal speech. Sentences such as **Em refereixo a que cal abaixar els impostos*, **Tinc por de que no ens basti el pa*, **Tot el problema consisteix en que no hi ha diàleg*, **No m'acontento amb que rebaixis el to* are avoidable by omitting the preposition or by inserting a noun between the preposition and the conjunction: ✓*Em refereixo que cal abaixar els impostos* 'I mean that taxes must be cut down', ✓*Tinc por que no ens basti el pa* 'I am afraid of bread not being enough', ✓*Tot el problema consisteix en el fet que no hi ha diàleg* 'The whole problem is that dialogue is lacking', ✓*No m'acontento amb el fet que rebaixis el to* 'I'm not satisfied just with you lowering your voice.' The option for inserting a noun is stronger when the clash is caused by a prepositional complement introduced by the preposition *a* and depending on a noun or an adjective, and rephrasing seems more suitable than a simple omission: **tenir dret a que els informin* 'to have the right to be informed' → ✓*tenir dret que els informin*, but more often ✓*tenir dret a rebre informació* / ✓*tenir dret a ser informats*.

As an exception, the preposition *amb* can be followed by the conjunction *que* when the subordinate clause appears in subjunctive, with a meaning close to conditional ('only by'): *Amb que m'insinuïs que estàs cansat ja en tindré prou per rellevar-te* 'If you just insinuate that you are tired, that will be enough for me to send you home.'

20.3.4 Infinitives preceded by a preposition

Prepositions can introduce infinitives when these are attached as complements: *Em va convidar a dinar a casa seva* 'He invited me to have lunch at his home', *Ser feliç no depèn de tenir molts diners* 'Being happy does not depend on having a lot of money'. However, in formal language, prepositions *en* and *amb* are rejected before infinitives, and normally replaced by *a* and *de*, the preference being for the former, although a few verbs (*amenaçar, bastar, tenir-ne prou, haver-n'hi prou* prefer *de*):

L'examen consisteix en un dictat, but ***L'examen consisteix en fer un dictat** → ✓**L'examen consisteix a fer un dictat** The exam consists of (doing) a dictation

Ton pare insisteix en aquestes coses, but ***Ton pare insisteix en dir aquestes coses** → ✓**Ton pare insisteix a dir aquestes coses** Your father insists on (saying) such things

M'han amenaçat amb l'expulsió, but ***M'han amenaçat amb expulsar-me** → ✓**M'han amenaçat d'expulsar-me** They have threatened me with expulsion / expelling me

Ningú no estava d'acord amb la proposta, but ***Ningú no estava d'acord amb fer el que es proposava** → ✓**Ningú no estava d'acord a fer el que es proposava** Nobody agreed with (doing) what was proposed.

However, remember that the preposition *en* can introduce an infinitive when it means *when* (see p. 148): *En arribar ella començarà la festa* 'When she arrives the party will begin'. *Amb* can introduce an infinitive depending on verbs of comparison such as *comparar*, *tenir relació* or *tenir a veure*: *No comparis el teu esforç amb córrer una marató* 'Do not compare your effort with running a marathon', *Això no té res a veure amb ser una persona honrada* 'This has nothing to do with being an honest person'.

See p. 150 for the causal meaning of the preposition *per* and a simple infinitive.

20.3.5 *Relatives preceded by a preposition and an article*

Relative *que* cannot be preceded by a preposition, and the combination is rebuilt as preposition + *què* if replacing an object, or preposition + *qui* if replacing a person, or, if an antecedent exists, in either case also by preposition + article + *el qual*:

La noia de qui parles no sé qui és
I don't know who the girl you are talking about is.

La casa de què parles no sé on és
I don't know where the house you are talking about is.

No conec la persona de la qual parles
I do not know the person you talk about.

However, *del que* is not a possible relative when an antecedent exists:

***La noia de la que em parles és filla d'una amiga meva** → ✓**La noia de què em parles és filla d'una amiga meva / La noia de la qual em parles és filla d'una amiga meva** The girl you speak of is the daughter of a friend of mine.

The only possible case in which *del que* can refer to an antecedent is when a noun has been omitted between the article and pronoun *que*:

> **✓No et parlo de la noia que vam veure, et parlo de la (noia) que viu al davant**
> I am not talking to you about the girl we saw, but about the one who lives opposite.

In all other cases the combination is a solecism, rather frequent in everyday speech.

20.3.6 *Unstressed pronouns*

It is quite usual to hear sentences where an expected pronoun *hi* or *en* is forgotten. The fact of Spanish lacking parallels to these pronouns may explain it. It is quite easy to detect the error when the pronouns replace adverbials:

> **–Vindràs a la platja?** 'Will you come to the beach?'
> ***–Sí, vindré** → **✓–Sí, hi vindré** 'Yes, I will come.'
> **–Véns de la platja?** 'Are you coming from the beach?'
> ***–Sí, ara arribo** → **✓–Sí, ara n'arribo** 'Yes, I'm back now.'

But omission occurs also in other cases, as with *en* replacing quantified or indefinite nouns:

> **–Han vingut molts turistes avui?** 'Have many tourists come today?'
> ***–Sí, han vingut molts** → **Sí, n'han vingut molts** '–Yes, many (of them) have come.'

The same can be said about the compulsory preposition *de* introducing an adjective qualifying a quantified or indefinite noun already replaced by pronoun *en*:

> ***T'he portat dos plats grossos i tres petits** → **T'he portat dos plats grossos i tres de petits**
> I've brought you two big dishes and three small ones.

Another observable frequent mistake is spreading the functions of the pronoun *ho* to replace the pronoun *el*. Remember that *ho* can replace sentences and demonstrative neuter pronouns *això* and *allò*, while *el* substitutes for determined masculines:

> ***El dinar ho pagarà ell** → **✓El dinar el pagarà ell**
> Lunch? He'll pay for it.

Appendix

Verb conjugation

This appendix accompanies section 7.1 on verbs, particularly section 7.1.1 on verb conjugation. The appendix offers the following:

- Full conjugation models for all inflected tenses, i.e. those where the main verb forms a stem and then different endings are added for different people.
- Full lists of past participles and gerunds (for creating perfect tenses and continuous tenses).
- Full regional variations – these are given after the model conjugation only where they differ from the model. Numbers 1–3 are for 1st–3rd pers. singular, 4–6 for the 1st–3rd pers. plural.

The endings are in **bold** for the model regular verbs, for ease of identification.

The following tenses have not been included here:

- all perfect tenses in the indicative and the subjunctive
- all periphrastic preterite and past anterior tenses in the indicative and subjunctive

The reason for this is that only the auxiliary verbs *haver* (to have) and *vaig*, *vas*, *va*, etc. vary from person to person, and there are no exceptions. See section 7.1.1 on how to form these.

Also, the conditional indicative (except for *ser*), is not listed here, which is entirely regular once you take into account that it uses the same stem as the future tense.

muntar

This is the model conjugation I (–ar) verb

Stems: remove the – ar from the infinitive **except for:**

- Future tense: use the infinitive.
- Imperfect subjunctive: use the same stem as the (simple) preterite.

Indicative

Present (1)	Imperfect	Preterite	Future
munt**o**	munt**ava**	munt**í**	muntar**é**
munt**es**	munt**aves**	munt**ares**	muntar**às**
munt**a**	munt**ava**	munt**à**	muntar**à**
munt**em**	munt**àvem**	munt**àrem**	muntar**em**
munt**eu**	munt**aveu**	munt**àreu**	muntar**eu**
munt**en**	munt**aven**	munt**aren**	muntar**an**

Subjunctive		Imperative
Present (2)	Imperfect (3)	munt**a**
munt**i**	munt**és**	munt**eu** **(4)**
munt**is**	munt**essis**	Impersonal forms
munt**i**	munt**és**	Past participle
munt**em**	munt**éssim**	munt**at**, munt**ada**, munt**ats**, munt**ades**
munt**eu**	munt**éssiu**	Gerund
munt**in**	munt**essin**	munt**ant**

Regional variations

(1). Bal.: 1 munt, 4 munt**am**, 5 munt**au**
N. Cat.: 1 munt**i**
Val.: 1 munt**e**

(2). N.W. and Val.: 1 munt**e**, 2 munt**es**, 3 munt**e**, 6 munt**en**

(3). Bal.: 1 munt**às**, 2 munt**assis**, 3 munt**às**, 4 munt**àssim**, 5 munt**àssiu**, 6 munt**assin**
N.W. and Lit. Val.: 2 munt**esses**, 4 munt**éssem**, 5 munt**ésseu**, 6 munt**essen**
Lit. Val.: 1 munt**às**, 2 munt**asses**, 3 munt**às**, 4 munt**àssem**, 5 munt**àsseu**, 6 munt**assen**
Val.: 1 munt**ara**, 2 munt**ares**, 3 munt**ara**, 4 munt**àrem**, 5 munt**àreu**, 6 munt**aren**

(4). Bal.: munt**au**

perdre

This is the model conjugation II (–re and –er) verb

Stems: remove the –er or –re from the infinitive **except for:**

- Future tense: use the infinitive for –er verbs, and the infinitive without the final –e for –re verbs. If the ending of the -er verb is stressed, the 'e' is elided and the ending becomes -r.
- Imperfect subjunctive: use the same stem as the (simple) preterite.

Indicative

Present (1)	Imperfect	Preterite	Future
perd**o**	perd**ia**	perd**í**	perdr**é**
perd**s**	perd**ies**	perd**eres**	perdr**às**
perd	perd**ia**	perd**é**	perdr**à**
perd**em**	perd**íem**	perd**érem**	perdr**em**
perd**eu**	perd**íeu**	perd**éreu**	perdr**eu**
perd**en**	perd**ien**	perd**eren**	perdr**an**

Subjunctive		Imperative
Present (2)	Imperfect (3)	perd
perd**i**	perd**és**	perd**eu**
perd**is**	perd**essis**	Impersonal forms
perd**i**	perd**és**	Past participle
perd**em**	perd**éssim**	perd**ut**, perd**uda**, perd**uts**, perd**udes**
perd**eu**	perd**éssiu**	Gerund
perd**in**	perd**essin**	perd**ent**

Regional variations

(1). Bal.: 1 perd
N. Cat.: 1 perdi
Val.: 1 perd

(2). Bal.: 4 perd**em** / (colloq.) perd**iguem**, 5 perd**eu** / (colloq.) perd**igueu**
N.W. and Val.: 1 perd**a**, 2 perd**es**, 3 perd**a**, 6 perd**en**
(3). N.W. and Val.: 2 perd**esses**, 4 perd**éssem**, 5 perd**ésseu**, 6 perd**essen**
Val.: 1 perd**era**, 2 perd**eres**, 3 perd**era**, 4 perd**érem**, 5 perd**éreu**, 6 perd**eren**

assistir

This is the model inceptive conjugation III (–ir) verb

Stems: remove the –ir from the infinitive **except for:**

- Future tense: use the infinitive.
- Imperfect subjunctive: use the same stem as the (simple) preterite.

Indicative

Present (1)	Imperfect	Preterite	Future
assist**eixo**	assist**ia**	assist**í**	assistir**é**
assist**eixes**	assist**ies**	assist**ires**	assistir**às**
assist**eix**	assist**ia**	assist**í**	assistir**à**
assist**im**	assist**íem**	assist**írem**	assistir**em**
assist**iu**	assist**íeu**	assist**íreu**	assistir**eu**
assist**eixen**	assist**ien**	assist**iren**	assistir**an**

Subjunctive		Imperative
Present (2)	Imperfect (3)	assist**eix (4)**
assist**eixi**	assist**ís**	assist**iu**
assist**eixis**	assist**issis**	Impersonal forms
assist**eixi**	assist**ís**	Past participle
assist**im**	assist**íssim**	assist**it**, assist**ida**, assist**its**, assist**ides**
assist**iu**	assist**íssiu**	Gerund
assist**eixin**	assist**issin**	assist**int**

(1). Bal.: 1 assist**esc**
N. Cat.: 1 assist**eixi**
N.W. Cat: 1 assist**ixo**, 2 assist**ixes**, 3 assist**ix**, 6 assist**ixen**
Val: 1 assist**isc**, 2 assist**ixes**, 3 assist**ix**, 6 assist**ixen**
(2). Bal.: 1 assist**esqui**, 2 assist**esquis**, 3 assist**esqui**, 4 assist**iguem**, 5 assisti**gueu**, 6 assist**esquin**
Alternative Bal. and lit. Val.: 1 assist**esca**, 2 assist**esques**, 3 assist**esca**, 6 assist**esquen**
N.W. and Val.: 1 assist**isca**, 2 assist**isques**, 3 assist**isca**, 6 assist**isquen**
(3). N.W. and lit. Val.: 2 assist**isses**, 4 assist**íssem**, 5 assist**ísseu**, 6 assist**issen**
Val.: 1 assist**ira**, 2 assit**ires**, 3 assist**ira**, 4 assist**írem**, 5 assit**íreu**, 6 assit**iren**
(4). N.W. and Val.: assist**ix**

sentir

This is the model non-inceptive conjugation III (–ir) verb

Stems: remove the –ir from the infinitive **except for:**

- Future tense: use the infinitive.
- Imperfect subjunctive: us the same stem as the (simple) preterite.

Indicative

Present (1)	Imperfect	Preterite	Future
sento	**sentia**	**sentí**	**sentiré**
sents*	**senties**	**sentires**	**sentiràs**
sent	**sentia**	**sentí**	**sentirà**
sentim	**sentíem**	**sentírem**	**sentirem**
sentiu	**sentíeu**	**sentíreu**	**sentireu**
senten	**sentien**	**sentiren**	**sentiran**

Subjunctive		Imperative
Present (2)	Imperfect (3)	**sent**
senti	**sentís**	**sentiu**
sentis	**sentissis**	Impersonal forms

senti	sentís	Past participle
sentim	sentíssim	**sentit**, **sentida**, **sentits**, **sentides**
sentiu	sentíssiu	Gerund
sentin	sentissin	**sentint**

Regional variations

(1). Bal. and Val.: 1 sent
N. Cat.: 1 senti
(2). Bal.: 4 senti**guem**, 5 senti**gueu**
N.W. and Val.: 1 sent**a**, 2 sent**es**, 3 sent**a**, 6 sent**en**
(3). Lit. Val.: 2 sent**isses**, 4 sent**íssem**, 5 sent**ísseu**, 6 sent**íssen**
Val.: 1 sent**ira**, 2 sent**ires**, 3 sent**ira**, 4 sent**írem**, 5 sent**íreu**, 6 sent**iren**

Notes

*Verbs with a stem ending in –ix–, –g–, –c– (which will turn into –ç–), –ss–, and –s– have a 'tu' form ending in –es, simply for reasons of pronunciation, such as *cuses*, *fuges*, and so on.

Irregular conjugation I verbs

anar

Indicative

Present (1): 1 vaig, 2 vas, 3 va, 4 anem, 5 aneu, 6 van

Future stem: anir–

Subjunctive

Present (2): 1 vagi, 2 vagis, 3 vagi, 4 anem, 5 aneu, 6 vagin

Imperative: 2 ves

Regional variations

(1). Bal.: 4 anam, 5 anau
(2). N.W. and Val.: 1 vaja, 2 vages, 3 vaja, 6 vagen

estar

Indicative

Present (1): 1 estic, 2 estàs, 3 està, 4 estem, 5 esteu, 6 estan

Subjunctive

Present (2): 1 estigui, 2 estiguis, 3 estigui, 4 estiguem, 5 estigueu, 6 estiguin

Imperative (3): 2 estigues, 5 estigueu

Regional variations

(1). Bal.: 4 estam, 5 estau
(2). This takes on all of the regional variations seen in *muntar*, with estigu– as the stem.
(3). Alternative Bal.: 2 està, 5 estau *and* estigau
Alternative Val.: 2 està, 5 esteu

Irregular conjugation II verbs

absoldre

Past participle: absolt, absolta, absolts, absoltes

Otherwise it is conjugated like *doldre*.

admetre

Past participle: admès, admesa, admesos, admeses

atendre

Indicative

Present: 1 atenc, 2 atens, 3 atén, 4 atenem, 5 ateneu, 6 atenem

Imperfect: 1 atenia, 2 atenies, 3 atenia, 4 ateníem, 5 ateníeu, 6 atenien

Preterite: 1 atenguí, 2 atengueres, 3 atengué, 4 atenguérem, 5 atenguéreu, 6 atengueren

Subjunctive

Present (1): 1 atengui, 2 atenguis, 3 atengui, 4 atenguem, 5 atengueu, 6 atenguin

Impersonal forms

Past participle: atès, atesa, atesos, ateses

Regional variations

(1). This follows the regional variations seen in *perdre*, with atengu– as the stem (which becomes ateng– when the endings start with an 'a' to maintain the hard 'g' sound).

atènyer

Impersonal forms

Past participle: atès, atesa, atesos, ateses

beure

Indicative

Present: 1 bec, 2 beus, 3 beu, 4 bevem, 5 beveu, 6 beuen

Imperfect: 1 bevia, 2 bevies, 3 bevia, 4 bevíem, 5 bevíeu, 6 bevien

Preterite: 1 beguí, 2 begueres, 3 begué, 4 beguérem, 5 beguéreu, 6 begueren

Subjunctive

Present (1): 1 begui, 2 beguis, 3 begui, 4 beguem, 5 begueu, 6 beguin

Impersonal forms

Past participle: begut, beguda, beguts, begudes

Gerund: bevent

Regional variation

(1). This follows the regional variations seen in *perdre*, with begu– as the stem (which becomes beg– when the endings start with an 'a' to maintain the hard 'g' sound).

cabre or caber

Subjunctive

Present (1): 1 càpiga, 2 càpigues, 3 càpiga, 4 capiguem, 5 capigueu, 6 càpiguen

Regional variation

(1). Val.: 1 càpia, 2 càpies, 3 càpia, 4 capiem, 5 capieu, 6 càpien

caldre *or* ***caler***

Conjugated like *doldre*, although only used in the third person.

caure

Indicative

Present (1): 1 caic, 2 caus, 3 cau, 4 caiem, 5 caieu, 6 cauen

Imperfect: 1 queia, 2 queies, 3 queia, 4 quèiem, 5 quèieu, 6 queien

Preterite: 1 caiguí, 2 caigueres, 3 caigué, 4 caiguérem, 5 caiguéreu, 6 caigueren

Subjunctive

Present (2): 1 caigui, 2 caiguis, 3 caigui, 4 caiguem, 5 caigueu, 6 caiguin

Impersonal forms

Past participle: caigut, caiguda, caiguts, caigudes

Present participle (3): caient

Regional variation

(1). Bal.: 4 queim, 5 queis
Val.: 4 caem, 5 caeu
(2). This follows the regional variations seen in *perdre*, with caigu– as the stem (which becomes caig– when the endings start with an 'a' to maintain the hard 'g' sound).
(3). Val.: caent

cerndre

Indicative

Present (1): 1 cerno, 2 cerns, 3 cern, 4 cernem, 5 cerneu, 6 cernen

Imperfect: 1 cernia, 2 cernies, 3 cernia, 4 cerníem, 5 cerníeu, 6 cernien

Preterite: 1 cerní, 2 cerneres, 3 cerné, 4 cernérem, 5 cernéreu, 6 cerneren

Subjunctive

Present (2): 1 cerni, 2 cernis, 3 cerni, 4 cernem, 5 cerneu, 6 cernin

Impersonal forms

Past participle: cernut, cernuda, cernuts, cernudes

Gerund: cernent

Regional variation

(1). Bal. and Val.: 1 cern
N. Cat.: 1 cerni

(2). This follows the regional variations seen in *perdre*, with cern– as the stem.

cloure

Impersonal forms

Past participle: clos, closa, closos, closes

Otherwise, it is conjugated like *plaure*.

conèixer

Indicative

Present: 1 conec, 2 coneixes, 3 coneix, 4 coneixem, 5 coneixeu, 6 coneixen

Preterite: 1 coneguí, 2 conegueres, 3 conegué, 4 coneguerem, 5 conegguereu, 6 conegueren

Subjunctive

Present (1): 1 conegui, 2 coneguis, 3 conegui, 4 coneguem, 5 conegueu, 6 coneguin

Impersonal forms

Past participle: conegut, coneguda, coneguts, conegudes

Regional variation

(1). This follows the regional variations seen in *perdre*, with conegu– as the stem (which becomes coneg– when the endings start with an 'a' to maintain the hard 'g' sound).

córrer

Indicative

Present (1): 1 corro, 2 corres, 3 corre, 4 correm, 5 correu, 6 corren

Preterite: 1 correguí, 2 corregueres, 3 corregué, 4 correguérem, 5 correguéreu, 6 corregueren

Subjunctive

Present (2): 1 corri, 2 corris, 3 corri, 4 correm *or* correguem, 5 correu *or* corregueu, 6 corrin

Impersonal forms

Past participle: corregut, correguda, correguts, corregudes

Regional variation

(1). Bal.: 1 corr, 2 corres *or* corrs
Val.: 1 córrec
(2). Val.: 1 córrega, 2 córregues, 3 córrega, 4 correguem, 5 corregueu, 6 córreguen

Also, there is an alternative second-person familiar imperative in Balearic: *corr*.

coure

Impersonal forms

Past participle: when meaning 'cooked', cuit, cuita, cuits, cuites

When meaning 'smart', cogut, coguda, coguts, cogudes

Otherwise, it is conjugated like *plaure*

créixer

Indicative

Present (1): 1 creixo, 2 creixes, 3 creix, 4 creixem, 5 creixeu, 6 creixen

Preterite: 1 creixí *or* cresquí, 2 creixeres *or* cresqueres, 3 creixé *or* cresqué, 4 creixérem *or* cresquérem, 5 creixéreu *or* cresquéreu, 6 creixeren *or* cresqueren

Subjunctive

Present (2): 1 creixi, 2 creixis, 3 creixi, 4 creixem *or* cresquem, 5 creixeu *or* cresqueu, 6 creixin

Impersonal forms

Past participle: crescut, crescuda, crescuts, crescudes

Regional variation

(1). Bal.: 1 cresc, 2 creixes *or* creixs
Val.: 1 cresc
(2). Bal.: 1 cresqui, 2 cresquis, 3 cresqui, 4 cresquem, 5 cresqueu, 6 cresquin
Val.: 1 cresca, 2 cresques, 3 cresca, 4 cresquem, 5 cresqueu, 6 cresquen

creure

Indicative

Present (1): 1 crec, 2 creus, 3 creu, 4 creiem, 5 creieu, 6 creuen

Imperfect: 1 creia, 2 creies, 3 creia, 4 crèiem, 5 crèieu, 6 creien

Preterite: 1 creguí, 2 cregueres, 3 cregué, 4 creguérem, 5 creguéreu, 6 cregueren

Subjunctive

Present (2): 1 cregui, 2 creguis, 3 cregui, 4 creguem, 5 cregueu, 6 creguin

Impersonal forms

Past participle: cregut, creguda, creguts, cregudes

Gerund (3): creient

Regional variation

(1). Bal.: 4 creim, 5 creis
Val.: 4 creem, 5 creeu
(2). This follows the regional variations seen in *perdre*, with cregu– as the stem (which becomes creg– when the endings start with an 'a' to maintain the hard 'g' sound).
(3). Val.: creent

defendre

Impersonal forms

Past participle: defès, defesa, defesos, defeses

Otherwise it is conjugated like *atendre.*

dependre

Impersonal forms

Past participle: depès, depesa, depesos, depeses

Otherwise it is conjugated like *atendre*

despendre

Impersonal forms

Past participle: despès, despesa, despesos, despeses

Otherwise it is conjugated like *atendre*

deure

Conjugated like *beure*

dissoldre

Conjugated like *absoldre*

distendre

Impersonal forms

Past participle: distès, distesa, distesos, disteses

Otherwise it is conjugated like *atendre*

doldre

Indicative

Present: 1 dolc, 2 dols, 3 dol, 4 dolem, 5 doleu, 6 dolen

Imperfect: 1 dolia, 2 dolies, 3 dolia, 4 dolíem, 5 dolíeu, 6 dolien

Preterite: 1 dolguí, 2 dolgueres, 3 dolgué, 4 dolguérem, 5 dolguéreu, 6 dolgueren

Subjunctive

Present (1): 1 dolgui, 2 dolguis, 3 dolgui, 4 dolguem, 5 dolgueu, 6 dolguin

Impersonal forms

Past participle: dolgut, dolguda, dolguts, dolgudes

Gerund: dolent

Regional variation

(1) This follows the regional variations in seen in *perdre*, with dolgu– as the stem (which becomes dolg– when the endings start with an 'a' to maintain the hard 'g' sound).

dur

Indicative

Present (1): 1 duc, 2 dus *or* duus, 3 du *or* duu, 4 duem, 5 dueu, 6 duen

Imperfect: 1 duia, 2 duies, 3 duia, 4 dúiem, 5 dúieu, 6 duien

Preterite: 1 duguí, 2 dugueres, 3 dugué, 4 duguérem, 5 duguéreu, 6 dugueren

Subjunctive

Present (2): 1 dugui, 2 duguis, 3 dugui, 4 duguem, 5 dugueu, 6 duguin

Impersonal forms

Past participle (3): dut, duta, duts, dutes

Gerund: duent

Regional variations

(1). Bal.: 4 duim, 5 duis
(2). This follows the regional variations in seen in *perdre*, with dugu– as the stem (which becomes dug– when the endings start with an 'a' to maintain the hard 'g' sound).
(3). Bal.: duit, duita, duits, duites

There is also the Valencian irregular second-person familiar imperative **dus** or **duus**.

empènyer

Impersonal forms

Past participle: empès, empesa, empesos, empeses

encendre

Impersonal forms

Past participle: encès, encesa, encesos, enceses

Otherwise it is conjugated like *atendre*.

escriure

Indicative

Present: 1 escric, 2 escrius, 3 escriu, 4 escrivim, 5 escriviu, 6 escriuen

Imperfect: 1 escrivia, 2 escrivies, 3 escrivia, 4 escrivíem, 5 escrivíeu, 6 escrivien

Preterite: 1 escriví *or* escriguí, 2 escrivires *or* escrigueres, 3 escriví *or* escrigué, 4 escrivírem *or* escriguérem, 5 escrivíreu *or* escriguéreu, 6 escriviren *or* escrigueren

Subjunctive

Present (1): 1 escrigui, 2 escriguis, 3 escrigui, 4 escriguem, 5 escrigueu, 6 escriguin

Impersonal forms

Past participle: escrit, escrita, escrits, escrites

Gerund: escrivint

Regional variation

(1). This follows the regional variations seen in *perdre*, with escrigu– as the stem (which becomes escrig– when the endings start with an 'a' to maintain the hard 'g' sound).

estrènyer

Impersonal forms

Past participle: estret, estreta, estrets, estretes

Regional variation

In Balearic usage, there is an irregular first-person singular present indicative **estrenc**. This then gives the irregular stem **estrengu–** for the preterite indicative, and the present and imperfect subjunctive.

fènyer

Conjugated like *pertànyer*

fer

Indicative

Present (1): 1 faig, 2 fas, 3 fa, 4 fem, 5 feu, 6 fan

Imperfect: 1 feia, 2 feies, 3 feia, 4 fèiem, 5 fèieu, 6 feien

Preterite (2): 1 fiu, 2 feres, 3 féu, 4 férem, 5 féreu, 6 feren

Future: 1 faré, 2 faràs, 3 farà, 4 farem, 5 fareu, 6 faran

Subjunctive

Present (3): 1 faci, 2 facis, 3 faci, 4 fem, 5 feu, 6 facin

Imperfect (4): 1 fes, 2 fessis, 3 fes, 4 féssim, 5 féssiu, 6 fessin

Imperative (5): 2 fes, 5 feu

Impersonal forms

Past participle: fet, feta, fets, fetes

Regional variation

(1). Bal.: 4 feim, 5 feis
(2). Bal.: 3 fe
(3). Bal.: 4 facem, 5 faceu
Val., N.W. Cat. and optionally Bal.: 1 faça, 2 faces, 3 faça, 6 facen.
(4). Note that this is regular, except for the lack of accents on the one-syllable forms. Alternate endings are used in different regions, as seen in *perdre*.
(5). Bal.: 2 fe, 5 feis

fondre

Impersonal forms

Past participle: fos, fosa, fosos, foses

Otherwise it is conjugated like *atendre*.

haver (auxiliary verb for perfect tenses and as a modal verb indicating obligation in **haver de** + infinitive)

See p. 63 and p. 67 for how to conjugate *haver*. When used as a modal verb (p. 204), the first-person present indicative has the alternative **haig**, and there are also the learned forms 4 **havem** and 5 **haveu**.

haver or haure or heure (as a transitive verb)

Indicative

Present: 1 hec *or* hac, 2 heus *or* haus, 3 heu *or* hau, 4 havem, 5 haveu, 6 heuen *or* hauen

Imperfect: 1 havia, 2 havies, 3 havia, 4 havíem, 5 havíeu, 6 havien

Preterite: 1 haguí, 2 hagueres, 3 hagué, 4 haguérem, 5 haguéreu, 6 hagueren

Future: 1 hauré, 2 hauràs, 3 haurà, 4 haurem, 5 haureu, 6 hauran

Subjunctive

Present: (1): 1 hegui, 2 heguis, 3 hegui, 4 haguem, 5 hagueu, 6 heguin

Impersonal forms

Past participle: hagut, haguda, haguts, hagudes

Gerund: havent

Regional variation

(1). Val.: 1 haga, 2 hagues, 3 haga, 6 haguen

N.W. Cat: 1 hagui, 2 haguis, 3 hagui, 6 haguin

jaure or jeure

Indicative

Present (1): 1 jac *or* jec, 2 jaus *or* jeus, 3 jau *or* jeu, 4 jaiem, 5 jaieu, 6 jauen *or* jeuen

Imperfect: 1 jeia, 2 jeies, 3 jeia, 4 jèiem, 5 jèieu, 6 jeien

Preterite: 1 jaguí, 2 jagueres, 3 jagué, 4 jaguérem, 5 jaguéreu, 6 jagueren

Future: 1 jauré, 2 jauràs, 3 jaurà, 4 jaurem, 5 jaureu, 6 jauran

Subjunctive

Present (2): 1 jegui, 2 jeguis, 3 jegui, 4 jaguem, 5 jagueu, 6 jeguin

Impersonal forms

Past participle: jagut, jaguda, jaguts, jagudes

Gerund: jaient

Regional variation

(1). Bal.: 4 jeim, 5 jeis
Val.: 4 jaem, 5 jaeu
(2). Val.: 1 jaga, 2 jagues, 3 jaga, 6 jaguen
N.W. Catalan: 1 jagui, 2 jaguis, 3 jagui, 6 jaguin

lleure

Conjugated like *beure* – although *lleure* is only conjugated in the third person.

merèixer

Conjugated like *crèixer*

moldre

Impersonal forms

Past participle: mòlt, mòlta, mòlts, mòltes

Otherwise it is conjugated like *doldre*

moure

Conjugated like *beure*

nàixer or *néixer*

Indicative

Present (1): 1 neixo, 2 naixes *or* neixes, 3 naix *or* neix, 4 naixem, 5 naixeu, 6 naixen *or* neixen

Imperfect: 1 naixia, 2 naixies, 3 naixia, 4 naixíem, 5 naixíeu, 6 naixien

Preterite: 1 naixí *or* nasquí, 2 naixeres *or* nasqueres, 3 naixé *or* nasqué, 4 naixérem *or* nasquérem, 5 naixéreu *or* nasquéreu, 6 naixeren *or* nasqueren

Future: 1 naixeré, 2 naixeràs, 3 naixerà, 4 naixerem, 5 naixereu, 6 naixeran

Subjunctive

Present (2): 1 neixi, 2 neixis, 3 neixi, 4 naixem *or* nasquem, 5 naixeu *or* nasqueu, 6 neixin

Impersonal forms

Past participle: nascut, nascuda, nascuts, nascudes

Also, when not conjugated with *haver*: nat, nada, nats, nades

Gerund: naixent

Regional variation

(1). Bal.: 1 nesc
Val.: 1 nasc
N.W. Cat.: 1 naixo
N. Cat.: 1 neixi
(2). Bal.: 1 nesqui, 2 nesquis, 3 nesqui, 6 nesquin
Val.: 1 nasca, 2 nasques, 3 nasca, 6 nasquen
N.W. Cat.: 1 naixi, 2 naixis, 3 naixi, 6 naixin

noure

Conjugated like *plaure*

ofendre

Impersonal forms

Past participle: ofès, ofesa, ofesos, ofeses

Otherwise, it is conjugated like *atendre*.

pàixer or péixer

Conjugated like *nàixer / néixer*

parèixer

Conjugated like *conèixer*

pertànyer

Indicative

Present (1): 1 pertanyo, 2 pertanys, 3 pertany, 4 pertanyem, 5 pertanyeu, 6 pertanyen

Preterite (2): 1 pertanyí, 2 pertanyeres, 3 pertanyé, 4 pertanyérem, 5 pertanyéreu, 6 pertanyeren

Subjunctive

Present (3): 1 pertanyi, 2 pertanyis, 3 pertanyi, 4 pertanyem, 5 pertanyeu, 6 pertanyin

Impersonal forms

Past participle: pertangut, pertanguda, pertanguts, pertangudes *or* pertanyut, pertanyuda, pertanyuts, pertanyudes

Regional variation

(1). Bal. and Val.: 1 pertanc
N. Cat.: 1 pertanyi
(2). Bal. and Val.: 1 pertanguí, 2 pertangueres, 3 pertangué, 4 pertanguérem, 5 pertanguéreu, 6 pertangueren
(3). Bal.: 1 pertangui, 2 pertanguis, 3 pertangui, 4 pertanguem, 5 pertangueu, 6 pertanguin
Val.: 1 pertanga, 2 pertangues, 3 pertanga, 6 pertanguen

plànyer

Conjugated like *pertànyer*

plaure

Indicative

Present: 1 plac, 2 plaus, 3 plau, 4 plaem, 5 plaeu, 6 plauen

Imperfect: 1 plaïa, 2 plaïes, 3 plaïa, 4 plaíem, 5 plaíeu, 6 plaïen

Preterite: 1 plaguí, 2 plagueres, 3 plagué, 4 plaguérem, 5 plaguéreu, 6 plagueren

Subjunctive

Present (1): 1 plagui, 2 plaguis, 3 plagui, 4 plaguem, 5 plagueu, 6 plaguin

Impersonal forms

Past participle: plagut, plaguda, plaguts, plagudes

Gerund: plaent

Regional variation

(1). This follows the regional variations seen in *perdre*, with plagu– as the stem (which becomes plag– when the endings start with an 'a' to maintain the hard 'g' sound).

ploure

Conjugated like *beure*.

poder

Indicative

Present: 1 puc, 2 pots, 3 pot, 4 podem, 5 podeu, 6 poden

Preterite: 1 poguí, 2 pogueres, 3 pogué, 4 poguérem, 5 poguéreu, 6 pogueren

Future: 1 podré, 2 podràs, 3 podrà, 4 podrem, 5 podreu, 6 podran

Subjunctive

Present (1): 1 pugui, 2 puguis, 3 pugui, 4 puguem, 5 pugueu, 6 puguin

Indicative: 2 pugues, 5 pugueu

Impersonal forms

Past participle: pogut, poguda, poguts, pogudes

Regional variation

(1). This follows the regional variations seen in *perdre*, with pugu– as the stem (which becomes pug– when the endings start with an 'a' to maintain the hard 'g' sound).

pondre

Impersonal forms

Past participle: post, posta, posts *or* postos, postes

Otherwise it is conjugated like *atendre*.

prendre

Impersonal forms

Past participle: pres, presa, presos, preses

Otherwise it is conjugated like *atendre*.

pretendre

Impersonal forms

Past participle: pretès, pretesa, pretesos, preteses

Otherwise it is conjugated like *atendre*.

raure

Impersonal forms

Past participle: ragut, raguda, raguts, ragudes, and Val. ras, rasa, rasos, rases

Otherwise it is conjugated like *plaure*.

resoldre

Conjugated like *absoldre*

responder

Conjugated like *pondre*

riure

Indicative

Present (1): 1 ric, 2 rius, 3 riu, 4 riem, 5 rieu, 6 riuen

Imperfect: 1 reia, 2 reies, 3 reia, 4 rèiem, 5 rèieu, 6 reien

Preterite: 1 riguí, 2 rigueres, 3 rigué, 4 riguérem, 5 riguéreu, 6 rigueren

Subjunctive

Present (2): 1 rigui, 2 riguis, 3 rigui, 4 riguem, 5 rigueu, 6 riguin

Impersonal forms

Past participle (3): rigut, riguda, riguts, rigudes

Gerund: rient

Regional variation

(1). Bal.: 4 reim, 5 reis
(2). This follows the regional variations in seen in *perdre*, with rigu– as the stem (which becomes rig– when the endings start with an 'a' to maintain the hard 'g' sound).
(3). Val.: rist, rista, rists *or* ristos, ristes

romandre

Impersonal forms

Past participle: romàs, romasa, romasos, romases

Otherwise it is conjugated like *atendre*.

saber

Indicative

Present: 1 sé, 2 saps, 3 sap. 4 sabem, 5 sabeu, 6 saben

Otherwise it is conjugated like *cabre / caber*, except for the irregular imperative 2 sàpigues, 5 sapigueu (and the Val. variant 2 sàpies, 5 sapieu).

ser or ésser or esser

Indicative

Present (1): 1 sóc, 2 ets, 3 és, 4 som, 5 sou, 6 són

Imperfect: 1 era, 2 eres, 3 era, 4 érem, 5 éreu, 6 eren

Preterite (2): 1 fui, 2 fores, 3 fou, 4 fórem, 5 fóreu, 6 foren

Future: 1 seré, 2 seràs, 3 serà, 4 serem, 5 sereu, 6 seran

Conditional: 1 seria *or* fora, 2 series *or* fores, 3 seria *or* fora, 4 seríem *or* fórem, 5 seríeu *or* fóreu, 6 serien *or* foren

Subjunctive

Present (3): 1 sigui, 2 siguis, 3 sigui, 4 siguem, 5 sigueu, 6 siguin

Imperfect (4): 1 fos, 2 fossis, 3 fos, 4 fóssim, 5 fóssiu, 6 fossin

Imperative (5): 2 sigues, 5 sigueu

Impersonal forms

Past participle: estat, estada, estats, estades, *or, less formally* sigut, siguda, siguts, sigudes

Gerund: essent *or* sent

Regional variation

(1). Bal.: 1 som
Val.: 2 eres
Archaic and in Alghero: 1 só
(2). Val.: 3 fon
(3). Bal. (optional), Val. and N.W. Cat.: 1 siga, 2 sigues, 3 siga, 6 siguen
Archaic (normally in idioms): 1 sia, 2 sies, 3 sia, 4 siem *or* siam, 5 sieu *or* siau, 6 sien
(4). Val.: 1 fora, 2 fores, 3 fora, 4 fórem, 5 fóreu, 6 foren
Val. and N.W. Cat.: 2 fosses, 4 fóssem, 5 fósseu, 6 fossen
(5). Bal.: 5 sigau

seure

Conjugated like *creure*

soler

Conjugated like *doldre*

suspendre

Impersonal forms

Past participle: suspès, suspesa, suspesos, suspeses

Otherwise it is conjugated like *atendre*.

toldre

Impersonal forms

Past participle: tolt, tolta, tolts, toltes

Otherwise it is conjugated like *doldre*.

tondre

Impersonal forms

Past participle: tos, tosa, tosos, toses

Otherwise it is conjugated like *atendre*.

traure or treure

Impersonal forms

Past participle: tret, treat, trets, tretes

Otherwise it is conjugated like *jeure* / *jaure*.

valer or *valdre*

Conjugated like *doldre*

vendre

Impersonal forms

Past participle: venut, venuda, venuts, venudes

Otherwise it is conjugated like *atendre* (with the third-person present indicative **ven**).

veure

Indicative

Present (1): 1 veig, 2 veus, 3 veu, 4 veiem, 5 veieu, 6 veuen

Imperfect: 1 veia, 2 veies, 3 veia, 4 vèiem, 5 vèieu, 6 veien

Preterite: 1 viu, 2 veieres *or* veres, 3 veié *or* véu, 4 veiérem *or* vérem, 5 veiéreu *or* véreu, 6 veieren *or* veren

Subjunctive

Present (2): 1 vegi, 2 vegis, 3 vegi, 4 vegem. 5 vegeu, 6 vegin

Imperfect (3): 1 veiés, 2 veiessis, 3 veiés, 4 veiéssim, 5 veiéssiu, 6 veiessin

Imperative (4): 2 veges, 5 vegeu *or* veieu

Impersonal forms

Past participle: vist, vista, vists *or* vistos, vistes

Gerund (5): veient

Regional variation

(1). Bal.: 4 veim, 5 veis
Val.: 4 veem, 5 veeu
(2). Val. and N.W. Cat.: 1 veja, 2 veges, 3 veja, 6 vegen
(3). Bal.: 1 ves, 2 vessis, 3 ves, 4 véssim, 5 véssiu, 6 vessin
Val.: 1 vera, 2 veres, 3 vera, 4 vérem, 5 véreu, 6 veren
Val. and N.W. Cat.: 2 veiesses, 4 veiéssem, 5 veiésseu, 6 veiessen
(4). Bal.: 5 veis
Val.: 5 veeu
There is also the familiar form **ves**, and the colloquial familiar form **vet**.
(5). Val.: veent

viure

Indicative

Present: 1 visc, 2 vius, 3 viu, 4 vivim, 5 viviu, 6 viuen

Imperfect: 1 vivia, 2 vivies, 3 vivia, 4 vivíem, 5 vivíeu, 6 vivien

Preterite: 1 visquí, 2 visqueres, 3 visqué, 4 visquérem, 5 visquéreu, 6 visqueren

Subjunctive

Present (1): 1 visqui, 2 visquis, 3 visqui, 4 visquem, 5 visqueu, 6 visquin

Impersonal forms

Past participle: viscut, viscuda, viscuts, viscudes

Gerund: vivint

Regional variation

(1). This follows the regional variations seen in *perdre*, with visqu– as the stem (which becomes visc– when the endings start with an 'a' to maintain the hard 'g' sound).

voler

Indicative

Present: 1 vull, 2 vols, 3 vol, 4 volem, 5 voleu, 6 volen

Preterite: 1 volguí, 2 volgueres, 3 volgué, 4 volguérem, 5 volguéreu, 6 volgueren

Future: 1 voldré, 2 voldràs, 3 voldrà, 4 voldrem, 5 voldreu, 6 voldran

Subjunctive

Present (1): 1 vulgui, 2 vulguis, 3 vulgui, 4 vulguem, 5 vulgueu, 6 vulguin

Imperative: 2 vulgues, 5 vulgueu

Impersonal forms

Past participle: volgut, volguda, volguts, volgudes

afegir

Irregular conjugation III verbs

In Bal. and Val. this can be non-inceptive, with a stem of **afig–** (with a soft 'g') when the stem is stressed, and **afeg–** when the stress falls on the ending. In other places, it is a regular inceptive verb.

cobrir

Impersonal forms

Past participle: cobert, coberta, coberts, cobertes

Otherwise it is a regular inceptive verb.

collir

This is a regular non-inceptive verb, except it has a stem of **cull–** when the stem is stressed, and **coll–** when the ending is stressed.

complir

Impersonal forms

Past participle: complit, complida, complits, complides *or* complert, complerta, complerts, complertes

Otherwise it is a regular inceptive verb.

cosir

This is a regular non-inceptive verb, except it has a stem of **cus–** when the stem is stressed, and **cos–** when the ending is stressed.

eixir

Indicative

Present (1): 1 ixo, 2 ixes, 3 ix, 4 eixim, 5 eixiu, 6 ixen

Subjunctive

Present (2): 1 ixi, 2 ixis, 3 ixi, 4 eixim, 5 eixiu, 6 ixin

Regional variation

(1). Bal. and Val.: 1 isc
N. Cat.: 1 ixi
(2). Bal.: 4 eixiguem, 5 eixigueu
Val.: 1 isca, 2 isques, 3 isca, 4 isquem, 5 isqueu, 6 isquen

There is also the alternative Val. preterite indicative: 1 isquí, 2 isqueres, 3 isqué, 4 isquérem, 5 isquéreu, 6 isqueren. This then gives the alternative imperfect subjunctive forms 1 isqués / isquera, etc.

engolir

In Val. this can be non-inceptive, with a stem of **engul–** when the stem is stressed, and **engol–** when the stress falls on the ending. In other places, it is a regular inceptive verb.

escopir

This is a regular non-inceptive verb, except it has a stem of **escup–** when the stem is stressed, and **escop–** when the ending is stressed.

establir

Impersonal forms

Past participle: establert, establerta, establerts, establertes

Otherwise it is a regular inceptive verb.

fugir

This is a regular non-inceptive verb, except for the irregular Bal. past participle **fuit, fuita, fuits, fuites.**

imprimir

Impersonal forms

Past participle: imprès, impresa, impresos, impreses

Otherwise it is a regular inceptive verb.

llegir

Conjugated like *afegir*

lluir

A regular non-inceptive verb (with a diaresis on the 'i' of verb endings where necessary to split the 'u' and 'i' sounds). However, when *lluir* (and verbs derived from it) are used figuratively, then it is a regular inceptive verb.

morir

Impersonal forms

Past participle: mort, morta, morts, mortes

There is also a Val. and optional Bal. form for the first-person singular present indicative **muir**, which is the used as the stem for the present subjunctive.

Otherwise it is a regular non-inceptive verb.

obrir

Impersonal forms

Past participle: obert, oberta, oberts, obertes

Otherwise, it is a regular non-inceptive verb, except for in Val. and Bal.:

Val. present indicative: 1 òbric, 2 obris, 3 obri, 6 obrin

Val. present subjunctive: 1 òbriga, 2 òbrigues, 3 òbriga, 4 obriguem, 5 obrigueu, 6 òbriguen

Bal. present indicative: 1 obr, 2 obris *or* obrs, 3 obri *or* obr, 6 obrin

oferir

Impersonal forms

Past participle: ofert, oferta, oferts, ofertes *or* oferit, oferida, oferits, oferides

Otherwise it is a regular inceptive verb.

oir

This is a regular inceptive verb conjugated like III.1 except for optional Val.:

Optional Val. present indicative: 1 oig, 2 ous, 3 ou, 6 ouen

Optional Val. present subjunctive: 1 oja, 2 oges, 3 oja, 6 ogen

omplir

Impersonal forms

Past participle: omplert, omplerta, omplerts, omplertes *or* omplit, omplida, omplits, omplides

Otherwise, it is a regular non-inceptive verb, except for in Val. and Bal.:

Val. present indicative: 1 òmplic, 2 omplis, 3 ompli, 6 omplin

Val. present subjunctive: 1 òmpliga, 2 òmpligues, 3 òmpliga, 4 ompliguem, 5 ompligueu, 6 òmpliguen

Bal. present indicative: 1 umpl, 2 umpls, 3 umpl, 6 umplen

Bal. present subjunctive: 1 umpli, 2 umplis, 3 umpli, 6 umplin

reblir

Impersonal forms

Past participle: reblert, reblerta, reblerts, reblertes *or* reblit, reblida, reblits, reblides

Otherwise it is a regular inceptive verb.

renyir

In Val. this is conjugated like *tenyir*. Otherwise, it is a regular inceptive verb.

sofrir

Impersonal forms

Past participle: sofert, soferta, soferts, sofertes *or* soferit, soferida, soferits, soferides

Otherwise it is a regular inceptive verb.

sortir

This is a regular non-inceptive verb, except it has a stem of **surt–** when the stem is stressed, and **sort–** when the ending is stressed.

teixir

In Val. this can be non-inceptive, with a stem of **tix–** when the stem is stressed, and **teix–** when the stress falls on the ending. In other places, it is a regular inceptive verb.

tenir or tindre

Indicative

Present (1): 1 tinc, 2 tens, 3 té, 4 tenim, 5 teniu, 6 tenen

Imperfect: 1 tenia, 2 tenies, 3 tenia, 4 teníem, 5 teníeu, 6 tenien

Preterite (2): 1 tinguí, 2 tingueres, 3 tingué, 4 tinguérem, 5 tinguéreu, 6 tingueren

Future (3): 1 tindré, 2 tindràs, 3 tindrà, 4 tindrem, 5 tindreu, 6 tindran

Subjunctive

Present (4): 1 tingui, 2 tinguis, 3 tingui, 4 tinguem, 5 tingueu, 6 tinguin

Imperative (5): 2 té *or* ten *or* tingues, 5 teniu *or* tingueu

Impersonal forms

Past participle (6): tingut, tinguda, tinguts, tingudes

Gerund: tenint

Regional variation

(1). Bal.: 1 tenc
(2). Bal.: 1 tenguí, etc.
(3). Bal.: 1 tendré, etc.
(4). Bal.: 1 tengui, etc.
  Val.: 1 tinga, 2 tingues, 3 tinga, 6 tinguen
(5). Bal.: 2 té *or* ten *or* tengues, 5 teniu *or* tengueu
  Val. and N.W. Cat.: 2 tin
(6). Bal.: tengut, etc.

tenyir

In Val. this can be non-inceptive, with a stem of **tiny–** when the stem is stressed, and **teny–** when the stress falls on the ending. In other places, it is a regular inceptive verb.

tossir

This is a regular non-inceptive verb, except it has a stem of **tuss–** when the stem is stressed, and **toss–** when the ending is stressed. In Bal. it is optionally conjugated as an inceptive verb.

venir or vindre

Indicative

Present (1): 1 vinc, 2 vens, 3 ve, 4 venim, 5 veniu, 6 venen

Imperfect: 1 venia, 2 venies, 3 venia, 4 veníem, 5 veníeu, 6 venien

Preterite (2): 1 vinguí, 2 vingueres, 3 vingué, 4 vinguérem, 5 vinguéreu, 6 vingueren

Future (3): 1 vindré, 2 vindràs, 3 vindrà, 4 vindrem, 5 vindreu, 6 vindran

Subjunctive

Present (4): 1 vingui, 2 vinguis, 3 vingui, 4 vinguem, 5 vingueu, 6 vinguin

Imperative: 2 vine, 5 veniu

Impersonal forms

Past participle (5): vingut, vinguda, vinguts, vingudes

Gerund: venint

Regional variation

(1). Bal.: 1 venc
(2). Bal.: 1 venguí, etc.
(3). Bal.: 1 vendré, etc.
(4). Bal.: 1 vengui, 2 venguis, 3 vengui, 4 venguem, 5 vengueu, 6 venguin
Val.: 1 vinga, 2 vingues, 3 vinga, 6 vinguen
(5). Bal.: vengut, etc.

vestir

In Val. this can be non-inceptive, with a stem of **vist–** when the stem is stressed, and **vest–** when the stress falls on the ending. In Bal. it is optionally non-inceptive with the stem used as **vest–** throughout. In other places, it is a regular inceptive verb.

Index